GLOSSY

AMBITION, BEAUTY, AND THE INSIDE STORY OF EMILY WEISS'S *GLOSSIER*

Marisa Meltzer

ONE SIGNAL
PUBLISHERS

ATRIA

New York London Toronto Sydney New Delhi

ONE SIGNAL
PUBLISHERS

ATRIA

An Imprint of Simon & Schuster, Inc.
1230 Avenue of the Americas
New York, NY 10020

First One Signal Publishers/Atria Books hardcover edition September 2023

ONE SIGNAL PUBLISHERS / ATRIA BOOKS and colophon
are trademarks of Simon & Schuster, Inc.

For information about special discounts for bulk purchases,
please contact Simon & Schuster Special Sales at 1-866-506-1949
or business@simonandschuster.com.

The Simon & Schuster Speakers Bureau can bring authors to
your live event. For more information or to book an event, contact
the Simon & Schuster Speakers Bureau at 1-866-248-3049 or visit
our website at www.simonspeakers.com.

Interior design by Silverglass

Manufactured in the United States of America

1   3   5   7   9   10   8   6   4   2

Library of Congress Control Number: 2023940310

ISBN 978-1-9821-9060-6
ISBN 978-1-9821-9062-0 (ebook)

Contents

PART 3: THE LAST GIRLBOSS

GLOSSY

The Crosby

Emily Weiss was crying. The two of us were sitting in the middle of the restaurant at the Crosby Street Hotel in Lower Manhattan. Normally, when speaking to a reporter, Weiss would be chaperoned by a coterie of publicists. But this wasn't a fawning magazine piece about her billion-dollar makeup company, Glossier, or its over-the-top stores that have been described as a "beauty Disneyworld." This was about a book. More specifically, the book you're reading now.

Glossier changed everything after it debuted in 2014, from where and how products are sold to the kinds of emotional and social messages promoted—the intangible products—alongside skincare and makeup. Glossier is not just a beauty brand but *the* millennial and Gen Z brand, one that launched on Instagram before it even had its first products. Working there had the same cachet as working at the country's most powerful tech companies. One former employee said of being recruited by Glossier in 2019, "I mean, this doesn't come along a lot. It's like a typical Mark [Zuckerberg] and Sheryl [Sandberg] case—if someone asks you to go sit on a rocket ship, you don't ask which chair."

Weiss is one of the most visionary and consequential business leaders of her generation. She also got an ignominious start in the public eye, cast on the MTV reality show *The Hills* while she was an intern at *Teen Vogue*. America circa 2007 was in the grips of a reality TV boom. Weiss was tall, white, and beautiful, and had a fashion pedigree. After "Hi," her first words onscreen were "We have a big day ahead of us planning." She could correctly pronounce "chinoiserie" and identify cottage roses. They called her the Superintern. Weiss does not like to discuss *The Hills*. "Oh my God, please don't talk about that. I went for, like, two days, and it turned into three episodes. It was the first time I had even been to LA," she told me when I profiled her for *Vanity Fair* in 2019. I, too, would cringe at being associated with a TV show best known for black mascara tears and someone called Justin Bobby, but it was a very public glimpse of Weiss as a power player in the making.

From her reality TV arc, she founded the beauty blog Into the Gloss in 2010. Its candid reviews and intimate interviews with a mix of celebrities and models and media types felt like being invited to a really cool cocktail party—or just gathering in the bathroom and trying on a friend's products. It was a hit. By early 2012, the site had more than 200,000 unique visitors per month, and by May 2016 that number had swelled to 1.3 million. Weiss didn't just want to be a new-media titan; she wanted to make products. In her quest to raise money she was initially passed over by about a dozen venture capitalists until she met with one woman who saw her potential. Less than five years after its launch, Glossier had a billion-dollar valuation. The proverbial unicorn.

Weiss didn't build Glossier to be acquired by a beauty monolith like Estée Lauder; she wanted to *become* Estée Lauder. "I want to be the beauty version of Nike," Weiss said. "I plan to, you know, like—just 'dew' it." If the beauty industry has an "It girl," one who radiates genuine self-made power as well as genuine mystique, it's probably Weiss. And it's all enough to make the company's success seem effortless. As of July 2021, Glossier was valued at $1.8 billion. But like the labor of applying makeup to make you look naturally beautiful, nothing about Glossier is effortless.

Even though Weiss has been compared to household names like LeBron James, Barbara Walters, Mary Kay Ash, and Steve Jobs, she was a recessive CEO. No one I've interviewed—and I've been in the room with a lot of famous people—has generated more curiosity about what they're really like than Emily Weiss. She has viewed her privacy as a kind of political stance. "If you're reading stories about male founders, it's very rare to have as much intrigue around what they're wearing. Although I occupy sort of a weird middle place"—between tech and beauty—"and women are so hungry to have more role models and know more about women who have achieved what they want in their careers. But for me, who's such a mirror for others . . . it's a funny thing. Because I'm so used to being the person who's curious," she said to me. We were standing in her apartment—the only time she's ever let a journalist into her home. (She said something to the effect that she couldn't exactly let in every writer who wanted to see where she lived.) "From the windows of Weiss's living room, you can see the Glossier office," I wrote. "That doesn't bode well for work-life balance, but she swears the proximity allows her to sleep in (she's not a morning person) and walk to work. It's a rental apartment, heavy on natural light, with the same white, pink, and red palette as one of her thronged pop-ups. In the bedroom, laundry is air-drying on a rack in the corner."

I was immediately intrigued by the collection of books she had in her living room. She had copies of *Bad Blood* about Theranos founder Elizabeth Holmes and *Principles* by Ray Dalio, the founder of Bridgewater; two separate hardcovers of Angela Duckworth's *Grit*; *Small Fry*, the memoir by Steve Jobs's daughter Lisa Brennan-Jobs; *The Everything Store*, about Amazon; *Powerhouse*, on the Hollywood talent agency CAA; Sophia Amoruso's *Nasty Galaxy*. Other titles were *StrengthsFinder 2.0*, *The Innovator's Dilemma*, *Mindset*, *Originals*, *Imagine It Forward*, *Sensemaking*, *A Mind of Your Own*, *The Secret Language of Relationships*. At least, that was what was in the white section, as her stacks of books were organized by color. I wondered if she had read every business book in existence. I wanted to note more, but when she came out of the bedroom, she caught me photographing them instead of writing all the titles down before I could get to the other colors. "Do you like my hodgepodge?" she asked. "You're looking at my hodgepodge of books, trying to discern what they say about me." Her confidence was striking. She seemed to always know what to say.

Weiss was clearly aware of the power of the CEO origin story. Jeff Bezos had his door desks. Steve Jobs had his garage. Jobs's biographer Walter Isaacson wrote, "So was Mr.

Jobs smart? Not conventionally. Instead, he was a genius. That may seem like a silly word game, but in fact his success dramatizes an interesting distinction between intelligence and genius. His imaginative leaps were instinctive, unexpected, and at times magical. They were sparked by intuition, not analytic rigor. . . . He didn't study data or crunch numbers but like a pathfinder, he could sniff the winds and sense what lay ahead." At that point in her career Weiss was figuring out her legacy and how she wanted her own story to be told.

When I left her home that afternoon in the summer of 2019, I walked directly to a bookstore in search of well-known start-up stories about female-led companies. There had to be something out there, but I came up short. Weiss was a player who understood the game when it came to image and the CEO, so she must have encountered the same lack of stories about women that I did. There were scant biographies about founders of beauty companies born in the early twentieth century like Estée Lauder, and a handful of books that were more about self-help like Sandberg's *Lean In*, but the gender disparity was startling. There was almost nothing about women CEOs in tech, let alone those like Weiss whose career touched on myriad industries and facets of culture. There was no one like her.

The gender imbalance was also wildly apparent in who writes books about figures in business. A sea of men! I knew that I could be the one to create a balanced view of Weiss and all that her company has innovated without sugarcoating her flaws. I have been reporting on beauty for nearly two decades for the most respected publications in the world. I have written about Weiss for the past ten years; I would describe our relationship as "warmly professional." In early February of 2020, we had a brief text exchange about how she should write a business book of her own and I should ghostwrite it. She told me I first needed to read *Brotopia*, but nothing more progressed once the coronavirus pandemic descended upon us a few weeks later. Glossier's story—her story—was important to tell, and I was determined to write about it. I started working on a book idea a few months later.

———

The Crosby was packed with people at noon on a Friday: rushing waiters carrying thirty-dollar chopped salads; the sounds of silverware clinking and ambient conversations from the Manhattan demimonde. Low-hanging light fixtures in crayon colors of green and red matched upholstered banquettes. Portraits of hunting dogs lined the walls, and the floor-to-ceiling windows opened onto a terrace.

The hotel was at the center of Weiss's world, just minutes away from her former apartment and Glossier's office. A lot had happened since the last time I had seen her in New York City right before the pandemic. She'd moved to Los Angeles and given birth to her first child, Clara. She said she didn't even know how to dress for New York anymore since she moved to Malibu, but Weiss, in an oversize striped oxford shirt and Salomon sneakers, looked great. She always did.

An old friend of Weiss's, Selby Drummond, a blond and willowy fellow alumna of *Vogue*, walked by the table. Weiss composed herself instantly: uncrossed her arms, stood up, and forced a big smile. They chatted about how Weiss was staying upstairs but looking for an apartment in New York to be more bicoastal. I was trying not to listen too closely, tuning out the easy banter of monied women talking about their lives.

I thought Weiss would be giving me another interview that day in October 2022; that we'd delve even deeper into her time as head of Glossier. But within minutes of sitting down, Weiss asked me not to record the conversation. She wanted to talk about how she'd learned about the title of this book in an article in the *Business of Fashion*, an industry publication, and my post about it on Instagram. The outside interest had been immediately apparent. When news of my book emerged, I had already gotten emails from former employees telling me, "I swear there's no dirt to dig up." I had also gotten DMs from Glossier fans begging me, "Wait, is glossier bad??? Tell me!!!!" Weiss didn't entirely agree with the book's direction, or that it should even exist at all. She did not enjoy having her professional life being put under a microscope.

"Will you be writing about my personal life?" she asked. She looked panicked.

"I don't know very much about your personal life," I told her.

There were rumors she was having a difficult maternity leave and feeling lonely in Los Angeles. A woman with money and the help of a couple of nannies who can travel with her (flying by her side in first class, a friend of a friend relayed), and a partner and family she is close to, is not exempt from that. That she was taking time out while she had a baby who was still so young and she wasn't even fully back at work said a lot. Weiss had an alarm set for when she had to go back to her room upstairs to nurse her daughter.

My decision to write this book was not convenient for her. Janet Malcolm famously wrote, "Every journalist who is not too stupid or full of himself to notice what is going on knows that what he does is morally indefensible. He is a kind of confidence man, preying on people's vanity, ignorance, or loneliness, gaining their trust and betraying them without remorse." I was genuinely wondering if I was—and continue to be—to put it bluntly, a complete asshole for writing this book and for putting this woman I respect through such anxiety and turmoil. Just because I was not also crying didn't mean I was immune to Weiss's pain. But also: this wasn't the first time she'd cried to me, or even the second. She had cried to me at her apartment as I interviewed her for the *Vanity Fair* profile, and she had cried to me while touring the Los Angeles Glossier store.

Weiss was a skilled operator, that much was clear, and that was one reason I was drawn to her. Sometimes dealing with her could feel like talking to the prettiest and richest girl you knew who deigned to give you attention, only to realize her goal was to get something from you. Yes, she stirred up old adolescent insecurities. Likening Weiss and her ilk to popular girls is for me to sort out. But it is not an inapt description. She could come off as steely one minute, and the next have an outpouring of emotion. Employees said she often choked up during interviews while talking about the company. She was preternaturally good at reading people and knew when to intimidate and when to wield her big smile. She could do this to people in the room, but she had the ability to do this to her customers too: Emily Weiss knew how to delight people, and to keep them wanting more.

Weiss clearly felt betrayed and wanted to talk about her feelings. I inferred that this exchange was more of a power struggle than a question of whether I was selling her out, that she was concerned with what having a book out about Glossier at this point in time might say to the world. A former employee said to me, "A book implies a cooling-down of some nature. I would like you to be like, 'I can't write this book yet, it's still going,'" meaning it was too early to write a portrait of the company. I told Weiss to take time to decide if she would cooperate further, whether that meant sitting down for another interview or just giving me contacts of people to speak to. We bid each other goodbye and she went upstairs to her child.

———

I thought Weiss was underestimating herself and her company. Glossier's influence far exceeds beauty. The company was at the center of so many issues that defined the era: racial reckoning, the labor movement, pandemic shutdowns, supply chain problems, and female founders falling (or being pushed?) from grace. The brand is also tied in with a change in distribution, the mass proliferation of direct-to-consumer brands, the change in products from things we buy to signifiers of personal values. Out of all the public-facing "girlbosses" of the 2010s—an unfair and demeaning moniker for young, mediagenic female founders of companies that often used messages of empowerment in their marketing, but a cultural moment nonetheless—Weiss is the only one who founded a scalable, billion-dollar company. Weiss didn't go to business school, and barely held more than an assistant job before founding her company at the age of twenty-five. Yet she's the only one who survived while leaders of brands like the Wing, Away, Reformation, and Refinery29 resigned or were replaced amid scrutiny of their business practices.

Apart from it being an exceptional business story, I was also fascinated by Glossier's impact on beauty, an industry that generates more than $500 billion globally every year. And growing—*Forbes* predicts that number will reach $800 billion sometime this decade. In the United States, we spend more on beauty than any other country in the world. In a *Forbes* list of the twelve richest self-made women under the age of forty, six of them made their fortunes at least partially in beauty.

How? I wanted to understand these questions and have spent the past few years trying to do so. Is Emily Weiss a business genius or a well-connected rich girl? How did Glossier cultivate such unprecedented brand loyalty to the point of spawning Instagram accounts for both Dogs of

Glossier and Boyfriends at Glossier? Did it scale too fast? In early 2023, a writer for the *Business of Fashion* asked dozens of people "with varying degrees of knowledge of the landscape": " 'What is the most important beauty brand?' and 'Who is the most important beauty founder?' of the past fifteen years. Besides Glossier or Weiss, none could name another brand or founder." Will it last?

PART 1

THE SUPERINTERN

A little over two weeks ago, I got married in front of 37 of my nearest and dearest in the Bahamas. It was a truly magical weekend—one I'll be reporting on in my next ITG post, once the pictures come in.

The real story, seeing as though this is a beauty website and I'm a beauty editor, is in the prep. Months of prep! So much prep. Not of the venue, guest list, or seating chart—that was fairly easy—but of my limbs, skin, wanted hair, unwanted hair, nails, muscles, digestive tract, lashes, and brows. Did I go overboard? Perhaps. Was it high-maintenance? Maybe. I did spend an inordinate amount of the fall on my back. But it worked. I was 8/10 happy with how I looked . . . pretty good!

—EMILY WEISS, *"THE LITTLE WEDDING BLACK BOOK,"*
INTO THE GLOSS, FEBRUARY 9, 2016

1

Emily Weiss's friend from high school remembered her simply: "Emily was a Manolo in a school full of Birkenstocks." In a senior year photo for the Wilton High School yearbook of 2003, she's shown, like most of her 226 classmates, posed against a tree from the waist up, wearing a black sleeveless turtleneck, smiling toward the camera like she's happy to greet you. Her brown hair is long and straight and she's wearing subtle rosy lipstick. That much is like her cohort. But her two senior quotes are not.

Calvin Coolidge: "Nothing in the world can take the place of persistence. Talent will not; nothing is more common than unsuccessful people with talent. Genius will not; unrewarded genius is almost a proverb. Education will not; the world is full of educated derelicts. Persistence and determination alone are omnipotent."

Graydon Carter, then the editor in chief of *Vanity Fair*: "Style is not about being fabulous or fashionable, but about being comfortable in your own skin. Get that right and everything falls into place."

Just to put Weiss's choice of words to mark her high school years in context, the girl whose photo is just above has quotes from both A. A. Milne, writer of *Winnie-the-Pooh*, and the Tom Cruise movie *Vanilla Sky*.

Weiss grew up in one of the wealthiest towns in Connecticut, the state that had the highest per capita income in the country for decades. Wilton is a place whose money is less showy than the rambling homes of nearby New Canaan or the grandeur of Greenwich. Wilton High School, where Weiss started in 2000, was predominantly white. And the teens there were normal in a small-town, all-American way that feels like something out of *Gilmore Girls* or *American Graffiti*: house parties, watching the sports teams play other schools, hanging out around Dunkin' Donuts.

Weiss considered herself a product of the American Dream. Her parents, Kevin and Nancy Weiss, were gold benefactors of the yearbook and took a congratulatory yearbook spread ("We love you—Mom, Dad and Austin" handwritten with a photo of Weiss looking about kindergarten age in a frilly dress and a big bow in her hair). Her father was an executive for the global shipping company Pitney Bowes; her mother stayed home to raise Emily and her brother, Austin. "[My dad] worked his way up from door-to-door salesman. . . . I feel like I take after him a lot," she told a reporter. Weiss was entrepreneurial at a young age. She bred guppies and tried to sell them to a fish store. She had a lot of pets as a kid: an iguana, a turtle, and a red-cheeked cordon-bleu finch, which is the same shade of blue as a Tiffany's box. At home her bedroom walls were painted that same Tiffany blue with cream detailing. (Which begs the question, did the bird or the Tiffany obsession come first?) Her mom liked a fresh towel every day. ("I still have towel shame from that," said a friend who spent the night.)

The rest of her school didn't quite see her as so normal. She arrived for her first day of sixth grade in an outfit modeled after Alicia Silverstone's character Cher Horowitz in the movie *Clueless*, which was popular at the time. "I wore thigh-high stockings to my first day of sixth grade with high-heeled loafers and, like, a full kilt with, like, a feather pen in this town where people were playing lacrosse," she said. Or they just didn't understand what she was all about. They shopped at teen-stalwart mall brands like J.Crew; Weiss had a barrel-shaped Louis Vuitton Papillon handbag and wore pointy-toed shoes, all of which were very sophisticated and fashion-forward for the suburbs. When she was in college, she said in a *Teen Vogue* story that "I wore a tulle and velvet fifties gown that I found in the costume closet at my school" to prom and noted that the de facto school uniform was Abercrombie & Fitch. People thought she was odd, she said, for wearing Bakelite beads and retro dresses to homecoming.

"We may share the same chromosomes, my mom and I, but we have never shared the same sartorial outlook," Weiss wrote in a Mother's Day tribute to her mother on Into the Gloss. Her parents supported her fashion obsession but weren't fashion people themselves. Some people are born to fashion, wearing the little Chanel jackets their moms no longer want, telling anecdotes about dressing up in their mothers' stilettos and wobbling around the bedroom. Others were born that way regardless of the contents of their mothers' closets.

"I remember the first time I thought, 'Maybe Mom doesn't know best.' I was five, at an uncle's wedding in Ohio, and I was sobbing hysterically behind a couch because my mom had dressed my three-year-old brother and me in matching plaid rompers (it could have been a dress but, for all intents and purposes, it was a romper) that had our names down the front next to huge felt duck decals." Who knows where it came from—cast-off issues of *Vogue* or *Elle*? pictures of supermodels on the beach?—but Weiss's interest not just in looking good, but in style, seemingly came from the womb. "I always just loved playing dress-up and I loved clothes and makeup, jewelry, creative art, making things. I think it's just part of who I am," Weiss said. "I'm so grateful that my mom really did accept . . . whatever the creative endeavors were, whatever the flights of fancy, the things that I wanted to create, or the plays I wanted to be in, the clubs that I wanted to join."

As a teenager, she had a modeling agent and booked jobs posing for *Women's Wear Daily* and *Seventeen*. In a 2002 issue of *Seventeen* she modeled a rash guard by Roxy; another issue featured her in an outfit of Frye boots, denim miniskirt, tights, and layered tanks. She posed for an August 2003 spread called "School Belle": "A countdown to looking gorgeous on your first day back," which included the tip to use a mixture of unflavored gelatin and milk as an at-home mask for removing blackheads. She appeared fresh-faced, with brown hair and eyebrows thick before that was fashionable. Her smile with her slight overbite looked the same.

You can see how her identity emerged. She was the perfect Connecticut girl to outsiders. But at school, she wasn't the cheerleader archetype. She wasn't even given the senior super-latives for Best Dressed or Shopaholic—other kids at school got these—but she was voted Most Likely to Be Famous. She also got Best Actress (the year before, the now very celebrated Paul Dano was voted Best Actor) and played a ditzy character in her senior play to great applause. She was popular enough to show up a little bit in her yearbook's pages mugging with a skeleton and a photo of her with "JUNIORS" written on her face for Spirit Week. She certainly wasn't shunned. She dated Sam Hyde, a clown type, a guy who didn't seem close to any of Weiss's friend group but went on to be a sort of right-leaning political provocateur. To Weiss, she was growing up in a town where no one really got her interests, so she tried hard to spend time in New York City, just a short train ride away. Then again, the heiress Lydia Hearst attended the same school. It might have been full of teenagers whose interests were more about school sports than Chanel, but Weiss's feelings of being different were self-created. "I had no idea what I was going to do with my life and had no plan, I was just living life," one former classmate said. "She seemingly had a plan."

There was drinking and house parties, just like most teen experiences, but there were darker elements to her classmates too. "Later in high school there were more hard drugs—heavy use of [OxyContin] and at least two kids who had overdoses and a bunch who went to rehab. There was access to parents' stashes and then moving on to buying street drugs," said one classmate. Weiss didn't engage with that at all. But in Colo-rado during spring break of her senior year, she and friends went out in Vail and were arrested for using fake IDs. Her parents, who were also on the trip, were distraught and debated sending Weiss's friends home early, not as punishment but rather to get the bad influence away. They didn't, but it created a rift in her friend group. It does reflect a sense of how she was raised, their answer to a foundational question of parenting: Do you teach your children to take responsibility and hold them accountable, or do you find every opportunity to blame the other kids?

At New York University, Weiss worked as if driven by an ambition that felt outsize and made her acquaintances feel lazy and her professors remember her so many years later. "I recall Emily from my photography classes. She was a beautiful young woman, a great student, and (clearly) a hard worker!" an NYU art professor emailed me. She also had an air of coming from something. A classmate who described their own background as "lower middle class get the hell out of small-town Florida" said that, upon meeting Weiss freshman year in the dorms, "I felt her pedigree—or whatever—she comes from fancy stock. I remember thinking, 'Oh shit, I'm going to compete with this?' I felt like a country bumpkin next to her. I had traveled and seen a lot but not in the same way; she seemed like someone who had flown first-class before. She flitted in and out of a room and seemed used to people's eyes on her. I really remember thinking this girl was used to being the center of everything." But college was also where Weiss met her core group of friends to this day. "Even when you're a student, it's still such a rat race as soon as you get to the city, because every single person who comes to the city is like, I'm a tiny adult. Like, I want to work and get an internship. Including me," said Weiss.

Facebook debuted in 2004, when Weiss was a freshman. She used the social media network in college enough that by the time she graduated in 2007, her senior year communications thesis was on the rather prescient topic of the risks of social media. She extrapolated that into why Facebook made her feel bad. She doesn't remember the details; she no longer has the paper. Weiss is fond of telling interviewers she's not an anecdote person.

While Weiss was still a high school student, she spun a routine babysitting gig into an internship at Ralph Lauren. She simply asked her neighbor, who worked for Ralph Lauren, for a job. "I remember saying to him, 'I love your kids but I would really love to work [at Ralph Lauren].'" That ability to boldly ask for what you want is something that's hard for most adults, let alone a kid in high school who was fifteen or sixteen. "I think it's just, 'can't hurt to ask,'" she said. "There's a natural curiosity you have that propels you to speak to people and learn about them and ask questions. And that's just how I am."

Her boss in the women's design department at Ralph Lauren was Whitney St. John Fairchild, who was impressed with her from the first day. She loved Weiss's energy and style and the fact that she showed up in clothes she had sewn herself, a skill her mother had taught her. She thought Weiss was glamorous. Weiss has since joked that her job was probably illegal, but St. John Fairchild said it wasn't entirely unusual to have younger interns or assistants. One of them, years before Weiss, was Soon-Yi Previn. Weiss worked at the offices on Madison Avenue for two summers, doing whatever tasks they had for her: running errands, helping models get ready for fittings, carrying clothes to meetings. She was charged with taking notes in a meeting with Ralph Lauren himself. "I was sitting in the room in the back and in the corner," she said. "Ralph turned to me—I think I'd maybe shaken his hand at one point, but he doesn't know me—and everyone just stops and he looks at me, and he goes, 'What do you think?'" She has no memory of what she stammered out, just that the world stopped for her.

She did learn some lessons in the corporate culture of fashion companies. There was a hot dog stand outside the Ralph Lauren headquarters, and sometimes she'd go there for lunch. "I was so excited about getting these hot dogs when I was in New York City, like, this is what you do," she said. Her coworkers were horrified. "They were like, 'Oh my God, what are you eating?' Like, 'Do not eat that.'" Weiss did seem to have more poise as a teenager than most people have as adults. While she certainly came from what might be called "a good family" that taught her manners and how to exist in the world and project a certain kind of class, she was also a product of her own creation. Few teenagers have the experience of both observing and interacting with adults in professional environments.

St. John Fairchild found herself cold-calling Amy Astley, the editor of *Teen Vogue*, to recommend Weiss for an internship. This was in the early days of the magazine, which launched in 2003. She was adamant and persuasive on her call to Astley: "I would never normally do this, but I have someone very, very special for you to meet. I have never been this impressed by a young person. You won't regret making time to meet Emily Weiss. She's so sophisticated." Weiss operated in a preternaturally mature manner. St. John Fairchild remembered that Weiss took her out to lunch on Madison Avenue at Nello, a power spot that happened to be close to the office, as a thank-you. Weiss was the only person Whitney St. John Fairchild ever sent to Astley.

"Whitney was right. Emily was very special, and I saw it instantly," Astley recalled. She was focused and confident and responsible and had a serious work ethic. But every high school in America has a few high achievers with similar traits vying for Ivy League college admission or fame or fortune. Weiss had that, but she had something else too. "She did not try to hide her light as young people often do," Astley said. "She was very polite and appropriate but spoke to me as an equal. This was unusual and impressive. She was only sixteen years old—I'm working off memory here—but very self-assured and direct." Astley hired her as an intern.

Eva Chen, who is now the director of fashion partnerships at Instagram, was then an editor in the beauty department at *Teen Vogue* and remembers Weiss during those years. "She had that X-factor. She was a college student who clearly had a plan, so pulled-together and focused, which was so different from me at that age."

Grace Mirabella, the *Vogue* editor in the 1970s and 1980s, sandwiched between the over-the-top personalities of Diana Vreeland and Anna Wintour, was a *Vogue* assistant herself and wrote in her 1995 memoir *In and Out of Vogue* about her experience in the 1950s of who gets jobs there. It's instructive for understanding the kind of world Weiss was moving in, even if it was five decades prior. The head of personnel at

Mirabella's time, Miss Campbell, "could judge if a woman was right for *Vogue* by the length of her legs, her cheekbones, and the way she tied her scarf. (The rumor was that being flat-chested helped too.)" Editors at magazines lived a hallowed life full of perks like free town cars, gifts of clothes, comped meals. Not only were they leading a dream life, but they were tastemakers. Editors were influencers before that was a term. The editors were, yes, from some of the so-called best and most storied families in America, such as Babe Paley, a *Vogue* editor from the high-society Cushing family who had been married to the Standard Oil heir Stanley Mortimer Jr. The editors were an elegant but colorful bunch, who were oft-divorced or lived in hotels (sometimes both, in the case of Paley, who once lived at the St. Regis Hotel with Serge Obolensky, a Russian prince)—people for whom being stylish and striking was preferable to something more staid.

Weiss regularly appeared in the pages of *Teen Vogue*: in a 2005 issue she was identified as a nineteen-year-old NYU sophomore scouring her hometown in Connecticut for thrift shop scores. Magazine interns at that time were universally unpaid or paid in free samples, taxi rides, and office lunches.

The kinds of people who could advance at magazine jobs were the ones who could work for free or very little. To be able to be an unpaid intern presumed either that there was family money paying your expenses or that you'd be able to meet the demands of the internship while working some kind of real job or jobs. At the same time, it was the sort of business where both looking good and having good connections were prized. A certain famous editor in chief was well-known for asking everyone she interviewed where they lived and tut-tutting if it was—*gasp*—as far afield as Brooklyn. *The Devil Wears Prada* was a hit book and film, and Weiss fit the mold.

Interns also had to navigate the hierarchy of which of them were championed by the actual staff. In media there were workhorses and show ponies, and magazine internships were no exception. Guess which ones got to represent the brand? You had to be either inexplicably cool, socially connected, or stunningly beautiful. Or, preferably, all of the above. Consider the case of the actor Chloë Sevigny, who was an intern at the teen magazine *Sassy* in the 1990s. An editor scouted her in downtown Manhattan for her incredible style, and she often appeared in its pages as a model. There was certainly a whole cadre of other interns, but Sevigny was the only one whose name and face readers knew. Weiss was *Teen Vogue*'s Sevigny.

A fellow intern from those years remembers that, while she knew about fashion and wasn't flaky like a lot of privileged daughters who scored fashion magazine internships, Weiss had a certain amount of chutzpah and would ask to take home, say, nail polish she liked. Which may sound minor, but to be an intern at *Teen Vogue* was often a complex dance of wanting very much to be noticed while simultaneously wanting to disappear. A fellow low-ranking Condé Nast employee said that Weiss wore Balenciaga heels to work. "She was dressed to the nines—she would dress better than the editors and she was still in college. I was like, who is this girl?" The assistant said she was envious of her and wished she could afford to dress as well but also thought she seemed cool. Another said, "At a party I saw her take a bite of a cheeseburger slider and throw the rest in a trash can. I thought, 'Okay, I guess that's what thin and pretty people do.'" This is a common refrain. Another former *Teen Vogue* intern said, "I was coming from Missouri pretty naïve and was like, how are all of these girls making thirty thousand dollars a year and wearing designer clothes? What is this secret club I'm not a part of?" Weiss didn't charm everyone at Condé Nast. "She's a weird girl. You would think someone who had the charisma and balls and vision of [Glossier] would be so loud and dynamic," commented an editor who worked with her, "but she was soft-spoken, not a standout." Another former editor said, "I lived in a sorority house, went to an all-girls school, but no place made me more thin than when I worked at *Teen Vogue*. I once got Chipotle for lunch and everyone looked at me like I had done something they had never seen before. Basically, it was a ruthless environment, and Emily had something that readers really wanted."

When Amy Astley, the founding editor in chief of *Teen Vogue*, was working on the second season of MTV's breakout reality soap *The Hills* with the producer Adam DiVello, America was in the middle of a reality television boom that began with MTV's *The Real World* in 1992, which told the story of "seven strangers who were picked to live in a house." In 2002, *The Osbournes* premiered, chronicling the ups and downs of heavy metal star Ozzy Osbourne's family. The show became MTV's most-viewed series ever and spawned a genre of voyeuristic reality TV about the lives of the rich and privileged. Meanwhile, the fictional teen drama *The OC* was a hit for the Fox network. MTV combined *The OC* with *The Osbournes* and a little of *The Real World* for *Laguna Beach*, a show about wealthy teenagers who lived, loved, and fought in a particularly photogenic part of the Orange County coast. The series was so popular that MTV devised a spin-off in which it followed its *Laguna Beach* star Lauren Conrad into her college years as a Los Angeles fashion student and intern at *Teen Vogue*. The show was highly manufactured: *Teen Vogue* barely had a West Coast office, let alone one with multiple interns.

DiVello told Astley he wanted to cast another young woman on *The Hills* with a totally different energy from Lauren Conrad and Whitney Port, the LA-based, slightly hapless *Teen Vogue* interns at the center of the show. Did Astley have anyone to suggest? "Yes, I did: Emily Weiss, our impressively put-together intern. I suspected she would be gold on-camera—and she was," said Astley. Weiss's debut on *The Hills* in 2007 begins with footage of her briskly walking in high heels, wearing a short flared skirt and black turtleneck, her long brown hair stick-straight, a binder in her hands. "Emily: New York Intern" flashes onscreen. She looks like some kind of insanely confident apparition who has come to show the laconic and provincial stars of the show what working at a magazine really takes. Most of America's first time experiencing the determination of Emily Weiss was on *The Hills*. She could have been the show's villain with her clipped diction and no-nonsense attitude, but she managed to be someone to root for against all the dummies on the show. She was so capable!

Reality TV, with its artificial candor, did herald the manufactured authenticity where people like the Kardashian clan unapologetically live their reality TV lives. But *The Hills* gave her a high profile, especially to scores of wannabe Emily Weisses at magazines. "Emily was the model they were all going after," said a former *Teen Vogue* editor. "They wanted to be a style muse, they wanted to be featured in the magazine. Whatever tiny blip of celebrity she had, they wanted that." When she would come back and visit the LA *Teen Vogue* offices, they were too nervous even to talk to her. She had to have a secret Facebook account because too many *Hills* fans were finding her on it. When Weiss showed up to her five-year high school reunion in Wilton, her classmates were impressed she even came.

The way Weiss handled her life after her arc on *The Hills* ended turned out to be a defining moment for her. She could have gone with her own reality show—something like Whitney Port's *Hills* spin-off called *The City*, where post–*Teen Vogue* she moves to New York to work for the demanding publicist Kelly Cutrone. "She could have done anything in reality TV after her star turn," said Astley, who held the *Teen Vogue* job for thirteen years and has stayed at Condé Nast, moving on to become the editor in chief of *Architectural Digest*. "But she was focused on a career in fashion with longevity and she wanted to be taken seriously. I respected that decision."

Weiss said in an interview that her dream then was to be

an editor in chief. "I looked at someone like Anna Wintour and that was incredibly inspiring to me." So after three years at *Teen Vogue*, she went off to work as a fashion assistant at *W* magazine. It was a trajectory that made sense, working her way up the glossy media ladder. At *W*, word spread around the office that the "chinoiserie girl" intern from *The Hills* was now a fashion assistant. *W* magazine shared a floor with *Women's Wear Daily*, a trade paper for the fashion industry. The divide between the staffers who reported doggedly on the denim industry and those across the hall who worked on cover shoots with Katie Holmes was stark.

There's a reason people live for books like *The Devil Wears Prada*: fashion media is a mean industry with an intense pecking order. Fashion magazines were the kinds of places where people couldn't get a supermarket sheet cake for a birthday at the office, but rather cupcakes someone's assistant took a car to pick up from Magnolia Bakery. "Emily existed in that universe. Her whole life was carefully curated," said a coworker. And still, even among the fashion crowd, Weiss was considered a bit odd, or at least on her own planet. "I know she is from Connecticut, but she dressed like a Russian oligarch's wife. She has incredible taste. Where she was able to get the funds to afford those clothes I never figured out," said one former coworker from those days. Something that movies never get quite right about the media world is that there are codes within codes. Fashion assistants should certainly dress well, with a Cartier bracelet and a designer bag and expensively maintained hair, but they should look like they're there to work, not to pose in front of a step and repeat at a gala. They shouldn't look like fashion victims or like they're trying to peacock. Getting that look right involves a lot of privilege—money, class, information—and it's another way to haze and mildly humiliate outsiders. A coworker said, "You had to toe this line where you had to be at once very on top of fashion and glamorous but also know your place or you were considered gauche. A different person would have picked up on that, but Emily didn't have that filter."

Weiss was looked down on by some of her peers for being too sophisticated. She didn't look like someone who would ever hang out at a dive bar, which was what the cool girls who lived downtown did. By 2007, she had rented an apartment from Jane Keltner de Valle, who worked in fashion at *Teen Vogue*. It was in a large building on Bleecker Street, a studio with a sunken living room. She persuaded the interior designer Tom Delavan to help decorate it. It didn't look like any other twenty-two-year-old's apartment. "It had blue taffeta curtains out of an Upper East Side, Park Avenue kind of apartment, and she had a beautiful blue velvet chair. Most people I knew had Ikea stuff. It was very done," said a coworker who had come over for a party. "I mean, it looked great. Anything she did she would do perfectly because she had a great eye."

Weiss departed *W* soon. "It wasn't for me—I realized very quickly that I really wanted to be part of the shoots, even if it was just packing things," she said, but coworkers said she was fired. "She was the kind of person who could never be a good assistant because she didn't know her place," said one.

"And the people she was reporting to were awful." Weiss then worked as an assistant to freelance stylist Elissa Santisi. "We pulled for American *Vogue*, for runway shows—it was a great education and experience. We went to Dubai, we went to LA a bunch of times," Weiss said.

Self-tanner would turn out to change the trajectory of Weiss's life. In 2010, she had been on a *Vogue* accessories shoot in Miami with the Dutch model Doutzen Kroes. The two were killing time in a trailer or van—there is a lot of downtime for these kinds of things—and Kroes casually told Weiss about a self-tanner she was obsessed with called Sublime Bronze ProPerfect Salon Airbrush Self-Tanning Mist from L'Oréal. Her reasoning came out in a tumble, the way talking about something you're enthusiastic about usually does, but it was also potentially influenced by the fact that Kroes was an ambassador for the brand. "She was like, all the other ones are crazy, but when you use this one, you exfoliate this way, and then you put it on . . . and doesn't smell and all of these things," Weiss said. She didn't think she cared about self-tanner but decided she had to try that one. So when she was back at home in Wilton, Connecticut, staying with her family, she picked up an $11 bottle at the local CVS pharmacy.

She wanted to write about it for *Vogue* and told a beauty editor it was her civic duty to spread the word. She wrote about the product ("This, I've learned, is key to the process: Mist with confidence"), and they published it, accompanied by a photo of Kroes bronzed and possibly naked on a beach chair in Miami, a towel wrapped around her hair and wearing cat-eye sunglasses. This was Weiss's first *Vogue* byline. She got to keep writing. "I'm totally going to channel the new streamlined, minimalistic seventies vibe with these Gucci pants," she wrote on *Vogue*'s website in July 2010 of a $745 pair of Gucci travertine flared pants. "I'd wear them with a body-con cashmere turtleneck and substantial but simple gold jewelry." For a young woman of her monied class and powerful social circle, what she was doing was, in a sense, typical of her cohort. She modeled in Derek Lam's lookbook and was photographed at charity dinners and was the subject of the kinds of magazine stories where they say what an employee wears every day. "At least half of my wardrobe is Alexander Wang. I've been a fan for years; I still wear his knitwear from the first collections!" Or, "These dresses are great because they're so versatile—they look great at the office with a neat little jacket (this one's Margiela), or out to a party. Perhaps the best part is that no one will be wearing the same thing!" A search of my email reveals a person whose then boyfriend had dated Weiss in college. She was fascinated by her, not least because she wondered who paid her credit card bills. (Living in New York long enough, you realize the answer is always a rich husband or, barring a rich husband, a rich family; there is usually no mystery.)

Weiss could have gone on to become a pampered fashion editor or a stylist who married well that nobody seriously expected to work hard or long enough to earn her own money. Weiss did want to start a business, which wasn't extraordinary in and of itself: there are scores of socialite types who do a turn as editors and then start children's clothing lines or stationery stores or bottle their mother's salad dressing; something they can say they're pouring their own creativity into and call it a career. No, that's too dismissive of her real talent: Weiss could have continued on at Condé Nast to become an editor in chief, as Eva Chen did when she was put in charge of *Lucky* magazine in 2013, or followed Chen's next career step and left to go work for a tech company a few years later. Instead, Weiss told Eva Chen she needed a word.

2

"She closed the door. I was like, oh, this is serious," said Eva Chen. Weiss had come into her office at *Teen Vogue* near Times Square in 2010.

She told Chen that she'd had an idea over the summer while she was on a beach in Connecticut with her family—and maybe it was crazy—to start a website that would show the beauty routines of the fashion industry and celebrities, stuff that she learned on shoots. She wanted to call the beauty blog Into the Gloss.

The late aughts was when personal style blogs and street style started to really take off. "I was reading Jak and Jil and the Sartorialist and I was just shocked because everyone was just [looking at style] from the head down—not treating beauty as part of style in a huge way, but sort of as the kid sister, the afterthought," Weiss said. The fact was that she couldn't find anywhere online, or even in print media, that gave her what she wanted when it came to beauty. "There's such little airtime dedicated to [beauty], that in many ways you're forced to deal with [it] on a more fundamental level every day than even what you're wearing."

Weiss bought a used camera for $750 and a domain for intothegloss.com. The website for Into the Gloss launched in September 2010 with a post on Nicky Deam, an Australian publicist in New York, who Weiss thought had cool hair and a good sense of style. Weiss took her photo and asked her about her fashion week beauty survival items. And there was a welcome letter: "IntoTheGloss.com is a blog dedicated to Beauty, from the Inside. No, not from within, although that's great too—Inside in this case means Inside the fashion industry and on the street," read the original About section, which was coupled with Weiss wearing a red lip color and a pair of black Wayfarer sunglasses, her hair loosely swept back. It looks now like a parody of a street-style shot, and the editorial tone could have used a professional touch, but in 2010 it was the epitome of cool.

Weiss knew right away she wanted Top Shelf to be the central column, in which a famous (or famous-ish) person chronicles her grooming tips and routine. The tone of Into the Gloss was voyeuristic, useful, and democratic. Part of that came from the setting. Into the Gloss was a one-woman show. Weiss would come to her subject's bathroom and sit on the floor and interview them and take photos herself, and then transcribe and work at night in her apartment. By day, she still worked at *Vogue*. The blog had the intimacy of doing someone's makeup. She thought making a person feel seen and heard was one of the greatest things you could do in life. "You're having a conversation, you're learning about them by touching their face," Weiss said. Everyone had some kind of beauty routine, even if it was bar soap—although the ones Into the Gloss ran tended to be more grandiose. "Regardless of how high-maintenance or low-maintenance a woman is, every single woman is her own expert," Weiss said. "What was really exciting about Into the Gloss was taking something usually done behind closed doors and that often made women feel very—you know, just the sheer act of exploring beauty or talking about their beauty routines made them feel quite uncomfortable."

In one segment, J.Crew executive Jenna Lyons may have confided she had a makeup artist friend bring her Canmake Cream Cheek back from Japan, but she also praised $1.80 Blistex Medicated Lip Balm. In her installment, Catherine Deneuve, the legendary French actress, said, "I always sit with my makeup person and talk about how the most important part of the look is the eyebrow." Lauren Santo Domingo, a former *Vogue* editor and a founder of the fashion website Moda Operandi, recommended Avalon Organics $9 shampoos and conditioners with a disclaimer that was too good to make up: "Not like I wash my own hair, I can't even remember the last time I washed my own hair." There were posts on how to become a morning person; essentials for taking on an airplane; universally flattering makeup shades. It's where Kim Kardashian said she's known to go five days without washing her hair. (Weiss was particularly proud that the photo she took was one Kardashian asked if she could reuse. For a while it was on her LinkedIn page.) Beyond the celebrity routines, one of Into the Gloss's most popular posts was simply called "How to Give Yourself a Brazilian Bikini Wax." The musician Courtney Love raved about a Bioxidea Miracle24 face mask that she got at the Sundance Film Festival, which she claimed made her look like she had just had sex for four days: "I'm on my last mask right now. I'm tweeting them tomorrow three times. I need more! They also have one for your hands, your feet, which I did last night. There's even one for your titties."

The specificity of products and enthusiastic tone of Into the Gloss were parodied to perfection by the writer Naomi Fry in the *New Yorker* in a Top Shelf from Jim Morrison of The Doors. "My favorite thing is eating some peyote, cracking open 'Thus Spoke Zarathustra,' and putting on something super-hydrating. Otherwise, I get sort of scaly. They don't call me the Lizard King for nothing!"

Weiss said when she was envisioning Into the Gloss, she started a notebook with all her ideas, and on one page she wrote down her top fifty names of people to cover for Top Shelf. "All of whom we've now shot," she said. That might have been an example of mythmaking. A magazine editor saw Weiss run after Bill Clinton at a fundraiser, assuming she was going to badger the former president to do a Top Shelf. And not every Top Shelf saw the light of day. They did one with Ivanka Trump tied to promoting her new bag company. Before it was posted, Donald Trump announced his candidacy for president, and they decided not to run it.

Top Shelf was the kind of signature column every blockbuster media brand needs. *Vanity Fair* has its Proust Questionnaire; *Cosmopolitan* has Why Don't You; *New York* magazine has the Approval Matrix. Weiss recognized the power of those diaristic franchises various media have always had for Sunday routines, food journals, culture diets. "You learn a lot about people when you're sitting on their bathroom floor, or on their toilet seat, riffling through their stuff," Weiss said.

Her most astute assessment was where power was coming from. She knew that magazine editors might be losing power but that their taste and influence remained to tap into, so she covered people like *Vogue*'s Sally Singer. She herself had experienced the intimacy that reality television offered and wasn't above featuring the Kardashians on her site, or their go-to hairstylist Jen Atkin (who became a successful beauty entrepreneur when she founded a hair line called Ouai and sold it for an undisclosed sum to Procter & Gamble in 2021).

Weiss was a born networker who wasn't loath to call up anyone she had met even in passing on her previous jobs and internships, such as a supermodel like Karlie Kloss or a makeup artist like Gucci Westman, who was so busy doing makeup for stars like Jennifer Aniston and being the creative artistic director for Revlon that she at first declined. "Emily kept asking me if she could just do pictures at home on the weekend. She was so persistent," Westman said. It worked, and in her 2012 Top Shelf she revealed that she used a $9.89 Roux touch-up stick on her gray roots.

The people the blog covered were chic, but what they talked about was accessible enough that it wasn't hard to understand. Their routines were demystified—not in a way that made them seem boring, but rather one that made you feel like you were let in on a secret. Who doesn't like that? Readers could buy the products that the British model and television presenter Alexa Chung used, which included Chanel Rouge Allure Incandescente 97 ("a good red" that she introduced the actress Liv Tyler to). For a lot of people, a moisturizer or a lip balm that a famous person also used was an accessible indulgence. Not everyone felt like there was democracy in the recommendations on how to look and stay beautiful coming largely from coastal and European beauty insiders. Someone who knew Weiss from NYU sighed when she saw Into the Gloss years after graduation. "I thought, 'She found her groove, this makes sense. It's aspirational and still weirdly making me feel at this age I'll never measure up and now it's through buying beauty products.'"

Into the Gloss's word-of-mouth recommendations from an array of people also offered a way for developers to do competitive research. "As a product developer I was researching the hot, nuanced, funky trends coming out of Into the Gloss," said a veteran of a large beauty company. "We were reading it to find out, what does Pat McGrath actually use? We'd go and research products that were mentioned and see if there was a way to commercialize it. No other place was opening the gates of what these people used."

The peek into how everyone else lives (or claims to live) is undeniably tantalizing. It was a brilliant idea for the brand and for engagement—comments were plentiful, between fifty and a hundred per post—and Into the Gloss was as good at it or better at it than most legacy magazines, which helped them get more famous subjects. A beauty writer at a competing website said they tried to come up with a similar franchise to Top Shelf but never could. On top of that, they were jealous of the edgy gamines, literary figures, and indie actresses Into the Gloss got to cover while they were stuck asking stars of Hallmark movies about what lip gloss they preferred. There were plenty of people employed elsewhere in the online media environment with a keen sense of who would be fun to cover, but that sphere of the internet was increasingly dominated by Chartbeat and other sites that could give a live count of website traffic. Numbers and affiliate links and advertising partnerships took precedence over what was cool. The main difference was that Weiss answered to herself.

Other media would repost an Into the Gloss interview with a quote or a recommendation, such as the eighteen-year-old model Lindsey Wixson admitting she prefers to do her own makeup. "Don't get me wrong, I'm happy to have someone do my makeup—I think everyone is—but it gets a little intense during fashion week." That helped the fledgling site gain a following. By early 2011, Into the Gloss had over 200,000 new users per month.

Into the Gloss had a steady build to success and stability. The media world and its business model of monetization through ads was one Weiss knew. She also had a unique ability to boldly ask people for things without the hemming and hawing and lead-ups and awkwardness most people attach to those kinds of asks. An editor once got a cold email from Weiss, writing that she'd noticed they had posted a job description similar to something she was looking for—a graphic design intern—and would she mind forwarding any résumés they didn't want. "I think that's the thing about Emily," said the editor, "is that she does stuff that with other people you would either ignore, or you would bristle at that, but she has the goods to back it up." Before Into the Gloss even launched, Weiss cold-called Kerry Diamond, an executive at Lancôme who Weiss knew championed digital marketing, about advertising every week for a month. "I remember talking to someone at Lancôme who was like, who does this girl think she is? But then she presented this great idea, and they bought advertising," said an editor at a rival publication. Lancôme spent $5,000 to be their first advertiser. "This was more money than I'd ever had in my life, and more money than I ever had in my bank account," Weiss said. That sounds unlikely for someone who routinely wore Gucci and Chloé, but she seems invested in her origin story.

For the first year Weiss worked at night and tried to do most of the shoots on the weekends because she still had her job with *Vogue*. Some colleagues thought Weiss had created Into the Gloss as a calling card to hopscotch several places forward in the media industry. She could make a name for herself at the blog, and instead of taking years to become a more senior editor, she could do it in a year. An acquaintance said she went for an interview at *Harper's Bazaar* around 2011 for a features editor job, which would have been a huge coup for Weiss to get in her mid-twenties. But Weiss decided she didn't want the job, and she left *Vogue* too. There was too much momentum at Into the Gloss to turn away from it. She decided to follow her gut.

"We had enough [advertising] partners that by the time we hit a year, I said, 'Okay, this is really a business now, this is working,'" Weiss said. The timing of Into the Gloss's debut was critical to its success. Even though beauty was considered a less splashy area to cover than fashion, the most lucrative advertising in media came from beauty companies because of the inherent accessibility of beauty products. The 2008 financial crisis and recession made consumers reevaluate their own spending habits and relationship to luxury.

Do you know what Dior sells a lot more of than dresses, or even handbags? Diorshow mascara, which retails for $29.50. It was and continues to be difficult to spend $3,500 on a cocktail dress, but a facial cleanser can be used twice a day. Even the most expensive echelon of $70-plus lipstick from Tom Ford or Hermès is an affordable luxury whose use can be amortized to pennies.

May 2012 was a turning point for Into the Gloss. It solidified from a small project operated out of Weiss's apartment to something more official. Weiss rented an office at 611 Broadway in NoHo, on the corner of Broadway and Houston, above the Crate & Barrel store. She also started to build out the team by hiring Michael Harper as digital director and Nick Axelrod—now Nick Axelrod-Welk—as editorial director. Weiss's brief stint at *W* was when she met Axelrod-Welk, who was employed as a reporter across the floor at *Women's Wear Daily* starting in 2007; prior to that he had worked at a small advertising agency and at Ralph Lauren. He had grown up in Brooklyn and in the Berkshires, his father a literary agent and his mother a lawyer. "He had these perfect liberal parents and was so cosmopolitan in a way," said a former friend from those years. He was charming and handsome and smart. He was a master of social codes too. While Weiss was considered fancy but odd by her *W* and *WWD* coworkers, Axelrod-Welk saw something in her that her cohort didn't. "He always had someone in his orbit and can be incredibly charming and fun to be with," said his friend. "He can also make you feel very important and special. He's very good at sniffing out who is important and who's on the rise."

Axelrod-Welk had been ready to leave legacy media. Then working at *Elle* as a senior fashion news editor, he felt like he was forcing his editorial voice. "What I found there, I would catch myself having spent a day writing in the voice of a woman. What does a gay man who doesn't wear women's clothes have to say about a personal style decision? You know, 'Oh my God, this is the perfect boyfriend sweater'—I was writing this copy that felt silly." He was a fan of what Weiss had created. "What Emily had smartly perceived was there was no receptacle or website of record for beauty street style," Axelrod-Welk told me. "What was beauty street style, that idea of a chic woman outside of La Esquina who was also a brain surgeon with a cat eye and the way she did it with some kohl she got from Morocco or whatever."

He took a huge risk, leaving a job with benefits for a start-up where he wasn't even paid at first. He had to borrow money from his family. But he had a vision. "What my strategy was—and overall taste with editorial—was not the insider writing about the insider-y thing," said Axelrod-Welk, giving the example of *Vogue*'s Hamish Bowles writing about the Belgian designer Dries Van Noten for people who wear Dries Van Noten. "It's not opening up anything." He wanted beauty outsiders whose writing he loved to turn their lens onto beauty. He wanted them to take it seriously but also to keep things fun and experimental, like having a writer for Gawker or *New York* magazine go to a fashion show and write about the backstage hair and makeup. There were even days when he was alone at the office and would try on mascara he'd never wear himself to see if it clumped.

He and Weiss became so inseparable those years that they got delicate matching "10" tattoos just above their elbows. They went on vacation together, including a 2013 New Year's trip to Tulum, Mexico, to see Grimes (years before she famously had children with Elon Musk) play at a concert in the jungle. They both hung out on the beach topless. Toplessness was a theme at Into the Gloss too. "And we shot everyone topless, you know, like we shot everybody with their boobs . . . like everyone was no-shirts," said Weiss. She seemed uncharacteristically more relaxed during those years. Style-wise, she was going through a kind of grunge-chic tomboyish phase. She cut her long brunette hair short and then bleached it blond and lived in Rag & Bone skinny jeans. "I'm probably not a fashion person, first of all because I wear basically the same thing every single day: jean shorts or jeans and sneakers, and I don't experiment in a huge way with my look or spend so much time these days trying to pick out my outfit in the morning," she said in 2013. "I'm much more about doing my creative projects but then also hanging out with all my college friends or going skateboarding on the weekends." On Into the Gloss, she wrote, "My musical inclinations are fine and dandy within the confines of my ears and my earphones, but don't sit well with others. Or, more precisely, when I'm sitting with others. Naked. . . . And so I ask you, dear readers, like a forlorn dude writing a letter to *Playboy* in the year 1983: what are the all-time best albums and songs to hook up to?" Weiss was enjoying the single life. Even if she wasn't hiding the people she was dating from the denizens of cafés and dinner parties, it remains something she has never commented on publicly. Weiss *The Hills* girl, Weiss the Ralph

Lauren intern, had evolved from covering the cool downtown set into becoming one of them. What allowed her to change was the success she had found on her own terms.

Into the Gloss relaunched in July of 2012, and "we basically tripled our traffic overnight. Now we get about 8.5 million pageviews a month, and about 300,000 unique visits," Weiss reported in 2013. Beyond just the early ad buy from Lancôme, Coty and Estée Lauder were among other big advertisers to buy custom sponsored or integrated content. A Harvard Business School case study reported that, with advertisers happy, Into the Gloss's "advertising revenue soon reached $5 million," although no date is given.

While Weiss was becoming a de facto businessperson who manages others at such a young point, she was reluctant to give up control. Even though in her introductory post she called Into the Gloss a blog, she was adamant with employees that it was not merely a blog but an "editorial website." She still did a lot herself. "Don't, like, make me sound like an asshole who tries to take credit for everything—because everyone did a zillion things. All I'm trying to say is I was very involved," Weiss told me.

Into the Gloss molded the aesthetic of an era: the status hand wash (Aesop Resurrection), the expensive exfoliating toner everyone swears will change your skin (Biologique Recherche's P50), the beloved French pharmacy cream (Embryolisse), the blackest mascara (Diorshow in Black Out), the hairbrush no one could live without (Mason Pearson). And its fans were not just readers; they were customers: beauty obsessives who were all too willing to discuss in exhaustive detail what kinds of products they dreamt of. Readers loved the social currency of being able to casually mention a cult brand like the natural German line Weleda in conversation. Into the Gloss had a different aesthetic than the jewelry and beauty photography that ran in magazines, neither Naomi Campbell eating pasta with massive Bulgari jewels on her hands nor the precise still lifes of Irving Penn. What was important to readers of the site was not just the portraits of people or the product shots, but what else could be glimpsed in their homes, recalling the quote from the socialist writer William Morris, "Have nothing in your houses that you do not know to be useful, or believe to be beautiful." There might be a few delicate gold rings in a ceramic dish, or the rose-and-blackcurrant-scented Diptyque candle that had been turned into a makeup brush holder when it was burned down. People even created a name for the photo of perfectly arranged beauty products: the shelfie. This helped propel the idea of beauty as less a necessary labor of being female and more a form of self-expression for anyone of any gender. But to go even further, it created a connection and a community. Into the Gloss was trying to create a club where your affiliation with a brand indicated your tribe.

In the heyday of Into the Gloss there was a tweet that was widely circulated among its readers. A man posted to Twitter that he wanted to date the kind of woman who had Biologique Recherche P50 exfoliating toner in her bathroom. What sounds indecipherable is actually saying quite a bit. This guy is referencing the prototypical Top Shelf. He is declaring online that he wants to be with a woman who knows about a $100 beauty product from a cult French brand. Not only that, but one who buys and displays it because it's a signifier of self and identity, just as much as subscribing to HBO for Sunday night shows or owning a Nespresso machine or an iPhone is. Those products we buy are a shorthand for what we want to say about ourselves, our status.

In the recommendations for Into the Gloss, Weiss identified a powerful change in the way people exchanged information. Everyone thought Jeff Bezos was doing something really outlandish when he allowed mere customers to review Amazon products in 1995, turning the internet into the world's most powerful review tool. "Unlike the valued book club reviewer, who may be cozily challenged by companionable discourse, Amazon's 'customer reviewer' goes uncontested and unedited: the customer is always right. And the customer, the star of this shoddy procedure, controls the number of stars that reward or denigrate writers," wrote the critic Cynthia Ozick in 2007 in a scathing critique of the peer review system in *Harper's* magazine. What Weiss was after was the dwindling divide between the expert versus the customer, which was similar to something Bezos identified with the online reviewer versus the critic. "But if you think about how women shop and how women speak to each other about beauty, it's not about experts. Most women buy products based on what their friends recommend," Weiss said. "This idea of expert versus customer doesn't exist as much anymore and I think people understand now that an advertisement you see in a magazine is not reality. People have trust issues with these giant beauty companies."

Into the Gloss captured so much of what was pivotal to

this new era of beauty: recognizing the power of personal affiliation, of embracing and monetizing the idea that this-is-what-I-use is deeply linked to this-is-who-I-am. Weiss's beauty blog defined the trends that are now the norm on social media, chiefly the trope of "get ready with me," which is now an established TikTok genre. "I got a master's in the state of beauty through Into the Gloss," Weiss said. "All the weird hang-ups people have about beauty, the double standards of beauty. How beauty can start conversations, how beauty can break down walls, and how beauty is something that every single person everywhere in the world deals with. It's really foundational to who you are and how you relate."

Weiss soon learned that Into the Gloss was like an all-access pass to meet all manner of powerful people. "I could not only meet Arianna Huffington but go into her bathroom and spend two hours with her, and then make her in turn feel really seen and heard. Because she reads the article that I edited painstakingly from four a.m. to eight a.m." That was the real brilliance of her plan. She found the door to high-powered people through something seemingly prosaic but actually deeply personal: their beauty routines. Somebody without Weiss's access and privilege couldn't have pulled this off. And yet it came across so much more "real" than any other website or magazine.

Was Weiss's stupendously type A personality biding its time for what was next? "There was no real strategy—and certainly not a business strategy," she told the *Business of Fashion* in 2015 of her initial plans with Into the Gloss, denying there was a product component in the works from the beginning. What exactly made her surpass the wealthy women I've interviewed who started ventures such as activist cashmere companies? The difference was her ambition. I had never seen anything like it.

Into the Gloss wasn't just a blog that built up reader loyalty but a test market for her next project. In the summer of 2014, in the twilight of the Obama years, when Kim Kardashian and Kanye West got married and Gwyneth Paltrow and Chris Martin introduced the world to the concept of "conscious uncoupling," Into the Gloss started teasing the launch of something new that would be called Glossier. Even the pronunciation was a mystery! Within a week, this mystery brand had 13,000 Instagram followers who kept refreshing their phones for updates, but it was just photos of pink flowers and color swatches and smiling faces. A mood board online.

But celebrating beautiful things on a uniquely visual platform was always going to mean selling beautiful things.

Kirsten Green thought she and Emily Weiss were just having tea at the Mercer Kitchen.

Green, a former retail analyst on Wall Street, was in her early forties. The founder of Forerunner Ventures, a venture capital firm that she had started just a year prior in 2012, she was conventionally beautiful, with big, bright eyes, auburn hair, and a warm smile. Green began by investing modestly (less than $1 million) and early in Dollar Shave Club, which would be acquired in 2016 by the personal care conglomerate Unilever for $1 billion. She had similar success with her Jet.com investment when Walmart bought it, also in 2016, but for $3.3 billion. All that was still in the future in 2013, but Green clearly had an eye for retail. Her fund would go on to be synonymous with successfully defining direct-to-consumer (DTC) brands of the era. In other words, a brand that sells directly to the end user, bypassing retail partners. Avon and Tupperware and Girl Scout Cookies are legacy DTC brands, but the category became synonymous with the rise of e-commerce businesses backed by Green: eyeglasses company Warby Parker, Outdoor Voices, the luggage company Away, the telehealth companies

Hers and Hims, and the haircare brand Prose, among others. I asked her in 2022 to describe her mega-successful portfolio's evolution. "A lot of DTC companies, I say in air quotes," she replied. But really, Green prefers to say that she likes companies that operate at the intersection of change, that disregard the rules of the past. In 2017, Green was number twelve on a *New York Times* list of the top twenty venture capitalists using performance as a ranking: the return on investment for a given fund's performance as a result of the underlying portfolio companies raising money at higher valuations, being acquired, or going public. This is all to say that Kirsten Green was and is a big deal, a rare woman in a very male-dominated field, a number that, circa 2013, hovered at less than 10 percent. She was a dream investor for Weiss.

Green knew of Into the Gloss and was intrigued by how, with just an upstart blog, Weiss was able to not only corral such a set of in-the-know beauty people, but also connect with them and her audience. She was impressed from a consumer standpoint and was curious about Weiss's plans. Hence the tea.

"I am not going to be able to tell you exactly what Emily had on, but it was obvious she was very chic—her whole poise, the way she held herself. I was immediately drawn to her confidence and her warmth," said Green. "I thought, 'Wow, I really like her.'" Green appreciated that Weiss was curious about what she did and wasn't awkward about what she didn't know. Green called her "a student of her audiences." Weiss asked great questions, and she really listened. There was something special in the way she was interested in what Green had to say; the quality of Weiss's attention gave a rarefied air to the meeting. Green felt on the edge of her seat and could tell that Weiss did too.

Weiss had never had a problem asking people for things, and showed Green what she had. Weiss knew she was onto something different and big with Into the Gloss. She had a lot of ideas about all the things her unique content and community could lead to, and she wanted Green's opinion. What she presented that morning in spring 2013 at the Mercer Kitchen was less of a pitch and more of a work-in-progress conversation about her plans.

Weiss's idea to expand Into the Gloss into something that could be monetized even further had been percolating for more than a year. "The way I was thinking about it was, how do you make an entire beauty company based on acknowledging that everyone is their own expert? You have an opinion about beauty that actually someone else will probably benefit from," Weiss said, giving the example of someone shopping at Sephora and texting a friend, "I'm in Sephora, should I get that thing you told me about?" She was frustrated that beauty brands were making products based on the needs of retailers like Sephora or department stores. Their real clients weren't customers, but retailers. These needs were based on things like seasonality and margin and shelf space but, Weiss thought, had very little to do with the customer, or at least not enough.

She had been sitting in bathrooms since 2010, listening to women talk about products. What if a beauty brand did that? What if you could ask a question about what your ideal face mask would be like and get a thousand responses from people who bought a lot of masks? Market researchers can ask consumers questions, but it's not so easy (or, for that matter, inexpensive) to ask a large number of exactly the right consumers. Weiss had created a forum where she could do just that. The consumer's path to purchasing was, increasingly, changing. The mall no longer reigned supreme; discovery through websites and social media seemed more enticing to people—and potentially more profitable.

Green was enjoying the conversation, but she didn't think Weiss's idea was fully formed. She was genuinely interested, and excited about Weiss. Investors like Green like to see that a thoughtful business stands behind a novel idea, but they're also looking for answers to questions such as: How big is the market? Can it scale? Can it be profitable? What's the competition? Exactly how much money needs to be raised? Green asked Weiss to provide a PowerPoint presentation about her idea at a later meeting to give her something more concrete to consider.

Weiss had managed to build Into the Gloss initially as a small business. It was a content company with Weiss functioning as a kind of editor or publisher, in the vein of what Refinery29 was doing for fashion or what Well+Good or Goop was doing for wellness. What she wanted for her next venture was something different. She saw it as a start-up. Weiss called that moment 10/10 on the Crazy Idea Scale. "To build a product company from scratch, it would take money up front. How much money, and what kind of money (bank loan? parent's loan? venture capital? private equity?) is a unique decision for every business . . . so we went with venture—the stuff fast-growth, tech-enabled companies like Facebook, Amazon, and Apple are made of," Weiss wrote on Into the Gloss in 2013.

All such companies—whether it's Uber, Seamless, Casper, or Glossier—share a format. Start-ups, it should be noted, are not to be confused with companies that just started. Nor are they small businesses, though they can start small. Rather, they are companies designed for fast growth. They have something to develop and bring to market, and they want to do it stat! They're most often associated with the tech sector, but they don't have to be. Many of the companies featured on Weiss's apartment bookshelves began as start-ups, Nike and Apple among them. They need to raise money to grow, so it's important for a founder to be the kind of person, like Weiss, who is good in the room, as they say in Hollywood—great at pitching herself and her ideas. In terms of funding, there are preliminary rounds, where founders and their friends and family (a.k.a. angel investors) can invest; then come initial investors, often rich people (a.k.a. "high-net-worth individuals" who contribute from their "family offices"). These are followed by a series of funding rounds usually led by venture capital firms like Green's; and finally, there's an "exit" for those earlier-stage investors, where the company goes public or is acquired. Oh, and many start-ups—like almost all of them—fail before anyone finds fame or fortune.

Finding funding for Glossier was not straightforward. Emily Weiss was well-connected in her New York fashion and beauty and media milieu, so she was able to enlist friends and mentors, including Ben Gorham, who founded the fragrance brand Byredo, and Jeanine Lobell, the creator of the makeup line Stila, for small initial investments. (No one would give the exact number, but financiers with knowledge of Weiss and Glossier estimated the total from angel investors to be less than $250,000.) Weiss wanted to start raising money from established venture capital funds for this larger project beyond the editorial aspirations of Into the Gloss. She was seeking a million dollars, based on little more than a hunch. "I believed that it was going to be scary," she said, but she also believed that "people were really going to love it a lot." Going the venture capital route would allow her to raise the money she needed, and to do it fast.

Karlie Kloss was a bona fide supermodel of the era and had appeared quite early in Into the Gloss's short life span, doing a Top Shelf in November 2010. She talked about her love for Crest 3D Advanced Vivid toothpaste and a face highlighter stick from Madina Milano she'd heard you could get only in Italy. In 2012, Kloss started dating Josh Kushner, the founder of the venture capital fund Thrive Capital. During the Into the Gloss days, around 2013, Kloss introduced Kushner (whom she married in 2018) and his business partner Nabil Mallick to Weiss. It was like a model-to-venture-capitalist pipeline. Into the Gloss built credibility with beautiful and interesting women who happened to be connected to wealthy men.

Weiss felt like an outsider to the world of venture capital. She wasn't a man and she hadn't gone to business school. "There's a lot of, like, 'Who do you know?' and 'Who did you work with?' And you're like, 'Hey, you guys want to build something together?'" Weiss said. The tone of the conversations, taking place in conference rooms or restaurants, was often nonchalant and natural, but there was also the underlying tension of whether they would actually invest. "So, like, originally they're just betting on an idea," Weiss said. And even if you meet with powerful people, you still need a product. Mallick was impressed with the first Glossier mood board with its photos of Kate Moss early in her career and girls eating big slices of watermelon. He saw Weiss's aesthetic vision, but Thrive didn't invest in the company right away. They wanted to stay in contact and keep a close eye on the company, and they would do one more thing: introduce her to Kirsten Green.

In hindsight, Weiss claims a level of naïveté about the experience. "I was like, what is VC money? I mean, let's not forget I went to art school, I did not go to business school, I did not work at a tech company," she said. Weiss has a tendency to speak in that manner—undermining herself. It's hard to tell if she's playing down her intelligence and ambition or if she really was that clueless and was following the advice of others. She has an almost irresponsible drive to show how little she worked to get where she is, but at the same time will bristle at your saying she is privileged. She is clearly someone with a lot of determination but who also wants the world to think she lucked out, which is something deeper to do with Weiss's inner beliefs about herself and self-mythmaking. But if she has any interest in modeling a path for younger women entrepreneurs, it's a strange stance that she doesn't take herself seriously. Or rather, tries to hide her work while also valorizing work itself. This is what feminist writers in books like *Reviving Ophelia* and *Playing Big* have talked about all along regarding women downplaying achievements in the classroom and now out in the business world. The problem Weiss found herself wrestling with was wanting to be both relatable and likable, which is a trap not just for female executives, but for all women.

Securing funding wasn't some foregone conclusion. She had plenty of conviction, but Weiss knew the odds of getting the money she wanted were against her. In 2018, she said, "Four percent of venture capital deals last year went to female CEOs, so four out of a hundred deals went to women. So already it's like, well, how am I going to fund this thing?"

Each meeting with a new firm was an exercise in whether serendipity might happen. Henry Davis, a Brit who had gone to Stanford Business School and was now living in Geneva, Switzerland, was working for Index Ventures, where a big topic of conversation was emerging sectors and themes coming up around technology and the internet. One of the things Index, and Davis in particular, was interested in was what he was calling "brand commerce," or the new wave of direct-to-consumer brands like Warby Parker, Harry's for men's grooming, and the clothing companies Everlane and Bonobos. Davis thought that the very concept of DTC companies had a lot of potential. This wasn't merely about having the best price. "That was a race to the bottom, and size always wins," he said. He spoke like a lot of business school alums, in dazzling, jargon-packed statements that reflected a great deal of confidence and were always on message. A DTC brand could have an innovative product, and the ability to engage directly with customers could change the way customers interacted with brands. Which was exactly what Weiss was pitching.

Davis had been making his way between Switzerland, London, New York, and the Bay Area, trying to meet as many people as he could working in that DTC space. It's a fine line between meeting with someone who speaks well with good ideas and knowing that they're worth taking a risk to invest in them. Everyone told him to seek out Emily Weiss, and in 2013 they had a meeting at the Crosby Street Hotel. Weiss's first pitch was not a beauty company. It was: "I'm going to build a social experience on top of my blog, I'm going to make Top Shelf shoppable." Weiss envisioned something that was social network meets e-commerce. An app was mentioned. "These were the giddy days when content was everything. Refinery29 and Vox were raising these huge rounds of funding," recalled Davis. Weiss was wondering if she should do a spin on Refinery29 but with beauty instead of fashion—really go in the media and content and advertising direction.

But then she told him something else she had been thinking about: products that work really well geared toward her generation and not her mother's. "I was like, that's the thing, do that," said Davis. It was seductive in the same way that talking about beauty recommendations was seductive, like being let in on a secret. It's no wonder Weiss found these venture capitalists compelling. Starting a beauty company is so expensive, it would be prohibitive to most people, especially with venture capitalists notoriously poor at championing female leaders and female-focused industries. It costs about $1.5 million from marketing to staffing to manufacturing to launch a beauty company, according to *Vogue Business*. Davis was excited by what Weiss said—but Index didn't invest. Davis insisted that he and Weiss were just talking, and that it was unlikely she would get a deal done with Index, which wasn't really making seed investments in New York–based companies.

Meetings were becoming something of a routine for Weiss. After giving her pitch in a conference room or a coffee shop about the community they had built at Into the Gloss, how she understood that they deserved a better brand, and that the beauty industry was huge and ripe for disruption, she would end by handing out products. "We had our little goody bags and would bring them to different rooms full of guys and have them get the bag and say, 'Oh, that's so nice, thank you. I'm gonna give it to my wife and ask her what she thinks,'" Weiss said. This incensed her. "I would say to myself, if some financial technology company came to me and pitched me, I wouldn't be like, 'Oh, I'm going to go ask my husband to explain this to me,' I would learn about it. I would be like, 'Show me your product, let me understand this. Let me put it on the back of my hand. Can you tell me about how people use this product?'" Some of them did, but a lot of them didn't. What about the people who absolutely didn't get it? I asked Weiss. "It's a part of life. Rejection is a part of life," she said. A dozen investors Weiss met with subsequently said no. Rejection is a common motif in founder tales. Jamie Siminoff, who founded the security system Ring, was rejected not just by the TV show *Shark Tank* but by so many investors, he claims to have lost count; the data storage company Adaptive Insights is said to have been rejected by seventy VCs. (Those companies both achieved unicorn status, proof that history is often written by the winners.) Weiss didn't seem sad or regretful but rather had the air of someone who had, in 2022, gotten to the easy part. But how did she deal? What were those emotions like? "Yeah, I mean, I don't really remember if I was up all night crying but I don't think so." This is how Weiss is a master of wielding vulnerability as a tool in her toolkit—she so often denies emotion but highlights emotions. "She was like, 'Oh, this is really crazy. I can't believe I'm doing this,'" recalled an employee at Into the Gloss. Weiss would go to a meeting and return to the office and update the crew on how it had gone. "I felt really endeared," the employee said.

Green, like some of the other VCs, thought Weiss's concept was all a bit murky—too many things at once, that Weiss should start with one to really build out a business. Green calls herself a yes person. It's ironic because the vast majority of the time she says no. In 2022 alone, she would see 6,000 pitches and make six investments. And she said no to Weiss. "I did not invest in the pitch Emily showed me that day or the days that followed," Green said. "It was compelling as a vision for the company, but it wasn't obvious how executable it would be out of the gate."

But Green wanted to take some kind of chance on Weiss. She had the success of Dollar Shave Club behind her and the luxury of working for herself, so she didn't have to answer to anyone. She thought of every investment as a partnership. So she didn't invest in the first pitch, or immediately thereafter, but together, over many long conversations over several months, Green and Weiss landed on beauty products as a starting point that made sense to take to market. It didn't hurt that beauty products could have as much as a 90 percent profit margin. Developing an app was an expensive and much more abstract endeavor. They didn't throw away the idea, but rather shelved it as a next phase of the company. Green agreed to invest $1 million in Glossier.

That money went toward rent on a larger office, hiring a chemist, buying inventory, building out tech components, and growing the Glossier staff—because Weiss was about to disappear while she developed her first line of beauty products. Into the Gloss's small staff was working in the office on Broadway in NoHo, and Weiss lived around the corner on Bleecker Street. "I basically was like, 'Guys, I'm gonna leave for nine months. Like, I'm literally gonna go have a baby. I'm gonna go to my apartment building and make Glossier.'" Not all of the staff really understood what was going on. Kim Johnson, an intern who had left to go abroad her junior year, had made her way back to Into the Gloss in 2014 when Glossier was being conceptualized—it didn't even have a name yet. "I had no idea what they were up to and eventually learned they were making products, and didn't think much of it," she said. "I was like, 'Awesome, you guys, go for it.'"

4

"It was a middle-of-nowhere place and we pulled into the parking lot, it's empty, there's a stray dog roaming through and tumbleweeds blowing," Weiss said. This was her inauspicious start to developing Glossier's first products. Their destination was an odd little mirrored building that blocked her view of anything or anyone inside. She almost wanted to just turn and leave—this couldn't possibly be the guy who was going to make their products, she told herself. Instead, she went inside and was greeted by a six-foot-four man Weiss described as a "jacked dad." And he was more enthusiastic about women's skincare than anyone she had ever met.

"We" in this scenario was Weiss and Alexis Page, her new director of product development. Since Weiss had zero idea how to start making products, Page was her first hire with her new venture capital. Page had grown up in South Buffalo, very into reading magazines as a means of discovery and fantasy and transporting herself away into more glamorous locales. Her grandmother and aunts lived together, and she'd go to their home to sleep over and watch Miss America pageants and play with their makeup.

Page moved to New York City at eighteen in 2000 to go to the Fashion Institute of Technology, choosing the advertising and communications program because it was the only one that didn't require a portfolio to apply. Through a roommate, she worked assisting some makeup artists backstage at a fashion show, who told her about FIT's cosmetics and fragrance marketing program, and she ended up getting her degree there. It was a relatively small department at the time, about twenty students, and Estée Lauder was a supporter of the program and assisted students with placements. Page got an internship with the product development team at Lauder-owned MAC Cosmetics; she stayed at MAC for a decade, creating formulas, shades, and seasonal collections, as well as heading up collaborations.

Weiss found Page by thinking about which beauty brand had the best and most popular products and who was developing them. Weiss's philosophy was to hire for her own weaknesses, to know what she didn't know and surround herself with the most talented people she could find. Page was at a Chloé fashion show, working backstage with a MAC makeup artist, which Weiss was covering for Into the Gloss. Weiss started pitching Page on coming to work for her new beauty line (Page's boss was right next to her). But it worked, and she went over to Glossier.

Page got a recommendation for a cosmetic chemist based outside Los Angeles who had supposedly developed some of the most blockbuster products with brands that were household names. Which was how Weiss and Page ended up flying out to California, getting a Hertz rental car, and driving in rush-hour traffic out to the farthest exurbs to meet the man who would help create their products.

Weiss likened the development process between them and the chemist to working with an architect. "One of us might go to them knowing exactly what we want with exactly the ingredients and the exact approach to sustainability and exact budget and might be super involved, and the other one of us may be like, 'I kind of want a white house,'" she said. "The development process was a back-and-forth of shipping samples across the country between each other with notes. And we would spend on average maybe two or three months or four months of shipping samples back and forth and riffing off each other." They'd talk about whether the coverage of a foundation product was too sheer or too pigmented or too viscous; if the texture of a balm was moisturizing or too tacky on the lips; if a spray felt sticky on the skin or absorbed quickly; or if a smell was weird in a bad way. At the lab, the chemist had a little room full of ingredients, called raw materials in the cosmetic chemist world, and Weiss particularly liked it when he'd open a jar and tell her to smell something or scoop out a cream. It was like being in a kitchen with a chef.

Even though the bulk of Page's experience at MAC had been in color cosmetics, Weiss knew she wanted to start out with skincare basics: a mist to prime the face, a light moisturizer, a salve that could be used on the lips or any particularly dry area of the body. The idea was that those three products would create a smooth surface on the face, filling in pores and texture, and it would finish with a very sheer skin tint to even out skin tone. "I wanted skincare as makeup," Weiss said. "I think what's really important about your skin and getting your makeup right is having this moisturized, glowy, fresh, even complexion. And then you take it or leave it with color products and treat them as decoration, not as a mask."

They called the four-product launch Phase One, which was a nod to the streetwear-style merchandise drop, but also a subtle allusion to this being the first phase—not the totality—of the Glossier plan. It was an $80 set made up of four products priced from $12 to $26: rose-scented Soothing Face Mist, a light Priming Moisturizer, a rich Balm Dotcom salve, and a Perfecting Skin Tint. Glossier's products were priced competitively, somewhere between drugstore and department store brands. Weiss said she wanted to rethink what luxury meant and what the luxury experience should give customers.

In order to understand the foundations of Glossier that Alexis Page brought to fruition, it's important to understand Clinique. The brand came onto the market in 1968, partly the brainchild of Evelyn Lauder, the daughter-in-law of Estée Lauder and wife of Leonard Lauder, who had seen "Clinique Esthétique" signs in France, and thought the name made the brand sound alluringly French and scientific. The line was developed under the code name "Miss Lauder" because it was to be youthful, on par with the energy of the women's liberation movement of the late 1960s. Their big idea was to marry the idea of youth with a layer of science and a sprinkle of customization. The brand was for you, not for someone you looked up to. For generations of people, Clinique was the first beauty purchase just for them, with a bonus hint of prestige. (And if you were lucky, you could spend enough to get a coveted gift with your purchase, a suite of mini products in a tiny travel bag.) It was an early way to indoctrinate oneself into the world of an adult brand, and something that could be all yours. In stores, the sales associates even wore white lab coats (and smooth hair and silver jewelry were preferred), and the core skincare product was a 3-Step Skin Care System—that now familiar green-packaged facial soap, the blue toning Clarifying Lotion, and the yellow Dramatically Different Moisturizer.

No company had tried to make a modern version of the Clinique system until Glossier.

"The word 'glossier' was thrown around as something we could have used when we were talking about what was the future of Into the Gloss," Weiss said. The word "gloss" had been mentioned as a potential offshoot, and Weiss liked the name Glossier as rhyming and riffing off the word "dossier." (One problem was that the pronunciation was never clear to anyone from the outset. When I first saw the word, I assumed it was "gloss-ee-er," like it was more glossy than Into the Gloss.) "I was always super inspired by magazines and media. And the reason I like 'dossier' is because it's a collection of stories, right? I was in a relationship with *Vogue*. I subscribed to *Vogue*. I had a subscription; I was a card-carrying member of *Vogue* magazine to the tune of twenty-nine ninety-nine a year, or whatever it was." The issue of

Vogue Weiss got in the mail each month built upon the previous month's issue, and each issue had a different signature section. "How could you create a brand that would have these products that build into your collection and you could follow along with each new product launch?" Her definition of "dossier" is of course imprecise, but even so, a dossier is a collection of documents about someone that, if reviewed, can tell you what you need to know to define that person.

At the end of 2013, Glossier had a half dozen employees. Glossier was the name of the as-yet-to-be-launched product line, but already Into the Gloss had been subsumed, operating as the editorial arm of Glossier. Into the Gloss was still all the public knew about and was updated with new content three to five times per day, five days per week. Tom Newton was taking photos, Axelrod-Welk was the head of editorial, and Annie Kreighbaum, a writer and editor whose beauty blogging had led Weiss to recruit her via a Twitter direct message, was providing content. Kreighbaum's post in January 2014 about the makeup and beauty rituals she did as a University of Texas Chi Omega House sorority girl was considered one of the best at Into the Gloss. ("Tell a young girl with a poor body image that something as simple as napping naked in a heated pod will help her look skinnier and clear acne, and she'll do it every day.") "I think they thought I was funny. A lot of beauty writing didn't have as much personality. It kind of comes naturally to me to overshare," Kreighbaum said. Besides Page, Weiss hired Henry Davis as Glossier's chief operating officer, also in 2014.

That was a magical time: Into the Gloss was at its prime and Glossier was being developed and there was a sense that everyone was building something together. Sometimes the office looked and felt like all the clichés from a movie montage about young people working together. Weiss drew furiously on whiteboards and amassed mood boards—all her life's work and interests over the past ten years collected on them. She has a photo of herself in front of the Glossier whiteboard with two green hard wax plugs in her nose. She was waiting for the wax to dry to wax her nose and pointing at a list of a dozen things that needed to be done to launch Glossier: raise money, build website, find chemist, make logo . . .

They moved the office down a few blocks to a very white space with lofted ceilings and floor-to-ceiling arched windows at 123 Lafayette Street in SoHo. "On every floor, employees radiate good health and subtle highlighter," wrote a BuzzFeed reporter. "This is the kind of office where an administrative coordinator or front-end engineer can, and does, double as a model for the company's Instagram account, FaceTime tutorials, and Facebook Live videos." A new employee might be met with a big hug, and whoever was the most free would walk them through a tour and onboarding paperwork, passing by other people in their twenties who were using a turkey baster to put together samples for the press or packing up samples for the stylist Stevie Dance's studio or sending them to Beyoncé. Someone else might be cutting out sticker sheets with smiley faces and *Glossier* written in script by hand. Glossier was growing but not at the rate of some other companies drunk on capital. "It wasn't 'We're hiring ten people a day to grow-grow-grow,'" said an employee who was hired before Glossier was formally launched to the public. The company was still small enough that they all shared one tiny bathroom that held one towel for drying hands. It always seemed clean, but finally someone asked in a meeting, "Is it really dirty?" Weiss replied, "I take it home every day and I wash it, bring it back." Recalled the employee, "And it was at a time where we were like, 'Do you have bigger things to do?'"

The young team burned through dozens, possibly scores, of Diptyque Baies candles. They did things like have drinks on a Thursday or Friday evening and then hold three-legged races around the desks. They frequented the bakery Maman, the bar Mr. Fong's, and the restaurant Lucky Strike. They were well educated, mostly veterans of the upper middle class who lived in Nolita, the West Village, Williamsburg, Greenpoint: neighborhoods that were certainly hip but thoroughly gentrified and central. They hung out together at work, after work, and on the weekends.

But the idyll didn't last for very long. Davis, installed as COO and soon promoted to president, was trying to build a real business for Glossier. Into the Gloss was more of a fun and creative endeavor, but it was aping the media and publishing worlds, which were already outdated, or at least lagging, forms of making money. Why be a media company when they could be a start-up? Weiss was intoxicated by tech venture capitalists and wanted Glossier to be shaped in their image.

Into the Gloss was a company where Weiss and Axelrod-Welk had functioned almost as an editor in chief and a publisher together, often sharing the spotlight. *Elle* called the two of them "the geniuses behind hit beauty-voyeur site Into the

Gloss." The *Business of Fashion* interviewed the pair as part of a series on "fashion's most influential bloggers and their business models." This upset Weiss: she was the one who'd founded Into the Gloss. And then Axelrod-Welk was upset that she was upset. Weiss seemed to be drawn to him until she wasn't. She could have benefited from a trusted second-in-command, but was it him? And did he want that? "She let her guard down and didn't realize it," said a former friend of both. "My impression about the split was someone around her shrewdly told her this guy was trying to take credit for something that was hers and she snapped out of it." He saw before Glossier even existed that Into the Gloss would soon be in its shadow and knew his position in the company pecking order would be very different. "The way he works is you're his friend until he doesn't need you anymore," said that same former friend. "One day Emily wouldn't be of interest to him. It may have been the first and only time he was outsmarted. It must have just hurt him so much."

There was only room for one face of Glossier. Weiss had meticulously planned the company but had done so largely without his involvement, to the point where she was attending meetings and dinners with potential investors without telling him. Axelrod-Welk read the writing on the wall and left Into the Gloss in mid-2014. It was soon after the debut of Into the Gloss x Warby Parker aviator glasses, a project Axelrod-Welk had championed and for which he and Weiss modeled, arm in arm. I recall attending the aviators' lavish launch dinner in the garden of the Waverly Inn, a few months before Glossier debuted, attended by Amy Astley, media reporters, and Annabelle Dexter-Jones, a future star of the TV show *Succession*.

Weiss debated surprise-launching Glossier the way that Beyoncé had dropped her self-titled album the year before. Instead, she teased the company for four weeks on Instagram. Emily Weiss launched Glossier in October 2014 with $2 million in seed funding led by Green and Ben Lerer of Lerer Hippeau and her angel investors. The original Glossier brand strategy statement was: "Born from content; fueled by community."

Weiss wrote a post on Into the Gloss to introduce Glossier.

> Glossier is about living in—and embracing—the now, not the past, and not the future. It's about fun and freedom and being OK with yourself today. It's about being nice to people and knowing that a smile begets a smile. Snobby isn't cool, happy is cool.
>
> Our credo is to follow our gut and rethink products, creating exactly the items that we want to see. Who are we? We are you, listening to everyone, absorbing all of this information over the years, and trying to get at the core of what beauty is—and needs—in 2014. Glossier begins with YOU, which is why our first products are all about letting your personality shine through . . . glowy, dewy skin.
>
> We're laying the foundation for a beauty movement: one that celebrates real girls, in real life. . . . It is the beginning, I hope, of a new way of looking at beauty.

Weiss was adept at making her pronouncements sound like a polished version of the way people talk, which isn't easy to do. But when she declares in the post that "the single guiding principle that I try to follow, assuming blindly that the rest will fall into place, is to operate squarely in the present" doesn't read well now. Only a person who has always had a safety net can say that. For the time being, her fledgling fans were just excited to go along for the Glossier ride. (In fact, Weiss helped deliver the first New York City customers' product via UberRUSH.)

At lunches and in group chats, beauty insiders sniffed that the products weren't remarkable, that they borrowed heavily from existing products. Some went further to say that they were inferior dupes (beauty-speak for a similar "duplicate"), that the Priming Moisturizer was just like Embryolisse Lait Crème Sensitive, an inexpensive cream carried at French pharmacies and found in so many editorial makeup artists' kits; that the Balm Dotcom was like Vaseline; and the Soothing Face Mist was similar to the Mario Badescu Facial Spray with Aloe, Herbs, and Rosewater. "I was not impressed by the performance," said a product developer at a rival company. "Alexis Page is a very talented product developer, but it was basically a Vaseline and a pretty basic moisturizer."

But that's where many experts—product developers, critics, marketers—falter when they try to talk about Glossier. The products didn't need to be revolutionary. Weiss once explained Glossier's appeal and success to John Donahoe, the Nike CEO. He had wondered aloud if it was because they simply had the most effective products. Her response was that he was looking at it the wrong way. Are Nike's shoes the absolute best for performance, and that's what makes it one of the most successful companies in the world? No, of course not.

Weiss shrugged when asked whether she felt competitive with other products. "How many lip balms do you own? Zillions," she said. "We're not saying we make the best of everything for everyone." The vast majority of beauty products are based upon existing products. How many variations of red lipstick are there, or concealers, or eye creams? The key to a product's success lies not in being something entirely new. What makes a product successful is a combination of performance, price, marketing, and packaging. Is there a perceived sense of prestige? Are cool and influential people wearing the brand? Because, frankly, there's not a great deal of difference on a chemical or ingredient level between many products, and many supposedly key or active ingredients have little scientific basis for their efficacy. Which doesn't mean that women who buy into the fantasy of Glossier or drugstore makeup on the lower end or department store brands on the higher end are naïve. Consumers certainly want products that work, but what they also need is a compelling story, a collective fantasy and aspiration they can tap into.

From the beginning, there were issues with the Skin Tint. Lipstick is the number one bestseller in beauty products, but foundation is where people spend the most and, as a bonus, they're usually loyal once they find one they like. Skin Tint was meant to be sheer. "I'm scared of foundation," Weiss said in an interview with *Elle* upon the launch. In the article's words: " 'You can't f-ck it up,' she says, working a generous dab of Glossier Perfecting Skin Tint—her answer to the foundation problem—into her bare cheeks and forehead. 'If this were a regular foundation, I would look like pancake face.'"

Even though it came in only three shades, the team thought that would suffice for the debut of Phase One and planned to expand the range later. It's expensive to launch with a huge color range for foundation. But the shades skewed very, very light, even for something so sheer. (I normally wear whatever the lightest shade of foundation is, and in the original Glossier Skin Tint I wore Medium, the middle of the Light, Medium, and Rich shade trio.) There were certainly people in the office—Page came from MAC Cosmetics and its massive shade range—or who were testing products who pointed out that the darkest shade wouldn't be dark enough, and could easily anticipate consumer backlash if they didn't offer a dozen shades. Their complaints were said to be noted, but Weiss didn't seem to pay them much mind. She won't ever comment on it directly; the closest I have come to hearing her point of view on the issue was an aside in a 2018 interview: "If we had a super-high-coverage foundation product then that would require us to make, you know, fifty shades or something or fifty-five shades or something like that, which would be almost impossible to sell online. I would have a really hard time, like, shade-matching myself. If there were fifty shades of something I would not know how to do that. Um, but what we can do is create, you know, a product . . . that's super intuitive, that's super easy to use, that doesn't deposit too much."

Some Weiss defenders say the mistakes were simply emblematic of an earlier, less thoughtful era. "Three shades was obviously a different time, I'll put it that way," said one former employee, cautiously dismissive. A few other employees used phrases like "in hindsight." As MAC and the later success of Fenty had shown, though, this was a major oversight, and a mistake in anticipating the needs of the customer. When you make just three shades, you are saying quite clearly whom you value as a customer and whom you're marketing to. Glossier could have waited until they had more shades to launch the tint. Phase One could have debuted with just three products—a sheer foundation felt like a bit of an outlier anyway. It was a baffling decision both from the position of inclusivity and for sensible business. This was particularly galling, as the beauty industry has historically been a place where women and people of color could achieve real financial wealth and power. It was months before Glossier expanded the Skin Tint to five shades. Fans continued to ask for an even greater range of colors. One prominent source was the Instagram account Glossier Brown by blogger Devin McGhee that showcased Glossier fans of color. McGhee told *Glamour*, "Women of color, black women specifically, spend more money than any other demographic on cosmetics. I believe this is mainly because we are constantly having to purchase multiple shades and mix our own to find a match. It can be discouraging and slightly taxing on our pockets." They expanded to twelve in 2019, and Glossier also did away with the naming conventions and just had the shades numbered.

The visual signifiers of Glossier were present from its inception. The first Glossier products came in a pink bubble-wrap bag with a ziplock that was meant to be conspicuous. It functioned as packaging, but also as unbranded merchandise that could double as a clutch. (So one would hope, since the original pouches were made out of a category of plastic that was difficult to recycle.) Jimmy Choo sold a similar clutch for $950. On some yoga retreats it seemed half the women kept their travel essentials in them, and other fans have exchanged nods in security lines at airports with fellow travelers who pulled out their liquids in the same Glossier pouch. For some they are a preferred and slightly chaotic way to file things: a pouch for receipts, another for stray phone and computer cords, another to hold masks and hand sanitizer during the pandemic. The company created them to be recognized by fellow travelers on the Glossier journey so they could find each other and share the same communal experience as in the comments section of Into the Gloss or on Instagram. Weiss could use the connections she leveraged at Into the Gloss not just to develop products but to work with influencers. Not just in the contemporary sense of the word, but also the previously influential: models, actors, magazine editors. Leandra Medine, the founder of Man Repeller and a friend of Weiss's, was spotted carrying a pouch in a street-style shot soon after the line's debut.

Glossier started as a digital company with its marketing focused on Instagram. Eva Chen, Weiss's longtime colleague and the director of fashion partnerships at Instagram, cited the company as an example of how best to use Instagram as a brand. "Their page was never product, product, product," she said. There were pink feathers or napping puppies. "You could close your eyes and imagine what a Glossier girl's or guy's bedroom might look like. It's not a basic fiddle-leaf fig, it's more interesting, like a bird-of-paradise." None of those tropes felt clichéd yet. "In 2013 and 2014, people were following brands liberally on Instagram, which was new," said Emily Parr, a former beauty publicist. "The look of packaging was newly important, and it was easier to amass a social media following then, and news, websites, and magazine websites were far less dictated by branded content than they would become in a few years—there's often a motive behind product-driven content now. So brands could tell their story in a way that didn't seem promotional."

To be a digitally native brand, let alone a beauty brand, was groundbreaking at the time. That meant that Glossier was thinking of its assets—photos of products, models, ads, e-commerce—for digital usage in a unified aesthetic. In other words, a user could discover a product on their Instagram page and then go over to the Glossier website to order it on its own product page, and the whole experience was designed to look and feel cohesive. Its product photography was supposed to be recognizable and look good across all channels. Right away the clean and codified look of Glossier was replicated far and wide, with many brands drawing their marketing content (or replicating it, if you want to judge it a bit more harshly) from Glossier: Sephora, Ilia, and Yves Saint Laurent ads all featured clean-faced young people who looked fresh and positive and perfectly imperfect. This is something the brand is well aware of. "We hear from models on set, makeup artists on set, and they text our team pictures of mood boards for other brands. And it's all pictures of Glossier ads," said Weiss. Does that make you feel proud, or do you get annoyed, or what is your reaction? I asked. "I mean, I don't know. I don't. We're always, like, on to the next." Weiss has expressed a version of that breezy refrain frequently. It's how she kept moving forward.

The signature shade for Glossier was a light pink. It wasn't the hue of a nail color or lipstick but rather the unifying color for the brand itself. Not quite as dusty a shade as a ballet slipper and more washed-out than a rose. "I remember two months before we launched the Glossier Instagram—which came before the company—and we were trying to think what to put as the avatar, and our designer made it that color pink, and it just stuck," said Weiss. "We just were like, that looks really good, that looks fresh, let's not make it a G, let's not make it a tiny Glossier, let's leave it pink and have that be the identity."

Leslie David, one of the designers working on Glossier, brought a palette of pastel colors to Helen Steed, the new creative director. Steed recalled, "If you're working with a palette of pastels, then you're not standing for anything. 'Let's reinterpret pink,' said Emily. Pink was more gender-neutral originally. As the brand continued to evolve, it was something we thought we should own."

This was 2014, and that shade of pink, which was a variation of Pantone's 705C, felt new and fresh just the way the Glossier brand did. Fans who followed Into the Gloss and Weiss to the next venture latched on to it. They called it #glossierpink on Instagram, tagging it when they saw it in the wild and giving it a distinct virality: rose quartz, sunsets, needlepoints of proteas, a Victorian home in San Francisco, vintage cocktail glassware, satin hair scrunchies. Sofia Coppola's movies of elegant melancholy were a common source. Some of the customers who were the biggest fans changed their avatars to Glossier pink, the way a superfan of Beyoncé might have their last name on social media be Knowles. "God, it was everywhere after that, but at the time it was unique in beauty and the product world," said Steed. "We had a sophisticated use of the color, this black and white with a touch of pink. It was such a soft shade of pink and we knew where to dial it up."

Glossier didn't own light pink in the public consciousness. It can't be separated from the deluge of pink that was happening in the middle of the 2010s. The fashion writer Véronique Hyland coined the term "millennial pink" in an article for the *Cut*, which she later expanded in her book of essays, *Dress Code*. "In the summer of 2016, I started to see a predominant shade bubbling up on everything that was marketed to me." The shade, she wrote, was particular. "It was a variation on the pink shade I'd always associated with girlhood, not necessarily my girlhood, but the concept at large. Instead of being the saccharine Barbie pink that brings to mind a disembodied squeal of 'Accessories sold separately!' it was a weirdly desaturated hue that seemed stripped of all associations with bubble gum and *Sweet Valley High* book spines." It was a shade engineered to signify femininity with an arched eyebrow—not just feminine but feminist, the equivalent of striking a power pose while wearing a pantsuit in the softest and girliest shade imaginable. Hyland called it "ambivalent girliness." It was both a declaration and a reclamation in one.

A crucial difference was where this specific shade of pink came from. This wasn't something filtered down from runways. The way colors diffuse from a top designer's show into a beauty collection into the mass market and drugstore is similar to the infamous trickle-down "cerulean" speech in *The Devil Wears Prada*. ("But what you don't know is that that sweater is not just blue, it's not turquoise, it's not lapis, it's actually cerulean.") Hyland named that light hue millennial pink because it was so squarely marketed to her generation. "Rather than being some dictated-from-on-high runway 'color of the season,' this was something aimed at the masses, backgrounding subway ads and front book covers as well as the windows of high-end boutiques," she wrote in *Dress Code*. It was on Glossier's branding, she noted in 2016, but also on the bags of the Swedish fashion brand Acne Studios, 2015 ad campaigns for Thinx period underwear, and the poster for Wes Anderson's *The Grand Budapest Hotel*, which came out in March 2014. It was on the covers of Sophia Amoruso's May 2014 memoir *#Girlboss* and Stephanie Danler's 2016 literary sensation about the restaurant industry, *Sweetbitter*. Pink was so ubiquitous for book covers for women that many female writers I know had to go into battle with their publishers over it.

For Glossier, Hyland said to me, "The color tied into both the start-up-y, girlboss roots of the brand and the 'cool girl' culture they sold. The inclusion of pink bubble-wrap packages and stickers had that charming whiff of juvenilia about it, but there was a distinctly millennial flavor to the off-kilter version of the hue, and a rejection of hyper-girliness in the 'no-makeup makeup' items that made up their offering."

On a wall in Glossier's conference room in the Lafayette Street office hung a framed white napkin with the beauty brand's guiding principles scrawled in red lipstick: "Inclusive, Innovative, Clever, Fun, Thoughtful." Not the most radical words, per se, or even words that matched what Glossier was actually doing. (How could a company that used "inclusive" as one of its core tenets have only three shades?) The Glossier slogan is "Skin first, makeup second, smile always" (the telling-people-to-smile part, in the post-#MeToo era, didn't age the best). Another motto they use is "Skincare is essential. Makeup is a choice. (Make good choices.)" The skincare was there for good habits and to promote clean and calm skin, and the makeup was for a little extra something. It would be barely there. Their aesthetic was laissez-faire: stains that come in tubes or sticks meant to be smeared on with fingers rather than artfully blended with an array of brushes. It was the pinnacle of no-makeup makeup.

Makeup made to lightly embellish is at the core of makeup history. Once, it meant using berries or other kinds of natural dyes to tint the lips and cheeks. Your lips, but better. Beauty is inherently unfair. Or rather, it's a reminder that the world is an unfair place. So, is makeup the equalizer? In the decade or two preceding Into the Gloss and Glossier's launches, beauty was a high-maintenance affair. It was the time of the perfect blowout, the Brazilian bikini wax (sometimes even bedazzled with crystals), and the "Bergdorf Blonde," satirized by novelist Plum Sykes, who gets her roots touched up every ten days. Heavily contoured faces were all the rage on YouTube, as were high-coverage foundations and heavy, drawn-in brows. Kylie Jenner was selling lip kits to mimic heavily lined, plump lips. Those who had time and money were dabbling in the 12-step Korean skincare routine. The Glossier ethos was meant to be a response to that, or at least something of a palate cleanser. It was underscored with words like "sheer" and "imperceptible." Skin was so moisturized—to the point of glistening—that they often got complaints that they posted too many photos of shiny girls. There was also an artificiality to it, as if people who used this brand were so effortlessly beautiful and chic that they need not put in effort at all.

Glossier really cracked the "effortless" code in terms of products for consumers. The idea they were communicating was: You're already fantastic, you've taken care of your skin, and now let's have fun. But not too much. "We believe that being yourself and being honest and authentic sells," Weiss said. "If you feel sexy, great. If you feel a little sad today, okay. If you want your freckles and scars to shine through, cool. . . . We're taking a chance that women will respond to this reclamation of beauty and their bodies."

Beauty standards can't be uncoupled from the business of beauty, which has always been, at its core, about the power of perceived positive transformation. I don't think we're ever going to stop wanting that. It's an innate longing we all have as humans. Zadie Smith might have written, "Any woman who counts on her face is a fool," but looking good is a great investment if someone chooses to make that investment. How a person looks can play significantly into their earning power over time—good-looking people are found to be paid about 3 to 4 percent more than their plain colleagues. But, in any case, what's wrong with wanting to spend time on one's beauty? In the 1990s, third-wave feminists championed the reclamation of items previously written off as girly and therefore insipid, such as slumber parties and high heels and pop music. Hadn't women come far enough that they could have hobbies—like applying a flawless red lip—and not be regarded as wasting their brains? And couldn't desire be just that—desire? Did makeup and skincare have to mean so much? The underlying question was: Which is a more honest way to use makeup?

Glossier's models were stunningly beautiful cool girls from the start. Coco Baudelle was a waitress in downtown Manhattan, newly arrived from her native Canada, who just happened to serve Weiss. "And I was like, you're my new muse," said Weiss. "And she really was kind of the original Glossier Girl." It launched Baudelle's modeling career, and she would go on to pose for Chanel. For those like Baudelle, who was shorter than the model average of five nine, and Paloma Elsesser, who wore a larger size than the typical size 2–ish model, Glossier campaigns were some of their first big breaks before magazine covers. Before casting from social media became the norm for model scouts, Glossier did it, or they scouted among friends and employees. (Weiss has, after all, always been phenomenally adept at approaching people and asking for things.) The company's models were racially diverse, young, and attractive, with gap teeth or bushy brows or freckles to show that they weren't too perfect. Many of them were found and cast because they tagged Glossier on selfies they posted on Instagram. However, none of them had awkward hair or acne or visible facial hair. These "real" girls were still held to a standard of beauty: Weiss was looking for character in their faces and for people who seemed comfortable in their own skin. Annie Kreighbaum's trick to scouring Instagram was to look at tagged photos, which give a more realistic idea of what someone looks like than those they post themselves. The user was the ad: Glossier crowdsourced so much of their imagery that they elevated their eager customer base to the (unpaid) position of campaign face. Or, at least, the most Glossier Girl version of the user. One former Glossier employee suggested to me that, at first, they secretly art-directed the selfies sent to them by their fans, to solidify and streamline the Glossier aesthetic. After a time, they no longer had to do that—after enough photos of users with dewy skin and thick brows gazing dreamily into the camera, their audience got it.

For the first Glossier shoot, "in order for the expressions not to be sinister, sinewy glances, they were throwing little pieces of bread at the models and the models were trying to catch it with their mouths," says Eva Alt, who worked in social media at Glossier. Glossier crowdsourced these effortless and chic "everyday girls" who were far from everyday. This democratic approach extended itself to office life; for their first ad campaign in 2014, Weiss asked staff to vote on their favorite images from the shoot using colored stickers.

Glossier didn't invent the perfectly imperfect model, but they built on an already successful framework. When Dove's Campaign for Real Beauty from 2005 debuted, it was groundbreaking, the idea of using "unconventional" women as models to sell products. The campaign was a sensation in the ad world just for showing gray-haired women or women with cellulite or women with a lot of freckles as being—*gasp!*—beautiful. That kind of love-yourself-the-way-you-are messaging seems normal now. But it didn't in the mid-2000s, when it was much discussed in the media and beyond. I remember a friend's boyfriend weighing in when he overheard us discussing it. We were two writers and he was just an average-looking guy who worked in a coffee shop, yet he still felt fine telling us that those real-life models would never catch on because men wanted ads with beautiful women.

The fact that the models cast by Glossier were quite conventionally attractive, mostly slim, presumably cis women seemed a little retro, or at least not all that progressive. "As someone who struggled with skin issues, it almost made me feel worse about myself," said a former employee, of the no-makeup makeup that Glossier espoused. "They're selling you this sheer tint and all these girls have perfect faces without acne. I thought, 'They are selling a concealer for people who don't have pimples.'"

The aesthetic could be seen as a rebuttal to Oscar Wilde's quote: "A man's face is his autobiography. A woman's face is her work of fiction." It was for people who were proud of their skin or just didn't want to spend the time loading makeup on their faces (is it any wonder that the slang for perfectly applied makeup is a "beat face"?). These were products that didn't want to inherently change you, but rather wanted you to thrive. With that comes the criticism that Glossier is makeup for people who already look like models, which I have been told dozens of times in my reporting. "It's just for pretty people who want the no-makeup look. It's like buying nothing to make yourself look the same," Ali, a nineteen-year-old Georgia-based makeup artist and influencer, told me. I, on the other hand, have always felt freedom in no-makeup makeup. I am inherently lazy about applying makeup, I don't feel like I'm skilled at it, and I don't like the heavy feel of a done face. The debate gets to the heart of the idea of the purpose of makeup: accentuating versus concealing; bringing out or covering up.

When Annie Kreighbaum trained new copywriters for Glossier, the first thing she would tell them was to forget everything, then open an email draft and pretend they were writing to their best friend. Yes, even Glossier's copywriting strategy had a no-makeup makeup approach. The brand's voice was that of your older sister—or, more accurately, the coolest friend who knew that trying too hard was antithetical to being cool. "I thought it was so cool and so cute and a new way of looking at beauty that felt like a language that hadn't been recorded," said a copywriter at a rival beauty company. Too many exclamation marks or words that felt too internet-y didn't work. And nothing that seemed like they were trying to sound like teenagers. "My other rule is to read what we wrote out loud, and if you wouldn't say that to each other, like, if you wouldn't say these words out loud, then don't write them," Kreighbaum said. "So, you wouldn't say, 'Your luscious locks need some extra TLC.'"

Weiss noticed that the big beauty companies had a top-down way of communicating with the people who bought their products. As beauty marketing has become less about gender and age boundaries, the differences in brands are largely about aesthetics and fantasies. Who do you aspire to be? Who are you at this moment in time? If the old guard of beauty conglomerates spoke to their fans in the form of celebrity ads or high-profile department store placements, as Weiss's millennial cohort came of age, they preferred a more casual and conversational approach.

Weiss knew that the Glossier voice needed to be nonchalant: "It doesn't have to be this big, scary, serious thing. Like billowing silk in the wind. Like whale sounds and the promise of eternal youth." It was about pictures and vibes as much as words: photos of a young Gisele Bündchen, Georgia O'Keeffe paintings, glitter. Followers know that if they leave a comment, Glossier will respond directly, usually with some emoji thrown in. As one fan put it: "Will gladly let u slide into my DMs @glossier." It was a more optimistic and empathetic way than beauty was usually marketed. And it was a smart way to reach the masses.

But even if Glossier had fans at other companies, it wasn't seen as real competition yet. An oft-repeated anecdote from people who worked at beauty companies was that their co-workers didn't even know what Glossier was—it was a brand that people loved, but it was still a cult phenomenon and had a relatively low level of brand awareness.

Weiss liked to say she wanted to create a lifestyle brand. Brooks Brothers is an American lifestyle brand that has been around since the nineteenth century. More recent additions include Coca-Cola, Playboy, Apple, Nike. Glossier was the first beauty brand to function as shorthand for the kind of person you wanted to be—the cafeteria table you wanted to sit with in the high school of life. Weiss wanted Glossier to be big enough that people wanted to wear the sweatshirt with the logo on it, and it worked. Glossier's pink hoodie had a pre-sale wait list of 10,000 names in May 2020. That's a bigger production run of a clothing item than many established fashion brands can lay claim to. Even Timothée Chalamet, the actor at the apex of young Hollywood success of the late 2010s, was photographed wearing a Glossier hoodie in millennial pink. He did get his for free when a fan in the Glossier office sent one to his management team. Glossier is about much more than aesthetic appearance; it has become a way for people to feel connected to bigger beliefs, to feel like their daily choices are having an impact, and that they are putting their money where their mouth is.

All that sunny inclusivity was a bit of a tone pivot from Into the Gloss's fashion and beauty insiders, and for Emily Weiss herself. I've long felt there was something particularly savvy about Weiss, who fit the cool and untouchable *Vogue*-style archetype to a T, creating a brand whose core message was so counter to that ice queen mold: sunny, nice, inclusive.

What made Into the Gloss work was that the site, Weiss, its subjects, all seemed a little cooler than you and like they inhabited a world closed off to most people, complete with SoHo headquarters and former models like Kelly Mittendorf. Or like the old Barbizon modeling school ads: "Train to be a model, or just look like one!" When she wrote in her post announcing the launch of Glossier that "snobby isn't cool, happy is cool," this marked a crucial change for Weiss's self-presentation, and a choice that would impact the future of her fledgling brand and her own life trajectory. (Although a former assistant pointed out that Weiss usually hated the word "cool.") Even the penmanship on address labels had to look right. One intern learned quickly that she "had to try to make it look like pretty/bubbly/friendly 'Glossier' penmanship." The message with Glossier was quite literally written out as "You CAN sit with us" in a chipper tone. Glossier had a double-edged sword of relatability. On the one hand, it promoted inclusivity and acceptance, but it had to remain still aloof enough, cool enough, to be aspirational.

Glossier pulled off a many-layered feat of branding and meaning. Into the Gloss took that seduction of beauty secrets passed from woman to woman in the bathroom of a restaurant or sniffed on a friend's wrist to anyone who found their website. Their profile subjects were a coterie of insiders with a great deal of cultural capital (and, in many cases, actual capital), but anyone could join in the community by posting to the robust comments section or just by buying, say, Homeoplasmine, the French nipple cream that worked on all chapped skin. That inherent tension and irony were present in Glossier as well when the company introduced its line; they made their spin on some of these cult products and brought them to the masses with an added smiley-face flourish.

The idea of a brand being your friend is never real. Nor is your boss your friend, nor is the founder of your favorite beauty company. This feels like a particularly female problem—no one believes they are "friends" with the head of Apple or Nike. Yes, there is the trend of the "friendly" company, but how many were founded by men? In fashion, Patagonia and the North Face, and in food, Ben & Jerry's? And before anyone says it "has to" be that way in beauty: nobody in their right mind thinks they are good enough to be friends with Rihanna, but they are still going to buy her makeup. Weiss was a founder, a manager, a woman with a lot on her plate.

It was a kind of disconnect that put off a lot of people. And Weiss's "Little Wedding Black Book" published on Into the Gloss in 2015 did not help. In it, she revealed the lengths to which she had gone (colonics, microcurrents to lift her butt, "subtle" hair extensions, which were detailed under the categories of wellness, body, face, even teeth) to look her best for her own destination wedding in the Bahamas, with thirty-seven guests and a honeymoon in Japan.

"So much prep," she wrote. "Not of the venue, guest list, or seating chart—that was fairly easy—but of my limbs, skin, wanted hair, unwanted hair, nails, muscles, digestive tract, lashes, and brows. Did I go overboard? Perhaps. Was it high-maintenance? Maybe. I did spend an inordinate amount of the fall on my back. But it worked. I was 8/10 happy with how I looked . . . pretty good!" It was the 80 percent rating she gave herself after all that effort that made it a target. It was lampooned as some kind of apotheosis of the extremes to which women go to look good. "One of the most superlative accounts of beauty-related futility the world has ever seen," wrote Charlotte Shane on the *Cut*. "Fifty feminist academics working for fifty years could not have concocted such a concise depiction of what is involved when one strives for conventional feminine perfection, not even if they were helmed by *The Beauty Myth* author Naomi Wolf herself."

This was a reversal of the persona she had tried to sell in the media amid the Glossier launch. It was tone-deaf, as if while trying to be the cool older sister, she sometimes tripped over the fact of her own privilege and pedigree. Glossier staff justified it as that she genuinely loved beauty, that she wanted to share all the stuff she was doing to get married because that was such a large part of her life at the time—she was trying to let everyone in.

All that talk about betterment reminded me of the promise of the Top Shelf routines, how they could be both heartbreakingly opaque and quite revealing at once. When, as part of her trial, Theranos founder Elizabeth Holmes had certain documents made public, one of them was a schedule scrawled on a piece of paper with such entries as: "4:00–4:15 wash face, change," "4:15–4:45 meditate, clear mind." When I read it, I was instantly reminded of Weiss's "Little Wedding Black Book." What was Weiss thinking, I wondered, while going to all those appointments? What was her emotional state? What, in her detailed chronicle, wasn't she telling us? There was a certain particularly cruel schadenfreude that internet commenters expressed toward the marriage itself. Her husband, the photographer Diego Dueñas, was someone she'd been with on and off since her early twenties. He comes from a niche-famous family: his sisters are Bianca Dueñas and Maria Dueñas Jacobs, both well-married, beautiful, and co-owners of a children's jewelry company. Their marriage was short-lived, and I wish luck to anyone who tries to get her to discuss it.

Weiss had marketed a version of "you but better" and "a seat at the table," but when it came down to it, was she just another prisoner of the beauty standards? Albeit one who had a lot of natural advantages in terms of looks, height, body, money, and access? In some ways her wedding post was refreshing in that it showed just what lengths our culture encourages women to go for their bridal moment; it was radically honest, whether she intended it to be or not. Talking about beauty routines was how she'd built her business. And trying them out was part of her job. For a website like Into the Gloss, the industry standard was that these services would be comped or discounted anyway. But she was taken apart for it. A woman showing the work that goes into the upkeep of the feminine shell is still taboo. The effort that the Kardashian-Jenner clan reveals or at least implies in their show and on social media is, I believe, part of their success. Women find that honesty refreshing. And Weiss showed some bravery in admitting that as a conventionally beautiful woman, a woman who has modeled and appeared on television, she still felt an 8 out of 10 after all she did. It's truly sad that she didn't feel a 10 out of 10. But can any woman?

Weiss was well aware of the backlash and seemed to view it as a symbol of remaining cultural gaps in female leadership. "No wonder you're fascinated," she said. "Does this make you frivolous? Does this mean you're not a deep person or a caring person or a socially conscious person? And there's no level of maintenance that's actually okay. I actually loved the dialogue, meaning, like, that's exactly the conversation around beauty that we should be having."

This was the moment, so early on in her company, that made her scale back personally. Even if she showed so little to the public in the early days, she still wanted the world to know she was not a dilettante but rather an unlikely disruptor, surpassing anyone else in her "rich kid" set. Now, as she settled into full CEO mode, she would show a different self to the public.

5

Glossier was finally ready to introduce its first four products to the world. Except the company had zero media strategy. Weiss was having lunch with a veteran of the publicity world, who asked her if she had hired anyone to run PR. Weiss hadn't—it was still a skeleton crew and they had never really needed PR before. The PR veteran suggested one of her mentees, Sarah Hudson, then working in tech PR, who described herself as perfect for the job because "I was the girl with under-eye cream at summer camp." She was hired to lead public relations and communications for Glossier about six weeks before the October 2014 launch. Hudson got the job partly based on an exercise writing down a list of people—tastemakers, influencers—she would want to gift products to. During her interview with Weiss, the staff was buzzing because Weiss had just shot Jenna Lyons of J.Crew for Top Shelf, which was considered a coup for Into the Gloss. Weiss started crying while talking about the team she had built, how close she felt to them. Crying was a big show of herself being vulnerable, earnest, overcome with emotion, and also a way to shift focus back to herself, even during an interview.

Hudson was by Weiss's side when they met with editors at the Mondrian, a hotel, to debut Glossier's products. I was one of the invitees. As they took me through all four products, I remember asking, "That's all?" and realizing that was rude, but I didn't entirely get the idea of phases or drops, thinking the four items seemed a bit spare and randomly chosen. If there was skincare, why no cleanser (or toner or sunscreen)? Why was there just one sort-of makeup product? Still, I had followed Weiss's career and knew the launch of the line would be a big deal.

The goal was to get press in tech-, consumer-, and beauty-oriented publications. Weiss frequently repeated versions of: "People often ask, 'Are you a tech company? Are you a beauty company?' And I say, 'Yes, we are.'" That is nothing new for the tech world. Jonathan Glick, the CEO of Sulia, called his own company as well as Medium, Buzz-Feed, Gawker, and Vox "platishers": both platforms and publishers. Skift founder, Rafat Ali, dubbed his travel news company "Mediata," for its hybrid of media and travel data analysis. But that was much more difficult for editors to understand about a beauty company. Or rather, with Glossier launching products, it was hard to see them as anything but. Tech editors didn't think Glossier's debut was a serious story, and beauty editors thought of Weiss as a competitor because of Into the Gloss. "I don't think we should cover the launch, I'd rather see if the line is successful before devoting a profile to her. As a tech story, I don't think she's yet successful enough or doing something that fascinating as to merit a stand-alone (a.k.a. not part of a trend) story. And as a beauty story, I think we need to see if her products get any real traction," wrote one editor, responding to a query about profiling Weiss for Glossier's debut.

Weiss was reluctant to answer anything remotely personal and often her answers sounded overly rehearsed or were boring, which, from the point of view of a journalist, made covering the company difficult. Weiss's own company struggled with her as a tool to get coverage in the press, or the right kind of press. Publications would pitch her a subject for a lifestyle story on her apartment or what was in her bag (which isn't dissimilar to Top Shelf), but she always declined. By 2015, Glossier had secured a profile in the *New York Times*, but Weiss wouldn't let the writer see her personal Top Shelf. "She would not permit this reporter into either her hotel bathroom or the one in downtown New York that she shares with her fiancé, an artist whose name she did not want published. She said there was not much to see in her bathrooms."

Most media stories led with *The Hills*, or mentioned her as the Superintern, and would comment on her outfits and demeanor. Weiss thought that her innovation and vision got lost and that the press used a gossipy tone to describe her past. But that's also how journalism works. The reporter profiling Weiss must assume readers know nothing about her or Glossier. To start with *The Hills* is to zoom in on something recognizable before zooming out to the rest of Weiss's real accomplishments. Her team hated seeing a story that led with a reference to *The Hills* because they knew she wouldn't be happy. If a writer asked something that diverged from the product launch they were focusing on, a publicist, who would be taking notes the entire time (which is, again, not unusual or off-limits but makes journalists uneasy), would sweep in and say, politely but very firmly, they preferred to stay on topic. Weiss's staff also tried to manage her own expectations. What reporters chose to write and what their editors wanted was, ultimately, out of their control, and the kinds of bullying tactics that some CEOs and their minions used were not the Glossier way of doing things. Instead, her communications team prepped Weiss in a way that was overly cautious. They compiled dossiers on writers interviewing her with links to recent articles they had written and information culled from online searches and scanning their social media profiles. Weiss was so concentrated on working, building, growing, that she often forgot that interviews and press coverage were going to take place, and staff had to ask her if she needed to take a minute to reset or change into a different shirt or brush her hair.

All the implied secrecy just made people want to know more about the company. Withholding info and even stonewalling the press is standard for tech companies, not female-founded beauty brands. The complications of covering Weiss were not hers alone. There still are not all that many portrayals of female ambition in popular culture. It was a double standard that people expected Weiss to be eager to participate in anything.

She did thrive in certain settings, such as a fireside chat she gave in January 2015 at the office of Harry's, the fellow DTC men's grooming company that was also backed by Kirsten Green of Forerunner. "The young employees scribbled her remarks in Moleskine notebooks, their heads cocked thoughtfully. (The 'fire' had been downloaded from YouTube and projected onto a wall). 'When I think of Into the Gloss, I think of you,' one female audience member said. 'How much push do you feel to live this ideal?'" a *New York Times* writer described the scene. "Wearing a knit cap with her sweater-and-jeans uniform and looking rather elfin for a would-be cosmetics mogul, Ms. Weiss had an easy answer. 'There's so much pressure on women to have it all together,' she said reassuringly. 'There's always this "next, next, next." I hope Glossier encourages women to be O.K. wherever you are. Just, everyone, relax!'"

Relaxing wasn't really what Weiss was projecting in her career. Her rise was parallel to the ubiquity of a new cultural term: the girlboss (and the 2014 bestseller *#Girlboss* by Nasty Gal founder Sophia Amoruso, a close friend of Weiss's). The breathless girlboss narratives purveyed in the many media stories bore a striking similarity to Weiss's, where a mediagenic woman, often young, conventionally pretty, thin, fashionable, connected, and white, comes up with a concept for a women-centric company. Weiss was lumped in among a cohort of aspirational millennial(ish) founders—including Audrey Gelman of the women's co-working space and social club the Wing, Outdoor Voices' Ty Haney, Leandra Medine of Man Repeller, Steph Korey of the DTC luggage brand Away, Yael Aflalo of Reformation, and Amoruso—whose real-world savvy and third-wave-feminist bent granted them a gods-among-women stature.

Girlbosses might struggle with fertility, marriage, and their bodies, which makes them accessible, but they're doing it as they're trying to become titans of industry, trying to reinvent or disrupt something, usually with start-up companies catering to women in a cheerful and nonthreatening way. But female founders—and, by extension, women in business leadership—are not a monolith, and many bristled at being seen that way in the public view. "What about all the CEOs working hard who were people of color, or didn't live on the coasts, or didn't have consumer-facing products?" one female CEO said to me with an eye roll when I asked her about the mania for girlbosses. This was a slim cohort of women. Pun intended—they were thin and pretty, but also just a small slice of women in business. Plenty of CEOs of that era did not court the limelight—Mary Barra of General Motors, Ginni Rometty of IBM, Michelle Gass of Kohl's—but they weren't young founders of consumer brands in the 2010s. The women who garnered the most coverage, like Weiss, didn't always seem to match the world they wanted you to buy into. And Weiss, for her part, hated the girlboss topic as much as she hates hearing about *The Hills*. But the girlboss narrative, as demeaning as it was, was a way to cover Weiss's unique position in the culture.

The girlboss did represent a fantasy for a lot of young women. Did any teenagers until the past decade ever dream of starting their own beauty lines the way they once might have wanted to start fashion brands? Becoming a beauty mogul, thanks to Weiss, or Gwyneth Paltrow, or any YouTube influencer coming out with an eye shadow kit, is seen as not just cool but possible. The new beauty leaders have an accessibility that the Lauders or L'Oréal's Bettencourt family simply do not have, no matter how many times I have read articles trying to show heiress Aerin Lauder as a regular person, even if her namesake perfume is excellent.

Weiss was an aspirational figure—she's someone other young women want to be—that makes her and her brand, Glossier, attractive to customers. Morgan Von Steen, who was hired as Weiss's assistant in 2015, said that "the girlboss tagline felt like a commercialization of something that was so innate to who she was. There was never a part of her that was pretending. It's just that she was an ambitious person who wanted to see through a vision."

Culturally or in business, the girlboss didn't come out of nowhere. Feminism in the 2010s was becoming a prominent force in pop culture but diluted; girlbosses were an unholy marriage of feminism and capitalism and meritocracy. Nabil Mallick, the venture capitalist at Thrive, saw it as an extension of the fad for leveraged buyout barons in the 1980s or tech founders who had started companies in their garages in the 1990s. This was just the latest way to fetishize executives. The girlboss era was a time of transition when young women started to want to be entrepreneurs as much as or more than, say, movie stars. Gwyneth Paltow is arguably more famous—and certainly more powerful and interesting—now as the head of Goop than she ever was as an Oscar-winning actress. Even though CEO of a beauty business is a profession that shares some glamour with acting, there's a power inherent to business that actors don't have.

To be a girlboss was to make business cute—a boy boss is a completely moot point and absurd. The term is offensive from the start, using the soft and literally infantile word "girl" to soften the blow of the perceived masculinity of the "boss." There's internalized sexism inherent in the term.

"Research shows that as women get older, and as women become more powerful, they are perceived as less likable. So by using that term 'girlboss,' there's a desire to be powerful but a fear of losing likability," said Alexandra Solomon, a professor who specializes in gender and gender roles at Northwestern University. To be a girlboss was to be powerful and nonthreatening at the same time. A sort of wolf in sheep's clothing, wrecking the system from the inside with some scented candles and pink décor.

But it also shows the limitations of this point in Glossier's trajectory. The story of Glossier, like the girlboss cohort, was tied to Weiss. There was an idolatry attached to her, but could that scale? Did they even want it to? The rest of the world didn't know who Emily Weiss was, let alone execs at rival companies. And besides, the public gets tired of a single narrative quickly, and it couldn't all be Weiss's face posing in Gucci with a Balm Dotcom, retelling the same story each time. Even the public tires of that.

To raise the kind of funding she wanted, or that she thought Glossier needed, it had to be about whether Glossier worked. So to grow the company, Weiss—as a self-made female entrepreneur, a girlboss, whatever—could not be the whole story. The story had to be something else. If this was going to become a legacy company, Glossier's products had to be able to stand on their own with customers long after Weiss was gone.

There was real doubt about what might happen after the novelty of the brand's debut died down. The first big product launch in 2015 after Phase One was two masks: Mega Greens Galaxy Pack, which was purifying, and Moisturizing Moon

Mask, which was hydrating. "We thought, 'Is this repeatable? Can we continue?'" said creative director Helen Steed. "The brand launch was a success because of energy and talk. We thought, 'Do we launch masks in January, a kind of post-holiday detox story?' Masks weren't as big initially as we wanted them to be. It didn't always hit the mark."

Henry Davis calls it the nuclear winter. How do you sustain and maintain interest? He was quick to clarify that he didn't mean that for Glossier: "I wouldn't call it that. It's exciting and new and we had to earn it and work very, very hard to stay in front of people to create content that was exciting and engaging. When you're new and have a small team creating things, it takes a lot of effort." But if he isn't willing to say it was Glossier's nuclear winter, I am. I remember unwrapping the masks and thinking they were just fine. Not bad, but not all that exciting. I thought I could get a similar affordable mask at any drugstore or the beauty aisle at the health food store.

"We see Glossier for what it is now, this phenomenon," said Von Steen. "But Emily didn't know it was going to work. For a long time she was going through the process of: Is this going to be a real thing?—and defeating that feeling and keeping going."

The narrative could be one of runaway success. Just after Glossier's first real Black Friday sale in 2015, Weiss and Davis kept calling the tech team and checking the dashboard of Looker, the software they used to monitor sales metrics. Sales were pouring in. They sold $250,000 worth of product that day. On the Tuesday after Thanksgiving weekend, Glossier employees gathered in their largest conference room, the one with the brand's core values on the wall, for their regular all-hands meeting. The leadership announced the news. Glossier was taking off. "I remember how wowed Henry was. We were like, 'Holy shit, two hundred fifty thousand dollars of product,'" said Von Steen, who didn't know if it was selling well or not until she saw the reactions. "In the later years I would always think about that number, because it paled in comparison just two years later. We would do that within the first half a day. By then, we were doing just frivolous numbers."

PART 2

THE MAKEOVER

Jessica: Can I ask you a question?

Helen: Sure.

Jessica: What color lipstick are you wearing?

Helen: Well, it's three different kinds. I blend.

Jessica: Really?

Helen: Yeah.

Jessica: Really, wow.

Helen: Would you like to know the . . .

Jessica: Would you feel comfortable?

Helen: Of course, I'd love to share. I start with Mac Viva Glam 3,
which is a great base, and I add Prescriptive Poodle on the
top. I finish with Philosophy Supernatural Nude, which is
more of a glossy kind of thing. Bit of shine.

Jessica: It looks just beautiful on you.

Helen: You should try it yourself. It would look gorgeous
on your complexion.

Jessica: The blending thing is a little labor intensive for me,
you know. I'm kind of looking for that one.

—JENNIFER WESTFELDT AND HEATHER JUERGENSEN,
KISSING JESSICA STEIN

6

If Weiss wasn't talking to the media about her inner life, it's hard to know who or how many people she really did open up to. She wasn't known to have many close friends. One former coworker said she seemed to have one old friend, Rochelle, she would bring to parties. "I spend all my time with basically five friends. We all met in Florence during study abroad," she said. She told me that in 2019 when I was visiting her apartment. The afternoon had been pitched to me as "Emily would love to host you at her apartment (this would be a first for a reporter) to . . . wait for it . . . make a frittata with her!" wrote her PR rep. "If you follow her on social you might have seen that this is a new hobby of hers. After reading the book *The First Forty Days* she's been cooking and hand delivering homemade frittatas to her friends who are postpartum." I found this whole endeavor contrived but also quite sweet of her.

"And I'm freezing my eggs," Weiss told me with a little smirk. She was wearing slippers with a skirt and an oversize button-up shirt from the brand Toteme, and I remember how real she seemed, for a moment. When I asked why, she pointed

out that her oven is also a microwave—"Isn't that awesome?"—
and started to heat onion and butter on medium heat. She
had brought the subject up but still came off as really uncomfortable discussing it. There are start-ups offering egg freezing,
some borrowing heavily from Glossier-style branding, but she
went to a doctor a friend recommended. "I was super bloated
and looked four months pregnant. I gained ten pounds during
a three-week period," she said. I felt lucky to be in her space
and didn't want to make her regret inviting me over for the
interview, but I could also palpably feel her wanting to tell a
story, but stopping herself from doing so.

There was, for once, no publicist present. They made a
big deal out of that to show me how much Weiss trusted
me or how much the company trusted me. In one corner
of her New York apartment was a bag of her boyfriend
Will Gaybrick's stuff. He lived in San Francisco, where he
worked for the financial services start-up Stripe, and before that
he worked for Thrive Capital. It was a long-distance relationship. "It is adult. Like, real," Weiss said. Does she have to be
in a relationship to have kids? Would she have them alone? "I
don't know that I want to talk about that. I think I probably
want to be in a relationship, but I don't know. I feel my way
into things. Things always change. And they always have
changed." She sounded icy but looked uncomfortable. That
was as much as she was willing to give. "If it's okay, I'd love
to keep the relationship talks to a minimum."

Weiss never mentioned her ex-husband, but she'd moved
into that current apartment alone, and started tagging Gaybrick in posts to her followers in January 2019.

I was already a few years into reporting on Weiss, used to having waves of contradictory feelings about her. I would not necessarily want to have someone in my home, Notes app open on their iPhone, snooping around, looking at what was on my shelves and then forced to do a faux-bonding activity with me. Afterward, all you could hope for when the piece came out was that the writer was flattering in their depiction of you. But every profile is written for a reason, and usually that is to promote something or sell something or both. I have participated in them as a subject myself. No one is obligated to answer questions they don't wish to, and Weiss was adept not only at cutting off conversation but at redirecting it toward topics that would benefit her and Glossier. But, above all else, Emily Weiss has a great deal of choice in what she does. If she and her team did not think it would be advantageous for me to be in her home, getting her to weigh in on her personal life in some small way, she would not be doing the interview. She is not someone who does things she doesn't want to do, but she also won't hesitate to make me feel a little bit bad—trashy, overly curious, unfeeling—for being there in the first place.

Her apartment, which rented for around $8,500 a month, was in a luxury doorman building at the corner of Spring Street and Cleveland Place, and was where the singer John Mayer once lived. It was heavy on natural light and had the same white, pink, and red palette as her offices. There was a book on tropical fish, which made sense (Glossier's conference room had a large fish tank before the fish either died or were removed and replaced with a photo of marine life). Over her low-slung bed, there was a Glossier photograph of lips that looked like a Marilyn Minter; outside in the living room, there was a genuine Marilyn Minter—a painting of a woman's face behind steamed-up glass. It felt like a chicken-and-egg scenario: Did Weiss model her lifestyle after the Glossier brand, or was the branding of the company an extension of her own tastes? Was Emily choosing to live in her own corporate branding? I thought of Ralph Lauren's Double RL Ranch in Colorado or Karl Lagerfeld's eighteenth-century Château de Penhoët in Grand-Champ in France. Powerful and creative people seem to have a way of building fantasy worlds to live in.

I once watched her then assistant Stacey as she was perched at Weiss's dining room table, answering emails. I asked Emily how many meetings she had a day. "Stacey, how many?" she called out, laughing. "I promise I won't get mad at you if you're honest." She wanted to be seen in the same league as other founders, by being so much in demand that her email inbox was overflowing.

Weiss had a sense of how people perceived her, and she knew she had to change how she presented herself to both her company and the world at large, to evolve as Glossier grew. In the early days she would change clothes in the office, furiously busy between meetings, not caring who saw her. But she had to pull back and put a wall up around herself. Which could be alienating for friends and employees and isolating for her.

For someone who had been famous, or at least recognizable, since she was in her early twenties, she was getting older in the public eye. Her features softened and she appeared more voluptuous, whether that was with age or weight gain or the targeted help of a good dermatologist or a surgeon. Now that she was in full founder mode, she stopped going to most fashion events. She gave up on having hair that required touch-ups every four weeks, so the platinum bob was gone. She let go of that edgier period of her life, or at least of the times like in late 2016 when she showed up to a Proenza Schouler fashion show wearing a Glossier pink superhero cape and Zorro-style pink mask straight from an office party for the launch of their serums, which all had "super" in the name. She dyed her hair back to its natural brown and grew it long. Gone were the skinny jeans and sneakers, and in their place were more powerfully adult designer clothes: Chanel sandals and Gucci sweaters and power suits when the occasion necessitated it. She wore fine jewelry from the designer Sophie Bille Brahe, who is Danish. Weiss loved Copenhagen, and sometimes got her hair cut when she was in Denmark, and has a relationship with the Danish designer Julie Fagerholt, who would send her boxes of clothing. There is a sort of parallel universe where Weiss became an influencer instead of a CEO, showing up at the Met Gala (she had never been) and doing sponsored social media posts. "I would be at the Valentino dinner right now with Pernille Teisbaek and all those girls, who I love," she said, then laughed and smiled a little dreamily, or in relief.

Even though she posted as frequently as you would expect of a young CEO, she was a more muted presence on Instagram. One could learn very little about her private life, or even her opinions, from her vacation selfies and broad support of reproductive rights. For a brief stint she was posting a lot about airplane food, whether business class—JetBlue Mint is the best, she said—or coach, with the foil packets of hot mystery meat. At the time it seemed like a suggestion someone had made to her to show a quirky side of herself or to devise a passion that followers could relate to. She straddled a line between being approachable and aspirational, normal and extraordinary. "She presents this air of being a normal person; in reality, she's not a normal person. She's a very well-connected founder who is worth several million dollars. But she looks like a normal person," said one observer. An employee swore she was unchanged: "She hasn't bought a yacht or anything like that."

Weiss was not the first founder of a company to take an assertive role in trying to change the way the public perceived them. Founders like Weiss, or the ones she shaped herself after, are big talkers. Showboats. Creators of their own worlds. They say they're changing the world, and they believe it, and they'll say it to anyone. Jeff Bezos started out as a dork wunderkind who changed the business world and has now evolved into a source of some controversy over the treatment of workers. Elon Musk went from a proudly neurodivergent wunderkind into a political bad-boy billionaire on the loose. Martha Stewart began as a type A entrepreneur moving at the speed of the Energizer Bunny, taking the lemons of homemaking and turning them into billion-dollar lemonade. Sure, she happened to go to prison along the way, but she managed to emerge seemingly more likable and with a little bit of street cred. In her eighties, she is known for having a friendship with Snoop Dog, a cannabis business, and a propensity for posting thirst-trap photos of herself that people take seriously.

The most obvious evolution was in Weiss's interests. She personally had invested in the Co–Star astrology app and, in 2020, joined the board of the sustainable footwear brand Allbirds. She had a gratitude journal she wrote in for five minutes each day. At one point around 2019, she cut the accounts she followed on Instagram down to a lean 555 but was fond of Blue Zones, an account of "longevity and happiness secrets from the most extraordinary populations on earth." Those are worthy things to care about, but a bit cliché, as if interests in nurturing longevity and gurus come standard when you become a tech queenpin.

It was a cultivated image, a measured and crafted persona fashioned after the Silicon Valley tech model of the founder-philosopher. Much posturing is accepted as standard practice for a rising-star company and its founder. The way Weiss spoke about Glossier—literally the language she used—began to morph. Even though she didn't have a business degree, she was becoming fluent in the patois of start-ups and MBA grads. "I've spent my life relying on light bulb moments and just jumping in full force," she told the *Business of Fashion*. "That's fine when you're making something on your own, but not fine when you're thirty-plus people and there are a ton of stakeholders, as well as knock-on effects of pretty much every initiative we take on." She used words and phrases like "assess" and "lightning speed" and "our focus is very much on the digital." At Disrupt SF in 2018, she said Glossier was "a psychographic rather than a demographic," and that it fundamentally made beauty products that were essential for everyone. When she spoke that way, Weiss came across as someone who wanted to appear like a leader more than act like the chief executive of the massive operation Glossier was growing to be.

"Wow, I wish I could have that every day," she said in a humbled and impressed tone that sounded mostly genuine, referring to the crowd cheering at one live interview for the podcast *How I Built This*. The audience of fans literally chanted "Glos-see-yay" as she entered. In that roughly hourlong interview, she mentioned Duckworth's book *Grit* at least three times. "People often ask me what amount of your success is attributed to luck? Um, I really believe in kind of grit, and I mean I didn't make that up, that's Angela Duckworth's and her book *Grit*, a very good book." A few minutes later, she said, "Back to that power of grit. . . . I think my personal superpower, if there's one thing that I think I'm really good at, I'm super curious." And again: "When I hear the word 'grit,' that's what it says to me is there's a resiliency to just, to just brush, shake it off, right? And, and keep going." She ended by answering a question about good advice by invoking a business book. "The Phil Knight quote from Nike of, like, 'Just do it.' I mean, it's as cheesy as it sounds," she said. "Be courageous. Be curious and be courageous because the worst—it's like my friend says about dates, it's either a good date or a good story. I think that's really good advice. Try things, it's going to help you grow and learn, you know, learn something, learn something about yourself."

Weiss hosted fireside chats at the Glossier headquarters, where she interviewed people such as Deepak Chopra, Disney CEO Bob Iger, Reddit cofounder Alexis Ohanian, Warby Parker cofounder Neil Blumenthal, Chobani founder Hamdi Ulukaya, president of Planned Parenthood Cecile Richards, Shake Shack's then CFO Tara Comonte, Spanx inventor Sara Blakely. Weiss would pull from her own contacts to see who she could get. Meant for education and enrichment, such sessions are par for the course at plenty of tech companies and start-ups. It was an impressive list of people, but some employees found them to be an elaborate vanity project, less for their own enrichment and more for Weiss to cement her founder status. Said one, "Emily would have her hair and makeup done by product development and then take a selfie in the bathroom and walk the people through the office."

Weiss was good at making people feel special, listened to, showing that she was present. She lived to hear from someone who was an expert on something she didn't know about. "Emily would always do this thing where, depending on which leaders she talked to, she would soak up whatever they said. After the Warby Parker talk, she went on a big kick where she would just quote him a lot, which was kind of funny because it wasn't always hyper-relevant to what we were doing," said a creative employee who attended many of the chats. Weiss would compare Glossier to Amazon for how people stole their packages from customers' doors and Shake Shack for their dedication to pleasing customers. "After talking to the Disney guy, she was comparing the showrooms to Disney World, in the idea of really exciting experiences in a couple select locations. And then the showroom employees were characters like Mickey Mouse, and meeting them is so cool and nice and awesome you might want to take pictures with them."

She was buying her own good press. Weiss often talked of revolutionizing beauty and seemed to relish any opportunity to compare herself to a legacy American brand or use the "Glossier is your friend" metaphor. In a blog post on Into the Gloss marking Glossier's second anniversary in October 2016, she wrote that she had to remind herself how young the company was "and to look at the time it's taken iconic companies like Estée Lauder, Apple, and Nike to become what they are today." To both journalists and employees, she also compared the potential of Glossier's trajectory to those companies. Once, in a meeting with Nike to potentially partner with them on a product, Weiss advised that what Nike was missing in its stores was curation, that customers shouldn't walk into a pop-up and see fifteen shoes. "Pick one that's the shoe you're going out with," she said. Glossier wasn't going to offer five types of something, and that was why people trusted them: they had a perspective. Weiss told the author of a Harvard Business School case study: "Girls take pictures of themselves with the [outdoor] ads and tag us. Can you imagine that happening with, like, Ford Motors?" She was happy to hear that people were stealing Glossier packages off people's front steps. She compared the pink bubble-wrap pouches to the visibility of Apple's AirPods. She referenced Apple when talking about concepts for retail stores. "I think a lot about the Apple Store," she said.

"About creating hubs where you can touch and experience a product, yes, but you can also connect with like-minded people." To the *New York Times* in 2015, she said, "What is the Steve Jobs quote—'Stay hungry, stay foolish'? . . . I think I'm probably pretty foolish."

She looked up to Ralph Lauren and also Airbnb. "They have a product which is like people's homes, but really what they have is this incredible community who are sharing with one another, and it's very sort of self-sustaining," she told me. "And I think of Glossier like an ecosystem, like people come in and they rarely leave." Like the song "Hotel California"? I asked, making a bad joke. She didn't seem to acknowledge it. "Yeah, it's a club that everyone can be a part of. And there hasn't been a beauty brand like that in a while. And one that takes its customers' involvement—that really relies on its customers' involvement. It's our lifeblood."

Any CEO of a company is busy, but Weiss spread herself thin. Her Google calendar, where her assistant kept her schedule, was a block of text: interviews, creative meetings, product development. She was traveling a great deal, once a month at a minimum, for fundraising or a speaking engagement or going to a new city or country that Glossier was looking to expand into. She liked to be involved in every detail of the company, from larger questions about fundraising to decisions as small as what color the font should be on a new product package. A bit of an echo of Anna Wintour's notorious "AWOK" sign-off that *Vogue* employees needed to get on virtually every aspect of their professional lives. Morgan Von Steen would try to schedule time for Weiss to have a break, like a quiet solo lunch or meditation, but she would invariably end up deleting it as the tide of the day went on. She made herself too available, answering texts early in the day and late at night and encouraging employees to reach out no matter what. She missed taking photos of people for Into the Gloss, less because she didn't trust anyone else to do it and more because she found it all so exciting. She had a hard time letting go of anything.

It's easy, perhaps too easy, to bury someone like Weiss in her own words. Was reading all those business books and constantly invoking them cliché? Absolutely. But I also think it was how she was processing her changing life. And instead of letting the press in on her own challenges, it was easier to talk more broadly about grit or lessons she had learned or to speak in analogies. Weiss, for her part, said that the ultimate lesson was that no book can tell you how to be a CEO. And being a young, female CEO came with a lot of challenges that older men weren't exposed to.

When it came to running Glossier, Nabil Mallick, the Glossier board member, said to me in 2019, "She did not necessarily understand the supply chain or the instincts around finances or how to lean into growth. The one thing she did have as a leader was curiosity." Being self-aware about her own gaps in experience was a good thing. In that sense, she was the anti–Elon Musk, totally measured and erring on the side of caution.

But when it came to thinking of Glossier in the big picture as a brand, Weiss was single-minded and dazzlingly confident. Employees past and present called her a guru or their idol or godlike, said that she was inspiring, that she was smart and hardworking and had nonstop ideas. "My head of comms will kill me because I'm going to say something really weird right now," she told one reporter, opening her eyes wide and pulling a self-deprecating face. "But I think about it a little bit like, how are religions scaled?" She believed Glossier could accomplish anything. But growing a brand was very different from leading a company. The problem was that, more and more, she conflated those two things.

Glossier was not the kind of company to have a staid off-site team-building event where the whole staff would be together. Instead, they had Camp Glossier. The very first one in July 2015 was a day trip. The still small team of three dozen employees went for a ride in three long canoes in the Catskills in upstate New York, paddling downriver while merrily squirting one another with water bottles. They had a spaghetti dinner and rode a bus home, dancing and blaring Fetty Wap, the rapper with a hit that summer, until they all fell asleep before arriving back in Manhattan.

Calling team-building "camp" was a popular enough concept at the time. The women's coworking space the Wing had one in the Adirondacks called Camp No Man's Land, and the coworking behemoth WeWork had a camp (also in the Adirondacks) that I had the unfortunate task of covering for the *New York Times*. At the WeWork camp, I expected wannabe power brokers to be making deals. The reality was markedly different. People I was interviewing told me they were on mushrooms while I was talking to them and returned to swimming in a lake in drizzling weather. It took no time to realize I was surrounded by dilettantish founders who were big talkers above all else, and at a camp that promised gluten-free food but delivered really bad cold-cut sandwiches and bare-bones cabins. There was alcohol everywhere and it was free, and hard drugs were barely hidden. I never saw sexual assault, but I overheard stories of such misconduct.

There's probably no better way to understand a company than by spending a few nights among employees who are drinking and loose, so I tried to attend Glossier camp while reporting a *Vanity Fair* cover story but was denied by Glossier's very kind but firm communications team: "We're not able to accommodate Camp Glossier (keeping it employees only)." A lot of it was the brainchild of Cherie Camacho, who was the team and culture manager. In 2016, she saw that a cover band for Train (of "Hey, Soul Sister" fame) was playing in the same town as the camp and got everyone on staff tickets. It turned out to be the real band. "It was a formative bonding experience. One of the most fun nights of my life. We would talk about that Train concert for years," said Morgan Von Steen.

Each year camp became more of a production. In 2017, employees were whisked away to Port Jervis, New York, two hours away in the western Catskills, to a former summer camp for inner-city kids turned Team USA sports camp for Olympians and World Cup athletes turned haute adult campground called Cedar Lake Estates that costs around $35,000 just for a summer weekend site fee. Some employees were designated as kind of camp counselors to keep up team spirit. Cabins were split among employees, but you were lucky if one of your friends from the office was rooming with you (probably to keep it from having a few key groups of longtime Glossier employees or from seeming cliquey). Employees got plenty of personalized merch, including swimwear from the designer Bruna Malucelli, and crafts included jewelry making with Roxanne Assoulin bead sets. A lot of merchandise items that Glossier would later sell, like the water bottle or the duffel bag, originated at camp.

The Glossier camp was a genuinely wholesome affair. Everyone organizing camp leveraged any connection they could think of to make events happen, texting people they knew who taught yoga or knew how to tie-dye. They tried to make the work-related events fun, like creating Glossier Business School, where groups of disparate employees from different departments—say, someone from design, someone from tech, someone from marketing—thought of a new Glossier product and put together a full campaign and made a production for it. Some of the ideas, like the sleep and overnight products devised by one team, seemed so good that some employees thought they should develop them. There were fireside chats. "I put my heart and fucking soul into trying to get Hillary Clinton to do the camp fireside chat," said Von Steen. "Through the executive assistants' network I got her assistant's email address and wrote this heartfelt email about how, after the [2016] election, it would mean so much to us yada yada, but ultimately she said no."

There were also pink cowboy hats, giant inflatable beach balls, giant inflatable flamingos, ice cream socials, rosé and tequila happy hours (alcohol flowed but no one brought drugs), and cooking classes on how to fry squash blossoms grown on-site. The highlight per my Instagram feed, interviews, and the one time I attended Cedar Lake Estates (in a journalistic but non-Glossier, non-WeWork capacity where I broke my ankle) was the Blob, a massive inflatable pillow–raft–bouncy castle contraption on their lake under the high dive. Dozens of employees in swimwear and towels gathered on the dock to watch. Some took slo-mo videos of all who dared the leap; others held up "You're Doing Amazing" signs (inspired by a Kris Jenner meme). There was a game night one year with a massive Jenga competition, a Texas-inspired hoedown, and a dance party with a live band that did Beyoncé covers.

Camp also showed glimpses of Weiss's awkward theater-kid side from way back in high school. At a karaoke night one year, she and the chief marketing officer, Ali Weiss (no relation), did a duet to Whitney Houston's "I Wanna Dance with Somebody (Who Loves Me)." Another year Weiss insisted on doing the full 5-minute-and-52-second rendition of "Bohemian Rhapsody," which didn't exactly land with her audience. One summer a dance to Drake's "In My Feelings" was going viral on social media, and Weiss was insistent that everyone at camp learn it and perform it together and put it on Instagram. No one else really cared, but she was the boss and she got some people to do it with her. Some campers jockeyed for attention, trying to get their bosses to go zip-lining with them for face time. Weiss would make an effort to sit with the younger employees. This was probably to get to know everyone, but it felt forced. "She tried to be cool with them," says an older employee who watched the failed bonding. "My theory is she's a deeply insecure person who wants to be part of the cool crowd. When she got up and left, they were all kind of laughing about it." But it was also a way for her to be loose and goofy, to let particularly newer employees see her being a little more normal and quirky.

Back at the office, Weiss would tear daily horoscopes from her subscription to the print edition of the *New York Post* and hang them in the elevator. It was an office-wide pastime; one Glossier employee in the design department, Nadine Jane, even went on to become a professional astrologer. "Someone who once read my astrology chart said beauty was central to my purpose," said Weiss, herself an Aries. In the early days of Glossier, she liked to ask potential job candidates about astrology, particularly about the rising sign (which is believed to say something about how you face or interact with the world). Employees were divided on whether this far-reaching astrology obsession was annoying or endearing. "This is so stupid, why do we do this?" was one text message. Another found it all very fun: "It was one of the reasons why I felt like this was a workplace where I was having so much fun and was truly different from where I had ever worked before." Noted one former intern of an event where interns could ask Weiss questions, "Nothing very interesting came out of that because it was just a bunch of college students asking her about her horoscope." A myth even circulated around the office about the extent of Weiss's reliance on astrology. "There was a rumor that there was some big decision made by her based on a horoscope," a corporate employee said. "But I don't think that would have happened."

As Weiss was settling into her role as CEO of a growing

company, she developed a signature question. "There's a series of questions that ascertain, like, how values-aligned people are. The question I often ask people is, 'Why do you work?' " she said. "Like, my job, I wake up every day thinking about how to make, how to do things that make people happy, bring people this sense of self-actualization, joy. There has to be more to it than just, 'Oh, I need to support my family.' By the way, I need to support my family too. But why do you choose this? What drives you?"

In the pandemic-affected days of a revived labor movement and the so-called Great Resignation, that question is even more poignant. But even pre-2020, there was something to the manor born about it. Most people work simply because they have to. It's not a choice; the "why" is most often because they need money to live and, as a bonus, a sense of purpose. I can't imagine many people would have a very powerful answer because, for them, it's a question on a par with why you pay for health insurance or why you brush your teeth. I asked her what kind of answer she was looking for. "I've never heard the same answer twice, and it's not because I think that there's any right answer. It's because it's a window into what motivates someone, and the reason it's important to understand what motivates someone is that building Glossier is not a job. Like, it might be someday, but I doubt it," she said. "Meaning someday we might be so large that there are certain jobs that are, like, just jobs. I don't think that that will ever happen. I hope it doesn't because I believe that building Glossier is a calling, and obviously I'm a founder, so I'm always going to believe something like this. I just think there are lots of places someone can go work if they just want a job."

Weiss could be extremely blunt in interviews, which jarred people who were meeting her for the first time. Candidates had to walk up the stairs to the second-floor office at 123 Lafayette Street and there was no reception, so they had to mill around until someone took notice and pointed them in the right direction. One job seeker had heard that Weiss would stare at her and ask intense questions, so she prepared so much that Weiss dismissed her a little bit, saying, "Well, you definitely know the answers," as if she were being robotic. Another would-be employee was asked which brands she thought were doing well. She mentioned a fledgling company to Weiss, who replied she hated it. The candidate went home, got Taco Bell, and cried. She was still hired— sometimes the point was more about Weiss asking hard questions than it was how you answered. Glossier fan Youn Chang, who held an MBA from Wharton, had worked as a global supply chain manager at Apple before being hired at Glossier. When she came to her interview with her hair dyed pink, Weiss asked if she had done it for the interview, hinting that she was trying to impress them. "I love Glossier, but not that much to dye my hair for this interview," Chang said.

Even employees who got hired found the interview process tedious. "It wasn't an interview at all; it was more of a speech about what it means to be a woman in tech and what it means to work at Glossier and how many people want this and if I'm not up for the challenge to not take it," said a former tech employee. Another said Weiss gave her a long-winded speech about how start-ups have no typical days and that working at Glossier required commitment and energy.

None of this was mentioned as objectionable so much as it sounded generic. "Emily's a great speaker. When you start at Glossier, it is inspiring," said another former corporate middle manager. "Then you just hear the same great stuff over and over again and you become a little wiser about it. 'Okay, I've heard this before. I know this is coming.' You don't trust what she says anymore." As Glossier grew, not every employee was going to see Weiss as a visionary.

Some Glossier staff did feel like they were working at the best place in the world. Employees could be young and inexperienced and be promoted within the company. Weiss could make quick decisions—she was decisive, especially when it came to anything on the creative or product side—and wasn't a micromanager. Instead, she would tell people to inform her when a project was in its final stages. At its best, Glossier was a job where no idea was too outlandish. Someone could say they wanted to build a rocket ship that would go forty thousand feet up into the atmosphere and then drop Boy Brow, and it wasn't too weird. "The culture of Glossier was that everything was doable, and everything was learnable," said a junior employee. Watching Weiss raise money and pull it off gave some of her employees a sense of confidence. "She made it look not easy, but she made it look achievable."

In 2018, they moved from the office on Lafayette to a building on Hudson Square, on the outer west edge of SoHo, that was known for housing a number of start-up companies. (One of their building's other tenants was Warby Parker.) It was a twenty-thousand-square-foot Glossier fantasia designed by the architect Rafael de Cárdenas, a former Calvin Klein designer whose other clients included Nike and whose signature is mixing cylindrical, almost undulating shapes with vintage pieces—in this case, Weiman Preview art deco chairs, which sell for around $4,200 for a pair; nesting tables by Gianfranco Frattini for Cassina; and a 1940s cast-iron garden bench. (At least one agency who worked with Glossier on designs for stores and offices thought the company was stingy with giving credit to outside architects and designers, and didn't take enough pains to make sure the press knew Glossier's physical spaces were a vision of many, not just Weiss.)

Weiss personally burned sage in the space before they moved in to cleanse the energy. Like so many office designs of the era, it was open plan with emphasis on communal spaces. There were conference rooms with girlbossy monikers such as Frida Kahlo and Michelle Obama. It felt forced. In the old office there had just been a photo of Beyoncé taped on a door and that was the conference room; now you had to go into your calendar app and schedule the Ina Garten room. The famous strong women conference rooms read like a demented funhouse for feminists. The Wing did the same thing; it felt a bit like these companies were playing with the ideas of equity and advancement for women, which is not the same as actually doing it.

It should come as no surprise that the dominant color in the SoHo office was Glossier pink: on upholstery, in the bathroom. It was in the Byredo Burning Rose candles that perfumed the air and in the colors of the roses favored by Brittany Asch of Brrch Floral, who did the flowers for the Glossier offices and Weiss's apartment. Someone who was an intern in the public relations department remembers learning a lot about flowers from watching Asch reflexing roses—florist-speak for turning some of the petals outward or unfurling them—as she prepared the arrangements. Another employee recalled trying to wash her hands before a meeting; it always felt like there were four cute girls with stems everywhere taking up valuable bathroom space, she said. The flowers represented a folly and an overly expensive obsession with external appearances. "They were pretty and interesting and weird, but at the same time it was like, why don't you give me a raise?" said one employee. Another former tech employee said her joke was that "I was going to mash one of those orchids with my hands."

The kitchen was large, with double-door clear glass refrigerators, the better to show off the lavishly stocked coconut waters and yogurts and fresh berries that were always perfectly lined up, labels facing forward. But like the flowers, the snacks were considered symbolic of the company's commitment to exterior appearance. "The organic everything was frustrating to me because they gave me, like, a six percent raise one year," said one disgruntled employee.

There was a huge closet, really more of a room, full of product samples sent to Into the Gloss, where employees (and sometimes the interns) would get in line and say what category of product they needed, whether a body lotion or a mascara, and an Into the Gloss editor would select one for them as a gift. The bathrooms, which were gender-neutral, were fully stocked with the Glossier line for touch-ups and had $29 bottles of Aesop's Post-Poo Drops in each stall. It was a similar lineage to tech giants like Apple or Google that built out their corporate campuses so well that employees would instinctively spend more time there. It's another way Weiss was a representation of the tech culture she so strived to be a part of.

At times working at Glossier could feel like a dream job; it could feel like you were special just for getting to work there. The mere mention of working at Glossier could make a stranger's eyes at a party light up and trigger eager questions about working there and what Emily Weiss was really like. Even as Glossier grew, it resembled the halcyon early days of the small team at Into the Gloss. Weiss wrote in September 2015 on Into the Gloss, "What was once me in my apartment with a cat and spotty wifi is now me and one united team of 38, covering three floors of a Soho office building (with spotty wifi). We have . . . exactly one photographer, two interns who got promoted to full-time hires, a former competitive figure skater in Marketing, an amateur astrologer in Creative, weekly happy hours where we eat Domino's pizza, product-naming group chats, conference rooms called Beyoncé, Rihanna, and Madonna, dogs named Marni, Buttermilk Biscuit, and Quincy." Glossier could be an idyllic place where employees bonded, going to dance classes together after work. Departments had budgets for activities and would go out for red sauce Italian food or hire a tarot card reader. They bleached their eyebrows in the company bathroom and did Instagram stories of employees testing out snacks. They chatted all day in Slack about celebrity gossip, but with people who were better than just strangers on the internet; these were people who were very smart and arch and funny. They had an Ask Glossier Slack channel that was like a real-time version of Into the Gloss. "You could be like, 'Hey, I'm looking for a dry shampoo for my hair. I get oily really fast and I hate the feeling of the weight of a dry shampoo,' and then, like, eighteen people will chime in and be like, 'You just tried this one?'" You could ask for a good place to go get coffee with a potential candidate. One employee who didn't come away liking her brief stint at Glossier still has tried and failed to re-create the magic of Glossier's Slack channels at every job she has had since.

Weiss said there was a no-asshole rule, but there was an environment of mercuriality around the office. She could also be hot and cold with her staff. "Emily was pretty approachable, especially for someone who seemed like such a cool girl," said an employee. "I had watched a bunch of interviews with her, I had watched *The Hills*. I thought she was going to be a little bit more lofty, and I was pleasantly surprised." The younger employees in particular revered her and were quicker to be impressed by Weiss and put her on a pedestal than somewhat older ones who arrived as veterans of big companies. "People that young are also easily intimidated by someone that's more powerful, right?" said someone who came to Glossier in their thirties from a large tech company, who pointed out that tech CEOs do the same thing, playing the line between employees revering them and fearing them.

"Everyone has Emily Weiss stories," another employee said. There would be whispers in the offices that she was being sweet that day, hanging out in the kitchen, grabbing a yogurt. Someone would chime in that Weiss had asked her how her day was going, so it was a good day. But she could switch, smiling at a staff member and then suddenly asking, very intensely, what was going on with a project. Or offhandedly make a comment about how a female staff member resembled her mom or that someone else was so much thinner than Weiss was.

There was a draconian no-mess, clean desk policy. Weiss was so bent on the company being seen as part of tech culture, rather than fashion or beauty, that the company got more and more strict about dress codes. The idea was that if celebrities or investors or famous thinkers were coming around for fundraising or fireside chats or board meetings, then employees should look neat and professional. But sometimes that was done in a way that felt passive-aggressive. An employee might see Weiss eyeing her shorts, see her speaking to a manager, and then be told that her shorts were too short. They weren't sent home to change, but it was embarrassing nonetheless. "It felt like a zoo, to be the Glossier girl and have a cute outfit," says a former employee. "Everyone starts wearing the same scrunchie and it's like, do I have to get that scrunchie now?"

Glossier might have made real progress in disrupting the beauty industry, but for employee culture and salary, there wasn't much beyond surface differences with most other companies. On Glassdoor, the anonymous website where employees can rate workplaces, there were plenty of critics of Weiss and the office culture at large. Low salaries were cited. Interns were paid low wages—at least one reported she made around $12.50 an hour, which is not enough to live on in New York City, or even in the suburbs, without supplementary income. But getting another job was difficult because interns were expected to work the same hours as the rest of the office. "No boundaries, even your social media is judged and commented on. People are just plain rude, probably because they're burnt-out and miserable," was a typical comment.

None of these things are real offenses, particularly in the era of real #MeToo criminality, which roughly coincided with the rise of Glossier. Office culture in general could probably benefit from some more formality in helping employees create boundaries between themselves and their careers. But Glossier was a company that was about democratizing beauty, whose brand was about showing up and being yourself. That set up a high expectation for how employees were supposed to rep-resent themselves and, in turn, be received. Employees were expected to embody the brand, only to be told that the way they embodied it wasn't quite up to par. That dynamic sets up a flawed, girlboss-style progressivism.

Close observers of the company, former employees, and friends of friends of friends whispered about the company being generous with one thing: signing nondisclosure agreements. More than one former employee remembered having to sign one as part of the hiring process. According to a 2017 paper by the *Vanderbilt Law Review*, about one-third of the workforce in the United States was bound by one. Whether those agree-ments are common, I have found, depends on the industry. In entertainment they certainly are, where someone might know something about celebrities of some stripe, or financial infor-mation pertaining to public figures, or could potentially spoil the plot of the announcement of a project. They're frequent at tech companies to protect proprietary information. That seems to be what Weiss was after. She was a person who clung to her personal privacy too. But perhaps the real reason was the sheen of having something to protect and something competitors wanted. Weiss may have wanted Glossier to seem like an office of brilliant, game-changing ideas and have the same renown as the tech companies she so looked up to.

"My low point was being cornered in a room and yelled at for forty-five minutes and crying and everyone watching me while I was facing the glass. My boss was yelling at me, and meanwhile her face was on [an ad on] the side of the building," someone who worked in marketing said, not naming the person in the ads who had terrorized her. Even some employees who were not satisfied at Glossier didn't want to make waves or get fired because working there was so good for their résumés. According to the same marketing employee, "People of color really had to experience messed-up comments. People who worked in retail single-handedly had to create pop-ups and be put in messed-up situations with lack of accountability, lack of diversity training, no real HR team." It's true that the HR department was something of a cobbled-together afterthought. "Firing people was not their strong point. There were hires we made that maybe weren't the best fit, but it's a pretty normal thing to have to learn how to fire people and get good at that," said someone who worked in that department. "When the team was that close, though, firing people was a big deal." Like who? I asked. "Early team members. I'm not going to name them by names, they might not want their firing to be in a book." Whether they were officially fired or not, two early hires ended their time at the company on a sour note. Annie Kreighbaum left, with subordinates who found her hard to work with and a poor manager. (Kreighbaum prides herself on not commenting about Glossier, including for this book. On her beauty podcast she said that she ignores such requests, invoking Mariah Carey's casual insult about J.Lo, "I don't know her.") Henry Davis departed Glossier in late 2018. "I had been there a long time," he said as his reason for leaving.

The company has an issue with cliquishness. An inner circle of employees who were closest to Weiss and had been there the longest, for many as their first jobs, were seen by the rest as favored. They also happened to be beautiful and have Instagram presence, almost like local celebrities whom Glossier nurtured. Some people called them the OGs. They were seen as more invested because they had been there from the beginning, but there was more to it than just seniority. As someone who was definitely not part of that crowd described it, "A lot was trying to capture that ethereal coolness. Glossier was the ultimate brand—we were selling 'Vaseline' for $12 for half an ounce—so it's all about the brand. Weiss knew that to some degree, and thought, 'I need to be inspired by people who are cool and interesting and that's how I'm going to find that sparkly magic dust.'" There was also a hierarchy not so far from the kinds of office hierarchies that Weiss came from in the fashion and media world. If she was consciously trying to replicate tech culture, she was unconsciously replicating Condé Nast. In those corporate cultures, the beautiful and pedigreed and charismatic stood out as employees who also functioned as brand ambassadors. It was no different at Glossier, just with a millennial generation spin: follower count on social media mattered; your skin could be imperfect if you were beautiful and it translated to relatability online; you could be chubby if you had a gorgeous face and dressed well.

Weiss's assistant Morgan Von Steen starred in a series of social media posts called "Your Daily Morgan." It began when she got a pumpkin spice latte from Starbucks and Weiss recorded her talking about her order. Weiss posted them daily, Instagram stories of Von Steen being awkward on camera. "People started to enjoy that and I was getting recognized by people from her Instagram stories, which I thought was strange. People started to follow me from that. They would send me customized 'Your Daily Morgan' merch," said Von Steen. She ended up with about ten thousand followers, including one man who messaged her on Instagram; they went on a few dates but remained very close friends.

Elevating your employees to the role of a cast of characters is smart for engagement. It's what magazines like *Jane* had done in the past, and Weiss put a social media spin on it. It's when some employees become stars and others are left behind that a quickly growing business could feel more like high school. Weiss thought she was creating a utopia in her office culture. Maybe, for some, it was. But she also replicated some of the worst aspects of the magazine and fashion world at Glossier. Frustrated employees would tough it out, or leave, but others would eventually speak up.

8

Glossier posted a five-star review of its brow gel Boy Brow that was titled "Literally stayed on through getting hit by a car": "I wore this to a festival and it stayed on through infinite sweat there. After the festival I got hit by a car on the side of the road and after getting pulled out from under a car and going to the hospital the only intact part of my makeup when I left the hospital was this brow product." (Glossier's caption was: "Maddy and her brows are ok!") For a period of time in 2015, Boy Brow had a 10,000-person wait list. Glossier was a success as a company, in hype and in funding. But with Boy Brow it had found a true hero product.

Weiss compared Glossier's products to the Harry Potter books: "You have all of these, this huge community of people who have read Book One, read Book Two. Can all discuss it, and it's their common thread, and they're waiting for Book Three, or whatever it is. And with our products that's really what's happened." She also worried if there was an end to those true fans. As much of a household name as she wanted Glossier to be, she feared that "the second you go outside of that and try to reach audiences that you have to pay a little bit more to convince them to come in, you run the risk of not being able to retain their engagement. They could transact that one time and then not want anything to do with your brand again. They don't want to be on your email list; they don't want to follow you on social; they don't want to evangelize or recommend your brand."

Her answer was to keep rolling out hit products. A team of high-level people across the company—Annie Kreighbaum, head of design Adriana Deleo, Eva Alt on social, Helen Steed the creative director, and those who worked under them— would post images to a shared iCloud for inspiration for the product launches. The creative team would build the world and the mood for the product, the developers would work on the product itself, Kreighbaum would build the story around the product, and Alt would share it with the internet. Boy Brow had images that were tactile, like the feeling of eyebrow hair on a face. "A lot of the references came from art and fashion and editorial from the '90s and early 2000s. It wasn't, like, perfectly curated," Steed said. "And it was never about looking at what other beauty brands were doing. It was like Irving Penn's Clinique photography from the '60s, not what Clinique is doing today."

Topics covered in product development and supply meetings included whether to go for more cost-effective and manufacturing-friendly versions (like a plastic label for a bottle), or a custom silk screen on a glass bottle. That latter version would be more customized, heavier, and higher quality but also more expensive, to the tune of 70 percent more. Weiss wanted the most beautiful and, more importantly, the most Instagrammable versions of products. For her vision of the Glossier customer, that was what was most fulfilling. The idea of unboxing—how a customer received and opened the package—was key. "We talked about how, from the moment they received the box, we wanted people to be super excited about it, and how to get there," said an employee who was in those meetings.

Weiss thought about new products like experiences. "We've always thought about it from the customer experience. And I'm a customer, everyone is a customer. So I think it's not rocket science," she said. Weiss was belittling herself but also positioning herself as someone who really understands customer desires in the way that her beloved lifestyle brands Nike and Apple did, setting Glossier apart from other companies and setting herself apart from other CEOs. She's not a regular CEO; she's a cool CEO. "I think it's just dedication and it's intentionality. And I think one of the things that I'm so proud of about Glossier is how intentional we've been. Again, intentionality does not equal perfection does not equal no mistakes."

Enter Boy Brow. It was a gel pomade with a hint of color that kept brows in place without feeling like the hairs got crunchy. It sounds strikingly like the combination that Glossier's original product developer, Alexis Page, used on her own brows, per her Top Shelf: a Mary Kay gel, the Brow Primer from Anastasia Beverly Hills, and Tom Ford Brow Sculptor. Magazines had advised to use a brown mascara, with most of the product wiped off the wand, to tame and color brows, and in the 1980s brands like Maybelline had a clear mascara many used on their brows. But to get the lush look of defined, thick brows, it was a genius idea to combine the three products

Page had been using. Boy Brow's campaign advised fans to "Brush your teeth, brush your brows, and then maybe brush your hair." Says Amanda Montell, a feminist linguist and author of the book *Cultish*, "I think of Glossier. When you buy Boy Brow, you're not just buying brow gel, you're buying an identity, a community, values, and that's what capitalism and consumerism is in the twenty-first century."

The timing of the launch was savvy—the product came out in 2015, the same time that the vogue for thick eyebrows was cresting with Cara Delevingne's signature bushy brows all over ad campaigns and magazines and vintage shots of Brooke Shields, ambassador of thick brows from the last time they were in style, all over Instagram's mood boards. It was a departure from the plucked, skinny brows of the 1990s and aughts. "Eyebrows on fleek," as the internet meme went. Thick eyebrows signified youth and contemporary culture and a divergence from any lingering hangover of grunge-chic. It was the beauty equivalent of fashion's boyfriend jeans: easy and lived-in, a little tomboyish, but also a little calculated in their marketing. (Whose boyfriend has jeans that are perfectly loose on you but fit in the waist?) A thick brow was where both the minimalist no-makeup types and those who championed a full face of makeup could find common ground. In the first quarter of 2016, Glossier sold as much product as it thought it would in an entire year. (The caveat to all this good news is that Glossier was and remains a private company whose wait lists aren't available to be audited or sales publicly reported other than what they offer up.)

Executive editor Annie Kreighbaum had the brows of Boy Brow, featured in the campaigns, looking slightly unkempt but lush. "Maybe my eyebrows are more famous than I am? I hear they do well on our paid ads," she told BuzzFeed. Another brow of the campaign belonged to Anna Gray, a vintage clothing dealer and occasional model. Her friend Jen Steele was working with Glossier to scout and organize shoots. Gray's Boy Brow shoot for online and social media took twenty minutes in Glossier's conference room on Lafayette Street. "It was so funny and scrappy," she told me. "I max made a thousand dollars."

The idea of the "hero product" is key to the beauty industry, not just in marketing, but in the emotional response customers have to it. Hero products are the signature bestsellers of a company, high or low. Examples of such products are Charlotte Tilbury's Pillow Talk lipstick (a neutral "your lips, but better" shade), Maybelline's Great Lash mascara, Nars's Orgasm blush, Dyson's $400 Supersonic hair dryer, Urban Decay's Naked eye shadow palette, Laneige's Lip Sleeping Mask, and Essie's Ballet Slippers nail polish. Weiss herself had her favorites: "You put on your bright red MAC Ruby Woo lipstick, but it looks cooler and more rock 'n' roll a few hours later when it's worn off. It turns into a stain that no [lipstick] can replicate."

One product that was more evergreen because it was less tied to a trend like Boy Brow was Glossier's Milky Jelly Cleanser, a face wash that came out in 2016 and remains one of their bestsellers. The creative process "was about the texture and the feel and running with that," said Steed. It was described as their first crowdsourced product, based off a 2015 Into the Gloss post asking, "What's Your Dream Face Wash?" "What would your dream cleanser look like? Smell like? Feel like? Do for you? Not do for you? Who would play this cleanser in a movie?" A reader named Ali had a typically specific and gushing, almost florid comment, of which there were hundreds—thousands if you add in the company's other channels for customer input: "Hate cleansers that give me a squeaky clean feeling so nothing too sudsy or astringent. For me, the best cleansers are ones that do deep cleaning work but are also very nourishing with a milk-like texture. I also am a fan of oil based cleansers that melt away the dirt. That may be because I have very dry skin though. *HERE'S THE THING* I really don't believe there's a one size fits all cleanser!" The company ended up trying out more than forty formulas for the cleanser before landing on the right one. But others said that Milky Jelly was a more expensive version of La Roche-Posay Toleriane Hydrating Gentle Cleanser.

Some products had splashy debuts. When Glossier launched the highlighter Haloscope, they posted: "What we wanted is that Krispy Kreme straight-out-the-oven glazed look . . . warm on the inside, a little wet and sculpted on the outside. That's what we set out looking to achieve in a new highlighter—something that gives the glow of supremely hydrated skin." (Hailey Bieber, the model and founder of the beauty company Rhode, has made the glazed-doughnut look her signature, as if she invented it, when Glossier used similar terms in 2016.) Twenty days later one of the highlighter shades, the opalescent pink Quartz, was sold out. Kreighbaum was a savant at naming products and shades in terms of what customers wanted to write on Instagram. Would it be easy to spell? It couldn't already be a hashtag. Most of the company's shade names were just one syllable. For Haloscope, she just made the word up. "The product had real crystals in it, so we were thinking, like, what's this word? It's not really hippie-dippie crystal, but it's kind of like sciency-girl crystal. You're not like an earth mother, really. But you're more like, you're into astrology still. Kind of like the new age hippie," she said. "And so, I was thinking horoscopes, and then I was thinking a halo of light, and then I merged the two words, Haloscope, horoscope, halo. And then I googled it to make sure it wasn't already a weird thing—and I saw that it's actually a tool that scientists use to look at light phenomenons. And I was like, that's what highlighting is!"

Other products were successful but more of a slow burn to success. For Bubblewrap, an eye and lip cream, the directive for the product team was "it has to be creamy but also bouncy." Stretch Concealer was a Glossier way (read: sheer) to add coverage or hide discoloration or dark circles or imperfections of any kind. "We're not telling you that you need a concealer. We're providing a concealer in case you want it," Weiss said to me. "We're trying to give you the tools to be able to make whatever decision you want." Jenna Lyons, formerly of J.Crew, told *Vanity Fair* her favorite product was Glossier Ultralip Tinted Balm in the sheer shade Lucite. Combined with a smoky eye, she compared it to "pairing a men's blazer with pearls."

Glossier grew by 600 percent year over year in 2016. That same year Weiss noted that they had about 60,000 people across the sold-out products who were on either wait list or back order, and they would be notified first. The company had been using very small vendors and asking them to increase their capacity every month to keep up with Glossier's huge demand. Employees working on pop-up stores would joke about how much the company was spending on them despite, or maybe because of, operational problems they faced. They were always running late and using air rather than freight shipping to meet their timelines, which was enormously expensive.

Weiss's answer to impatient fans frustrated that Boy Brow was sold out was to compose a post on Into the Gloss about the difficulties of scaling a business like Glossier. Reflecting back on the post, she said, "The primary goal of that was, yes, to communicate why they're sold out, but also, if I'm a customer, I might not care why you're sold out, I might just want my Milky Jelly Cleanser. So what I really wanted us to do was just apologize, because it's our fault, I mean, we're the company. So the most important thing that came out of that was saying that we're really sorry. We miscalculated, the demand has been really crazy, and here are the three things we're doing actively to fix it." They managed to resolve their supply chain issues eventually with the help of Youn Chang. When they were able to restock lipsticks and concealers—those reportedly had a combined wait list of 30,000—they celebrated with breakfast sandwiches, parfaits, and cupcakes topped with fondant the color of, yes, Glossier pink and tiny versions of their Generation G lipsticks.

There were other mistakes and setbacks. The Generation G lipstick had to be reformulated a few times after customers said it was too drying and that the slim packaging looked too cheap. Glossier's sunscreen launch was delayed a year because the formula kept crystallizing in its bottle. The company that manufactured their concealer and lipstick in California "basically dropped us to do Kylie Cosmetics and that fucked our supply chain for six months," an employee said. Caroline Hirons, the British beauty writer and influencer who is known for her painfully frank reviews, said that after she tried Glossier's Solution, an exfoliating acid toner meant to compete with Biologique Recherche P50, she hated it: "I used it and it stung my face and I took pictures because I had sort of um well, it's more like a hive reaction but it felt like a burn around my nose." It was her most-read post.

Another aspect of the hero product discussion is introducing it to consumers—how do companies do that successfully, especially if the product's concept is unfamiliar, in a crowded marketplace? What's particularly impressive is the vast majority of Glossier customers were ordering these products online without any kind of samples. Weiss had made successful inroads into cracking the online retail code of how to get customers to buy things without trying them out at department stores or drugstores first. Or were Glossier girls such evangelists that they were imploring everyone they knew to try out and buy their favorite ones? This was, after all, a line engineered to make you feel like part of an elite but friendly clique.

The company experimented with ways to nurture its superfans. In fall 2015, when they were still at the Lafayette Street office, their forty top customers were invited to come for "a night of mystery product testing, pizza, rosé, and g.IRL talk with other members of the Glossier community and CEO and Founder Emily Weiss!" (The invite also came with a nondisclosure agreement.) They were launching their first flavored balms and the lucky guests were invited to taste flavors and choose the first. (Inspired by Lip Smackers and its cult classic Dr Pepper flavor, Glossier ended up launching with mint, rose, and cherry.) They ordered Rubirosa pizza, and the women who came liked each other so much that one left saying, "I think I just met my best friend here." They stayed so long that the tired employees were trying to find a polite way to get them to leave.

Soon Glossier opened up the penthouse floor at the Lafayette Street office on Fridays for any fans to come shop the showroom. One Barnard student frequented the showroom because it felt like an accessible, low-stakes way for her to participate in the New York beauty scene. She liked that it felt intimate and secret with five or ten people shopping there total, usually other young women around her age. Sometimes she'd recognize one of the fellow shoppers or the staff from Instagram. The showroom performed so well that it generated sales higher per square foot than an Apple Store, with a 65 percent conversion rate. A former employee told me that once an influencer asked if she could bring her lamb to an event.

The crew of fans from the lip balm tasting wanted to stay connected to one another, so Kim Johnson, an intern turned ad sales employee, told them about a new app called Slack, where they could all stay talking online. First it was the initial top forty customers from that pizza party; then it expanded to include top commenters. The channel immediately took on a life of its own, birthing friendships among beauty obsessives—some flying across the country to meet and visit each other, even attending each other's weddings. They sent thousands of messages a day, and recommended and discussed all manner of beauty products, but they also talked about their jobs and their lives. It was finally the dream of Glossier's friendliness—the cool but nice girls—materializing. Occasionally they were given products to test and encouraged to talk openly about the pros and cons on the dedicated Slack channel. Once, someone didn't like a product she'd tested and posted about it on her own social media, which caused quite a stir among the group, who were protective of Glossier and seemed to feel it was akin to airing family business.

Beyond just the Slack channel, Glossier experimented with whether they should have paid partnerships with professional influencers; a customer loyalty program; and paid media spending, which could include anything from traditional advertisements to direct mail to wheat-pasted posters to paid social media posts. They tried a representative program in summer 2016, something like throwing Tupperware-style parties for products. Could the Glossier Girl be the new, extremely online Avon Lady? Rather than a multilevel marketing company like Avon, this program was about sharing a sale. They noticed that they were getting product referral likes for a lot of revenue from just a few hyper-enthusiastic customers who had the link to Glossier's referral code (one anyone could get to pass a 20-percent-off coupon to a new customer) in their Instagram bios. Could they reward these loyal customers and make them more money? The program started out with just ten or fifteen users who were given their own Glossier landing pages, so someone would navigate to, say, glossier.com/rep/amy. There the rep would show off her favorite products in a routine, and anyone could shop all Glossier products from there. If someone bought anything from that page, the rep would get about 10 percent and the customer would get a percentage off her first order. The reps would get invited to meet Weiss or to try out new products. The Glossier team also worked with reps on content creation, sending out guides explaining the best way, for example, to take a selfie to show off a blush.

There is power in those kinds of connections. A gay teen could find a gay adult rep to ease him into buying glitter for the prom, or someone with rosacea might like hearing from someone else who deals with it on which products are the most soothing or the best at covering redness. But the company couldn't figure out how to best incentivize the process, whether it should be cash, or limited-edition products or merchandise, or store credit, or access to Weiss herself. "Anyone can buy customers, not everyone can earn them," Henry Davis said.

The product that most typifies this era was their first fragrance, You, which in 2022 sold a million units, or one every 43 seconds. When it came out in 2017, You, which was marketed as unisex, had a milky Glossier pink bottle and an undulating form with a blast of clear red on its cap. It was actually quite risky for a first perfume because it lacked a top note—the main first hit that the nose detects, and what most fragrances are known by. Instead, it was heavy on base notes of ambrette and musk in order "to smell mostly like you." It was also Weiss's favorite product to develop. One night she and their perfume developer were among the only people left in the office, around seven thirty. "She was unboxing all the new samples that had just come in," Weiss said. She thought they were on version thirty-four, and they were all lined up when Weiss came out of the conference room from whatever meeting she was wrapping up. "I remember breathing in the air and being like, 'That's it. That's the one. What is that?' And she was like, 'Oh, it's like this new sample we just got.' And I was like, 'That's Glossier You.'"

This was their perfume version of no-makeup makeup. It was ingenious and funny. It felt like a joke the surrealists might have made. They launched it with a surreal pop-up—excuse me, they called it an "offline experience"—focused on just one product. That felt like a throwback to Weiss's art school years, a Glossier folly. It was a theatrical experience decorated to resemble something between a boudoir and a funhouse where you went into a phone booth and pressed a button and a hand in a red latex glove would spritz you or do a dance move or hand you a rose. It was delightful to experience and to participate in—employees would take shifts being the hand. The two-week engagement ended up lasting all winter.

Fragrance can take a long time and a lot of money to develop, but the margin is incredible if it's a hit. People are loyal to fragrance in a way they aren't to virtually any other product, and fragrance marketing can live for years and years without being refreshed. I think of my ex-stepmother who still wears L'Eau d'Issey as she had when it was originally introduced more than forty years ago. Scent is closely tied to memory, and it has an emotional component that not even a product like cleanser or sunscreen that often needs to be replenished has. Men buy it for women as a gift in a way that doesn't happen for lipstick. You was a hit. In 2018, Glossier won the FiFi—the Oscars of the fragrance world—for it, making it a critical darling; it remains one of their best-selling products. It remains my personal favorite Glossier product, and the company has slowly started to expand the line with a candle and a deodorant in the same scent.

It didn't seem to matter that the You pop-up could have sold other Glossier products. Or that Glossier didn't really have stores, or that it was makeup for people who didn't want to (or need to) wear makeup. "Our creative team at Glossier is kind of like the modern-day MGM," Weiss recalled telling Marie Suter, who was hired as the company's creative director in 2018. "I'm serious. We can set the norms for what beauty imagery is, which photographers you shoot with, which people you put in campaigns." That sounds grandiose, but in those years it felt like the company could do no wrong, and no path was off-limits.

9

Emily Weiss was wearing a tuxedo with no shirt underneath. She greeted VIP guests as they walked up a red quartz staircase to find five-foot-tall tubes of Boy Brow ready to pose with and a party photographer ready to capture it all. The air was lightly scented with Glossier You, and the mood was buoyant by design at the opening party in November 2018 for Glossier's first permanent Manhattan flagship store. There were magazine editors there and Glossier employees, but the highlight in terms of celebrity wattage was when the crowd parted so Weiss could more easily lead Serena Williams and her husband, the Reddit cofounder Alexis Ohanian, on a tour of the space. The next morning Williams posted a snapshot of the night to her Instagram account with the caption "Bossed up with @emilyweiss." It felt like a microcosm of the company's success.

Inside, Glossier's boutique on Lafayette Street in SoHo, where their former office was, had been transformed. Weiss viewed the stores as a physical unboxing that needed to please and surprise customers. The flagship was built to incite maximum Instagram engagement. One room was called the wet bar and was set up like a women's public restroom with skincare products lined up next to the sink and large mirrors on the wall. Another room had a red banquette in the shape of lips. The space felt like being inside a really fresh-smelling vagina. (Which was a theme for that decade—Goop used a vagina theme for the premiere party of its Netflix show *The Goop Lab*, which also had a vulva episode. Were we in peak vagina?) You might as well call it a propaganda machine. A glittery and pink and pleasurable one. Weiss called the flagship store "Adult Disneyland."

This was the peak and pinnacle of Glossier, the moment when Weiss was sending out the signal that they were fully committed to the big time. The brand amassed even more high-powered fans as the financial market began taking it seriously. Beyoncé, Serena Williams, Michelle Obama, Alexandria Ocasio-Cortez, and the US women's soccer team during their apotheosis as role models were all members of "Generation G." Reese Witherspoon wore Glossier makeup to the Oscars. They were minting smiles and money.

Weiss graced the cover of *Time* magazine as one of the Next 100 Most Influential People in November 2019. That was after she had been on the cover of *Fast Company* and *Entrepreneur*, and made *Forbes*'s 30 Under 30 list. She occupied a cult of personality even among her own girlboss cohort. Leandra Medine said, of her media company Man Repeller's inception, "I think it started with Into the Gloss because I was like, 'Oh wow, look at how Emily is, like, growing her one-person blog into a media company, I can do that too.' And then after she launched Glossier, I was like, 'Hmm, I don't know about that.'"

From a financial standpoint, Glossier was continuing to gain steam—and gaining the attention of venture capital firms as it pursued its next rounds of funding. Weiss and Henry Davis would find themselves out at Sand Hill Road, the unassuming suburban road that winds through the particularly monied western parts of Silicon Valley—Palo Alto, Menlo Park, Woodside—where many venture capital companies had offices. So many that it had become shorthand for them, the way that "Madison Avenue" was for advertising or "Savile Row" for bespoke tailoring. One of my first jobs out of college was working at a book publisher there for a few months before it had to vacate its office for some large and storied financial institution to take over. It's not flashy or densely populated but rather spread out in a way that feels desolate, the mid-century architecture low-slung and deceptively suburban for the power that lies inside. "It's not by design the most welcoming place. That's changed a little bit," said Davis. "We were in a Honda Civic and always filling the pink pouches before meetings."

There was a Series A round in November 2014 just after the original Glossier launch that raised $8.4 million. Davis characterized that round as "idiosyncratic," in that some of the people they met with simply did not get it. "There are very few innovative companies where everyone agrees it's a good idea," said Davis. "Thrive and Nick Brown at 14W got it. They were in New York and that makes sense, and they had built a relationship with Emily since the seed round. They've heard what you're saying you're going to do and seen you deliver." Glossier had shown promise, but in late 2014 it was largely unproven. If I couldn't get a New York magazine editor to assign me a profile, I can only imagine the hurdles of getting a check. But Weiss was good in the room, and that early on, a lot of fundraising was about getting people to believe in her potential. Weiss was always good at selling herself, but she had gotten better at selling her sharpened vision of her company's plan. The gross profit margins for beauty are high. Glossier's were about 80 percent, according to more than one former employee. As face wash does not cost a lot to make—the real cost is in the marketing—and beauty companies have the potential to scale, both of which are attractive to venture capitalists. The money allowed them to expand office space, add forty employees, and launch a dozen products.

If funding had been tricky in Glossier's initial seed rounds, it was getting easier. The company was fresh off a splashy spring 2016 subway advertising campaign with pink ads that read: "Everyone says they're 'low-maintenance' (it's okay neither are we)." But the ad initially debuted on the subway with a huge typo—"say's"—and was photographed and shared on social media. One can only imagine the intensity of Weiss's reaction. It was still treated by fans as a celebration. Glossier employees handed out five hundred pink roses one morning to commuters who posted things to Twitter and Instagram like "Adorbs, brilliant!, the perfect subtle spring vibes I needed" and "OMG THERE ARE @glossier SUBWAY ADS. GOD SAVE MY CHECKING ACCOUNT."

In fall 2016, Glossier raised another $24 million in Series B financing. (Weiss would rate this 6/10 on the Crazy Idea Scale, while Series A had been 8/10. As in her "Little Wedding Black Book," she enjoyed giving things grades and ratings.)

Twelve out of twelve investment firms Weiss pitched signed on, and the round was led by IVP, which had previously invested in Twitter, Netflix, Snap, and the Honest Company. "Beauty is about a quarter-trillion-dollar industry, and the majority of that market consists of products made by stodgy, slow, offline companies that sell through third-party retailers. These are companies that only hear from their customers through focus groups and outsourced surveys. Product development is limited by shelf space constraints and quarters-old sell-through data," wrote Eric Liaw, Roseanne Wincek, and Louise Ireland of IVP about their commitment to Glossier. "Glossier knows not only where to find women, and how to ask them what they want, but also how to listen to their fan base." For her part, Weiss wrote on Into the Gloss in a funding update that she knew Liaw "was our guy when he texted me a #maskforce selfie with his face covered in the Mega Greens Galaxy Pack as we were getting to know each other." The money would go toward opening permanent retail spaces, developing and launching new products, and a vaguely worded commitment to invest in technology "because we think every woman should have the ability to be connected through her beauty knowledge, opinions, products, and routine."

Into the Gloss was a victim of vacillating company priorities. As Glossier grew, Into the Gloss shrank. Weiss at one point said that they didn't need Into the Gloss anymore because it was competing with Glossier—the diverse array of product recommendations made on Into the Gloss was cannibalizing Glossier's products. The solution was to all but shut down the site in order to minimize the readership and drive

Glossier products. The editorial employees of Into the Gloss were sort of their own entity within the company, so, without much to do, they were assigned to work on marketing or other copywriting jobs, which annoyed the career copywriters. But then, as if turning on a dime, that idea to minimize Into the Gloss was overhauled, and once again, around 2018, Weiss wanted to recommit to it and hire big-name journalists like Leah Chernikoff from *Elle* and Ashley Weatherford from the *Cut*. But at that point, the site had lost a lot of momentum it would not manage to regain.

For its Series C in early 2018, Davis took calls from the bathroom of his wife's hospital room as their twins were being born. By that time, venture capitalists knew what Glossier was and the business had taken off. It was a competitive enough round that Glossier got to choose who they wanted as their financial partners, which is far from the usual case. The Series C round added $52 million in investment. That same year, Bloomberg reported that Glossier had crossed into $100 million in revenue and brought on one million new customers.

The unveiling of the flagship store was in a sense a celebration of doing things their way, or rather Weiss's way: having stuck to a direct-to-consumer approach that's worked for them to have total control over how the customer experiences the company. They had methodically built up their content on Into the Gloss and brand awareness on Instagram, both driving customer loyalty and community, but they needed commerce for revenue. The company found that shoppers who bought from the showrooms tended to keep buying from them rather than go back to digital for their next purchases.

Glossier was launching its retail experiences at a time when the interactive experience was catering to social media. Color Factory, the Museum of Ice Cream, the two competing Van Gogh immersives are all vaguely cultural experiences that are really elaborate backdrops for photo ops. The Glossier store felt like a classier version of that. A brick-and-mortar store like Target that was essentially a big box, this was not. Rather, it was the kind of physical retail space that doubled as a cost-effective advertising and public relations generator, at once utterly enthralling as well as accessible to a new generation of consumers—one that retail analysts might reasonably have thought would never be into shopping IRL.

I have attended Glossier's original flagship store on multiple Saturday afternoons, with Weiss and without, when it averaged 50,000 visitors per month and the line to get in ran halfway down the block and customers were offered Invisible Shield sunscreen and spritzes of rosewater spray to help ease the wait. Up the stairs and inside, there were tweens teaching each other how to apply mascara, mothers and daughters comparing swatches of eyeliner on their wrists, and strangers going over their beauty routines with each other as they sampled cleanser. There was no counter, no waiting in line to pay. It was wholesome, and heartwarming. One friend of mine predicted that girls will age out of Build-A-Bear workshops into Glossier stores.

Not so long ago, the be-all and end-all of commerce was the department store beauty counter as a destination for women to bond, to reinvent themselves, to play. One of my favorite places to shop is Paris's Le Bon Marché department store, to which all grand (and less than grand) department stores owe their existence. Émile Zola used it as the setting for his 1883 book *The Ladies' Paradise* about Denise, a girl from the country who comes to Paris to work at a department store. Zola called such stores "cathedrals of commerce," where shopping was both a leisure pursuit and a sacred one. The midcentury British novelist Barbara Pym set a memorable scene at the beauty counter in her book of spinsterdom, *Excellent Women*. "I longed to be in a crowd of busy women shopping," muses her prickly heroine Mildred Lathbury. "There was a mirror on the counter and I caught sight of my own face, colourless and worried-looking, the eyes large and rather frightened, the lips too pale." That sort of poor self-reflection stokes the desire to find something to fix it and to treat herself. "The colors had such peculiar names but at last I chose one that seemed right and began to turn over a pile of lipsticks in a bowl in an effort to find it." The shade she chooses is Hawaiian Fire, an orange-red. The bossy saleswoman, who calls her "dear" (better, she muses, than "madam"), thinks she should choose Sea Coral or Jungle Red. She leaves with the Hawaiian Fire, exhausted but triumphant. The lust, the delight, the guilt, the mortification, are all things we can relate to. *The Muppets Take Manhattan* has a similar scene of finding selfhood via the beauty counter. In the 1984 movie the assertive Muppet Miss Piggy works on the beauty floor at Parfumerie, where she and coworker Joan Rivers wear frilly light-pink coats that look like a combination of eighteenth-century clothes and the scientific panache of a lab coat. "It's French, it's feminine, it will help you grab one of those rotten, stinkin' men,'" shouts Miss Piggy, who is fresh off an argument with her frog beau Kermit. Rivers tells her, "You could use a little rouge," and applies some makeup to perk her up, the beauty counter being a place of gossip, of emotion, and of wish fulfillment. But also aggression.

In the summer of 2019, I observed a meeting at the Glossier corporate offices about the retail pop-ups. Five people, including creative director Marie Suter and Adriana Deleo, the head of design, were packed into a tiny conference room in their SoHo headquarters—Weiss had deemed the first room too cold—reviewing plans for a store set to open in Boston. At least, I think it was a meeting. I couldn't shake the feeling the whole time I was there that this was just a pantomime of a meeting they were performing for a journalist's sake. Glossier had just wrapped up the pop-up in Seattle. "Did I show you guys the tweet?" Weiss took out her iPhone and passed around the photo. "This is the line outside Glossier Pop-up Seattle on the last weekend. It's a full city block long."

The Boston store was going to be spread out over eight rooms, but she paused to muse over renderings of a space devoted to Generation G, their lipstick. "More than the title, Generation G became the value system that Glossier creates throughout this new generation of people. You could be fifteen or you could be, like, sixty, but if you believe what we believe, then you're a part of Generation G," she said. "We can really own that here. The Generation G room."

"Maybe we can add some text," Deleo suggested.

"Yeah, that's a good idea," Weiss said, tapping her fingers on her mouth. "Instead of, like, 'You look good,' maybe—"

"'I'm Generation G,'" Suter supplied, sipping a ginger ale with a paper straw. Weiss nodded.

Melanie Masarin was originally in charge of retail. A veteran of American Eagle, she'd first started talking to Glossier about working with international when they were a hot downtown brand in 2015 and had some expansion initiatives. (Having launched on Instagram, Glossier had plenty of international fans from the beginning, but they couldn't get products. The company started shipping internationally to Canada and then the UK in 2017 and was said to be setting up a London office.) By the time Masarin, who's French, got her green card and was able to work, Glossier had already shifted gears. They decided they were no longer going to prioritize international business but still wanted to hire her. "I was the director of retail and there was no retail," she said with a laugh. "Warby Parker was going into retail. Everyone was asking us."

So Masarin worked on pop-up stores, where she soon had a real-life peek into Glossier's fans. She routinely met girls who had driven five or six hours just to see the products in real life. In Baltimore, a group of girls came before the store was open to the public. "They were training the team and I couldn't send them home, so we gave them a tour of the flagship and some bags," she said. In San Francisco, she persuaded Weiss to let her do the pop-up at a fried chicken restaurant. In Toronto, a cross-section of ages and genders waited in line for the doors to open as if it were a rock concert. The pop-ups weren't just a good excuse for press or a good moment for Instagram; they created a burst of new customers in that market who stayed Glossier customers even after the store's run ended.

They would scan Instagram for each new market and find a half dozen or so fans with the most engagement with Glossier. Then an employee would be dispatched to befriend them in order to tap into their community and understand what life was like for the people they wanted to sell to. They would invite fans for coffee or lunch or mixers. Glossier even threw a birthday party for one girl on a *bateau-mouche* in Paris. Retail was supposed to be hyper-localized, so London's pop-up was a massive house and Seattle had an elaborate plant installation from the landscape designer Studio Lily Kwong. There were later pop-ups in Ireland, Sweden, Denmark, and Paris, which had a wheat-paste poster campaign that read "Liberté, Égalité, *Glossier.*"

Retail employees were called offline editors, in a confusing nod to the editorial world (those in customer service were "online editors"), and wore light-pink jumpsuits with stickers that declared their preferred pronouns. The job listings for retail were posted on Instagram—a savvy way to hire existing fans—and were treated like casting calls. The first round was a self-taped video, like an audition. A lot of them consisted of Weiss superfans who said she was their idol. Hiring managers found this endearing, although they didn't always understand the point of gushing about the CEO over touting their own qualifications. If a candidate made it to the second round, there was a phone call with a store manager. The biggest red flag at that stage was a reluctance to talk—a surprisingly large number of candidates wouldn't pick up the phone and would respond that they'd prefer to do the interview over text message, which didn't bode well for a job in retail. The third round was in person. The one for the Los Angeles store, for instance, was held in the lobby of a West Hollywood hotel, where a group of girls largely in their twenties, obviously there for the Glossier interviews, milled about wearing clothes like green velvet Rachel Antonoff jumpsuits. One guy came dressed in all the Glossier merch—sweatshirt, bag, key chain—he had collected at pop-ups to show the depth of his devotion.

They were asked questions such as "Why do you want to work at Glossier?"—an echo of Weiss's "Why do you work?"—and "How do you envision Glossier benefiting from your experience?" That makes it sounds like Glossier's hiring department, and Weiss, don't really understand that most people take jobs, especially retail jobs, because they need the money. It's not a deep question for them to ponder, even if there are plenty of pretty and talented people who know there will be a bit of prestige with getting the job. It's a larger failing of both tech and California-style woo-woo culture—a demon baby of both those things. I imagine no one asked Morgan Von Steen when she was working at Cold Stone Creamery, saving up to intern in New York City, how she envisioned the ice cream store benefiting from her service. Weiss had envisioned Glossier retail employees as akin to career waiters at an old-school haunt like Balthazar in Soho or the ones at Café de Flore in Paris. "You walk into an old institution and it's their career and they know the menu and the place and it's their home," said Amy Snook, who worked in communications at Glossier. "But the problem is, most people don't look at retail jobs like that." The pay at Glossier's retail shops was competitive, around $20 per hour depending on the level of seniority and the city, with benefits if they worked full-time, but that usually wasn't the Gen Z or younger millennial workforce.

The lucky few who made the cut got to experience orientation, Glossier-style. They passed around a Body Hero lotion and made orgasm noises over how good the white flower scent was. "They just needed to convince these twentysomething girls this was the best scent ever to sell products. I loved it at the time, but it now smells overly synthetic and gross to me, which is an apt metaphor for my experience," said one retail employee.

To work in the Glossier store felt like joining a sorority or becoming a Playboy Bunny if it was still cool and not creepy. They were offered free facials by nearby salons, and bakeries in the neighborhood would send over cupcakes for the crew. The other editors were each other's new best friends, their favorite group chat, their future bridesmaids. They were the people they went with to rooftop bars or Shake Shack or to get vegan Mexican food.

The stores had a standard operating procedure for celebrities or VIPs or anyone famous who came in (the definition of fame getting murkier each year), with the manager told to make sure the person had a good experience, and to use their own judgment if someone asked for free products. Once a thirteen-ish Apple Martin, daughter of Gwyneth Paltrow and Chris Martin, came into the New York store and piled up a bunch of products, then had her credit card declined. She shrugged it off casually and slunk over to the elevator empty-handed. Another time Leandra Medine came into the LA store. "She poked around like everything was radioactive and left," one retail employee said.

The culture of the Glossier stores in particular spawned fan accounts, all of which Weiss followed. Dogs of Glossier and Cats of Glossier. Glossier Sticker on a Lighter was a meme account whose bio reads: "On your bedside table between your Aesop hand cream and Diptyque candles." Bianca Garcia, who was a college student when she started the account after she wasn't hired for an internship on Glossier's creative team, said, "I compare Glossier to the Soho House online but without the pretentiousness." There were pictures of supportive but bored partners at Boyfriends at Glossier. "I get a lot of DMs asking, how do I find a Glossier boyfriend? I say you don't just find them, you have to work to shape them," said Dani Barrett, who started the account on Instagram when she lived across the street from the Glossier store in Los Angeles. It was a joke—she thought the endless lines to get into the store were ridiculous. Still, fans took it seriously. Barrett would get around a hundred DMs a weekend, including from girls who sought relationship advice, screenshotting exchanges with the guys they were dating. (Glossier later paid Barrett to make the company a few memes.)

Not everyone who worked retail was on equal footing. Whether Emily Weiss personally followed you was a source of competition, and extra points if she commented on your posts. "A month or two in, we were having our morning meeting and were informed they were going to have a photo shoot starring our offline editors," says one former editor. "It was like getting Tyra Mail on *America's Next Top Model*." They all tried to submit the most beautiful yet carefree selfie. The most beautiful girls were chosen, and the ones with the largest social media following.

And then there were the regulation pink jumpsuits, which Weiss preferred to be buttoned all the way up with a rolled cuff at the ankle. In the first pop-up launch Glossier did for retail, its sales staff wore custom-dyed pink lab coats à la Clinique. "We always talked about taking something utilitarian and making it Glossier," said Weiss. The baggy coats made everyone lose their figures, so sometimes they wore them unbuttoned with a shirt underneath, or tied at the waist—anything to change it up. There was an informal competition over who could tie the arms around the waist the tightest. One girl was celebrated among her peers for being able to loop the sleeves around her waist twice.

The offline editors had some of the most grueling jobs at the company. With music like Charli XCX constantly blaring and long lines of teenagers, panic attacks among the editors weren't uncommon. On the first day the Los Angeles store was open, customers were cranky but excited after waiting in line to get in. One new employee's breath was getting shallow as she tried to recall which shade of Boy Brow a particularly demanding customer had just asked to purchase. The head of retail said, "Listen, we are selling Boy Brow. We are not curing cancer."

But some employees, especially working in locations outside New York, thought their corporate bosses seemed like a bunch of big-city women with a lot of their own money and fancy clothing. "I think the biggest issue or problem for the editors was interpersonal, like, 'The manager is treating me unfairly,'" said someone who worked in Glossier's people team.

"I brought an HR person for [customer experience] and retail whose background was in that." Weiss's philosophy for HR seems to have been about extracting themes, not so much about solving individual problems. That could have been reasonable for a rapidly growing company in theory but not a great way to retain happy employees in practice. So if someone had a concern about how to get promoted or an issue with a difficult coworker, that wasn't a priority until it became a theme; if many people had problems with the same coworker or several people had trouble understanding promotions, then that was something they needed to address. But the bottom line was, HR had no clue as to the kinds of issues offline editors had to deal with from customers while they were on the floor.

The stores were a picture of success. "But ultimately, it's about how are we winning people's hearts? The beauty industry, historically, won people's dollars by making them feel like they weren't enough. When Glossier launched, we made people feel good about themselves and want the products," Weiss said. Weiss thought having too many physical retail locations was expensive—and it was, the way she wanted it done. She wanted to translate that feeling of community the showrooms engendered and bring it back to digital. That was more scalable than having stores in midsize cities and college towns. The key for Weiss was control. A Harvard Business School case study quoted Weiss: "All of the other direct-to-consumer brands who only sell via e-commerce tend to cap out in terms of customer acquisition at a certain point. So, they do a partnership with Target. At some point, you realize that you can't be a contained ecosystem any longer," she said. "But I don't necessarily believe that has to be true. The glass ceiling for DTC brands just represents the diminishing marginal returns of acquiring customers online. But, we think that's a paradigm of e-commerce that doesn't need to exist. How can we break past this inflection point without leaving our own ecosystem?" Control was something Weiss prized in her company, so it is no wonder she even wanted to control how Glossier's customers purchased products. That adherence to DTC sounded smart when the case study was published in early 2019, but it was a stance that soon started to feel unwavering and overly stubborn.

Retailers like department stores and multibrand beauty stores like Sephora very much wanted Glossier to make products available via wholesale. Sephora, owned by the French luxury conglomerate LVMH, first opened in America in 1999. Everything was black, including the lacquered interior and the single glove each employee wore in a flourish that was a little surrealist, a little hygienic. (Even at the corporate office, employees were to wear black, white, gray, or red.) Ulta Beauty, a similar concept, was founded in 1990 in Illinois, but it didn't really compete nationally with Sephora until much later. These chains sold both high-end and low-end brands in their stores without making a big distinction between them. To get into even more cities, Ulta partnered with Target, and Sephora with Kohl's. Indie brands that focused on quality and ingredients got placement they would never have been granted at a department store. This seems innocent enough, but it was a major hinge moment that began to break down the power structure the beauty industry had so relied upon. The old guard of companies absolutely remains, but Sephora and Ulta paved the way for the decentralized industry as we know it today. Being a direct-to-consumer brand like Glossier requires a lot of cash on hand to find customers, and it was easier to acquire customers before Apple changed its privacy policies in April 2021, which limited the tracking capabilities of digital advertisers and enabled users of iPhones to opt out of data sharing, sending online marketing and customer acquisition costs through the roof. And while Glossier had been successful in getting customers to buy products well before there were any physical retail locations to sample them, DTC is ultimately limiting for a founder with scale goals the size of Emily Weiss's—because how else does she sell more product? The perks of wholesale are plenty, and fairly straightforward, but there are also incredible costs. Large retailers take 60 percent of the MSRP, plus brands pay for all the fixtures, training of staff, samples. Glossier did have a short-lived pop-up at Nordstrom in late 2019, with pink counters and signature flower arrangements and editors wearing pink jumpsuits. In keeping with Weiss's advice to Nike about being unafraid of having a perspective and choosing for the customer, they sold just one thing: the fragrance You. In reality, it seemed to cause some customer confusion about why they couldn't buy Milky Jelly Cleanser or Balm Dotcom there as well. And for Weiss, the experiment with Nordstrom could be seen as proof that Glossier worked only in its own self-contained spaces.

Glossier reached a valuation of $1 billion in March 2019. They reached it after closing a $100 million Series D funding round led by the most legendary Sand Hill Road firm, Sequoia Capital, an investor in Apple, Google, PayPal, Zoom, Reddit, and Snap (and also Sam Bankman-Fried's tarnished crypto company FTX). Weiss compared being funded by Sequoia to being accepted into Harvard, and Glossier was only the firm's second investment in beauty after Charlotte Tilbury in 2017. "Raising the hundred million is a strategic decision on our part to facilitate even bigger, faster growth of the company," Weiss said. "It is fuel in the tank, it's like going to a gas station and getting, like, what's the best kind of premium gas? That's what we just got." Glossier had just become a unicorn.

10

Emily Weiss visibly squirmed when I asked her about the billion-dollar valuation in summer 2019. "That is, like, a decision of the company and what you think you're valued at," she said. "It's, like, a decision that ultimately whoever's paying for it, the venture capitalist prices it, right? They're the ones who decide. It doesn't mean anything. It's like a stock price. Stock prices go up and down." I was surprised that she was reluctant to discuss unicorn status. I tried another tactic, asking her how she celebrated moments like that. Do you cry? Do you do a little dance? Did you go out to dinner? "Honestly, it's kind of like back to business, that's how I feel," she said. That echoed the nonchalance of "we're always, like, on to the next" when I asked about Glossier's many copycats. I couldn't believe she was downplaying this moment. "It is exciting, and of course I was super happy, and I'm really happy for the team, but . . . what are people going to say tomorrow? How are we continuing to make that number? It's not a static number. The numbers can go down in a month, the numbers can go up in a month, you know? Raising money is not success; raising money is fuel for success." I wondered to myself whether that was something she'd read in her pile of business books, like in *Shoe Dog* when Phil Knight recounts the day Nike went public in 1980. "The world was the same as it had been the day before, as it had always been," he wrote. "Nothing had changed, least of all me. And yet I was worth $178 million."

At the Glossier office, there were to be no unicorn cupcakes or merch to celebrate their billion-dollar valuation, which seemed out of character for a company that had made a step-and-repeat backdrop and had employees wear cocktail attire to celebrate the launch of a holiday beauty assortment. "It was not a moment. Emily always had a philosophy of valuation is not an indication of success, capital was for the future, and celebrating what you've already achieved," said a former employee who remembered Weiss at the weekly all-hands meeting after the valuation saying that success was in what they had already delivered, and what was tangible, like product launches and social media impressions.

Glossier was one of just twenty-one female-led companies that were christened unicorns in 2019. Others in Glossier's class included Away, Rent the Runway, and the RealReal, a marker of a new generation of powerful female-founded and female-focused companies. It would be all too convenient a narrative to say that Glossier's success made it easier for subsequent female-led teams to get venture capital funding, but that wasn't the case. Less than 2 percent of venture capital investment went to all-female founding teams in 2021 (itself a five-year low), and Black founders received only 1.3 percent of venture capital funding in that same year. "I do want to believe that with every success story, all of those start to build collective confidence that leaders come in all shapes and sizes and forms," said Kirsten Green. "But we are still in a prove-it-to-me phase. It's not equitable. It's not fifty-fifty. We're not at parity yet."

Glossier wasn't the only beauty company to achieve a billion-dollar valuation—so did Drunk Elephant, a brand that bills itself as "nontoxic," which had taken off at Sephora; IT Cosmetics, which made its name for skin-coverage products; Augustinus Bader, whose The Cream sold for $290 for just 50 ml; Tatcha, a Japanese-inspired brand; Charlotte Tilbury, a cosmetics company founded by a famous British makeup artist; and Kylie Jenner's Kylie Cosmetics. Around the same time that Glossier had its major cash infusion, the large beauty conglomerates like L'Oréal and Estée Lauder were on something of a buying spree, gobbling up independent companies. Charlotte Tilbury, Sequoia's first beauty investment, was sold to the Spanish conglomerate Puig in 2020 for a reported $1.2 billion. Unilever bought Tatcha for an estimated $500 million, and Shiseido bought Drunk Elephant for $845 million. It didn't always go well. Rodin Olio Lusso, which was bought by Lauder in 2014 for an undisclosed sum, was a brand championed by Into the Gloss. It was started in 2008 by Linda Rodin, a tall and lithe silver-haired former model and stylist who started making a face oil in the bathroom of her Manhattan apartment and sold it in art deco–inspired packaging. She was a street-style favorite, with a very cute silver poodle named Winky. Lauder expanded the line, as is customary upon an acquisition, launching lipsticks and hand and body creams. It was not a success, not to early fans, not to critics, and not financially. Lauder quietly shuttered the line in 2021.

From Glossier's inception, the company was an acquisitions target, or at least one constantly talked about among interested parties and industry gossip. By the time it was valued at over $1 billion in 2019, Glossier had raised so much money that very few companies could afford to acquire it. Or the better question was, of the parties that could afford to buy Glossier, whom would Weiss approve of? When I was reporting the *Vanity Fair* story in 2019, a beauty editor told me she'd heard Disney was buying Glossier. Disney? That same year a friend who was a Glossier fan texted me to ask: Was Walmart buying Glossier? I'm not even sure that one was a rumor so much as wishful thinking. As early as 2015, Weiss brushed off any rumors, saying, "We've just gotten started launching a brand that can really stand the test of time and is built well. We have a ways to go before we consider something. It's certainly flattering, but we really just have our heads down." In 2018, she said, "Typically when you sell to a larger conglomerate, it's because you need more distribution because the benefit of . . . being a L'Oréal or an Estée Lauder company or something like that is that they have this vast network of retailers. . . . We don't need that. We create our own channel through our digital platform." In 2019, she said, "I hear a new one every day" but admitted it's "a very inquisitive space." One former employee said there was some grain of truth: "From a year or two in, there were people interested in acquiring the company. Whatever rumor was based in some reality at some point."

The products Glossier manufactured could be beloved and important and household names. But that could also be one part of something larger. And what does the potential scale of a beauty company like Glossier look like? Weiss frequently received messages on Instagram with their own brainstorming. "People are like, 'I want a Glossier razor, I want a Glossier tampon, I want Glossier condominiums.'" It is unclear if they were joking, but Weiss shared their propensity for grandiose ideas. At one point Weiss really wanted Glossier to design a bra, and she always did want to design a hotel. (Which isn't so far-fetched considering that Bulgari, Armani, and *Elle* have hotels and Ralph Lauren has restaurants.) So what would hers look like? In 2019, she wouldn't elaborate on that. "Mainly our business will be beauty for the foreseeable future. It's just about reaching more people. We have very, very low brand awareness, even in the United States, but we're still young." That might have been a slip in her perfectionism. "Relatively low" seemed more like it, but then again, Weiss was never someone who graded on a curve or gave points for effort. "If you look at a company like Nike, I mean, that's what is possible for our future," she continues. "It's just about, how quickly can we get there, and in what order?"

Going back for more rounds of fundraising simply because the company could get more capital seemed like an investment hamster wheel. "Why did Glossier even have to be a unicorn? Who decided to go after all this investment money? What's the point of doing this stuff? I mean, I can gather it was probably to raise more money or to get a higher valuation," one former Glossier executive wondered aloud, speculating that Weiss had investors she trusted who encouraged her to keep growing the company bigger and bigger.

The first several rounds of funding went to obvious things like recruiting top talent or leasing larger office space. "When you raise money early, it's building on foundations to put in place that we think are a strong economic story," said Henry Davis. Glossier was exemplary for its user experience. With its strong web design, Glossier had proven it could sell beauty online to enthusiastic customers, which made it a very hot company in the eyes of both the media and finance sectors. Technology was a big part of that. Glossier's polished web design was not a generic online store checkout experience; all of it was custom-coded. As Glossier's product line grew, it required more time, workers, and, ultimately, money to maintain. But that didn't require a $100 million Series D funding round.

Weiss wanted to establish Glossier as more than a beauty product company; she wanted to prove that it could be a disruptive tech company. What it produced wouldn't be beauty or lifestyle products but something even less tangible that was potentially more valuable. "It arguably sounded more special or different to be a tech company," said Kirsten Green of Forerunner. "At the end of the day everyone is using tech, so I don't know what a tech company is anymore. I think the better way to interpret 'we are a tech company' is they wanted to lead with innovation."

Glossier wanted a technology offering to really set them apart. Part of Weiss's original pitch to Green had been a nebulous social commerce–meets–social media network for beauty fans. In a conversation onstage at Disrupt SF in the fall of 2018, Weiss and Green talked about the network as forthcoming, as something that combined Glossier's strength in direct-to-consumer sales with their active community. "It is still sort of hard to search for the best mascara," Weiss said. "The leading paradigm of what an e-commerce experience gives you is one of efficiency and breadth of product." If Glossier's name was on the app, that had a built-in community and press strategy.

One iteration of the app development was a community app through which users could connect, like a real-life, live version of Into the Gloss's Top Shelf and comments sections. It would be a place for Glossier's community to converse with each other, make plans to see each other at retail stores; they could more easily tell Glossier what they wanted and the company could develop products for them and show how to use them. Someone suggested a component that could help people with shade-matching for their skin tone. Another version of the app that was developed was around the idea of recognizing products, whether it was in a photo of a user's medicine cabinet or a live-streaming makeup application (like the popular genre of "get ready with me" videos); products could be automatically detected and purchased through Glossier.

The app was not just a resource for users to find and buy products but a source of data on their habits. That alone could potentially justify the company's aggressive fundraising and unicorn valuation. "The future of beauty is tech" is the kind of thing Weiss said with great conviction. She was a leader who relied on her intuition, but she couldn't land on what Glossier as a tech company meant. She wanted to be seen as in the same leagues as tech founders, but tech was her blind spot. The difference between making a physical beauty product and a tech product couldn't be more difficult. The development of a blockbuster beauty product like Milk Jelly Cleanser involved an eye for detail and storytelling. Tech is often about iteration and strategy and getting a rough early version out in front of people as quickly as possible. Perfectionism was a liability.

Not a single person I interviewed could answer whether the app had been given an actual name. "It felt like there were constant plot twists," said one former creative employee. "We want to be Estée Lauder with sub-brands—no, now we're making an app! Come up with names for our social media network. And it was like, 'What social media network? What's going on?'" Glossier's company culture was secretive, but particularly around the app development there was a marked lack of communication. Employees had little idea of what was going on on a larger business level in terms of strategy. One day a decision would be made about the user experience or a minute design detail, and the next day Weiss would say in a meeting that she had reconsidered it overnight, and coworkers could sense each other's internal groaning at the flip-flopping.

In early 2018, after the Series C round of funding, Glossier announced that it had acquired Dynamo, a Montreal-based tech company with which Glossier had worked from the brand's inception. Cofounder Bryan Mahoney became the CTO of Glossier in 2017, and most of the Dynamo team stayed in Montreal and became Glossier employees. One-third of Glossier's employees, around fifty people, were in the tech departments. One of their strategies to become a tech company was to hire for it, and they recruited aggressively in 2018 and 2019. Keith Peiris, a former product manager at Facebook and Instagram, was one of the first Glossier employees to come from a blue-chip tech company. Peiris lasted only six months at Glossier and was replaced by Facebook alum Maykel Loomans. Melissa Eamer came from holding various positions at Amazon for nineteen years to be the COO; another Amazon veteran, Pawan Uppuluri, replaced Mahoney as CTO after he left in 2019. Weiss also hired Vanessa Wittman, from Dropbox, as chief financial officer, and Diane Vavrasek, from Jet.com, as the chief people officer. (Weiss was averse to the term "human resources.") Hiring big-tech execs sent a strong statement that Glossier was making rigorous, data-driven decisions. These splashy hires were feathers in Weiss's cap, but none of them stayed very long.

The HR department was busy trying to redo titles, levels, and salaries to remain competitive. Some major hires were even offered interior designers for their apartments to lure them to New York City. "You get to a point where you want to attract major talent—Amazon, Facebook, Instagram execs— you have to figure out creative ways to get them to come on board," said one employee. Glossier couldn't compete in salaries with those companies, so they offered "middle-to-top-of-the-market" equity packages and hoped the prestige of working there might be enough.

Something very real that Glossier could uniquely offer was a staff filled with women in power. "There were female CFOs, VPs of products. What other company executive leadership table could you look around and everyone is a woman?" said the employee. Outside of the company's leadership, 50 percent of the engineering team was female, a number unheard-of at most companies.

Glossier was suffering from a culture clash. The kinds of celebrations and flourishes its culture was built on didn't always work with the new tech team. Once, to celebrate a web redesign, Weiss hired a magician. "Don't put these introverts in a situation where they're forced to engage with a magician who's, like, calling up people from a crowd," said one insider. "We would have just wanted some food."

Glossier functioned as two different companies that were in fact on two different floors: one for tech and one for basically everyone else. Tech department employees feared being trapped in the elevator with Weiss. Not because she was icy or because there was an unofficial rule that she was to ride the elevator alone, but because they dreaded her sunny disposition. They felt doom and gloom about the app, while they viewed her as optimistic to the point of ignorance.

11

"In reality, it was incompetent leadership and decision-making that really sunk that ship. Not a lot of people wanted to take accountability for what went wrong, but I see Play as the product of greed," said one employee who worked on Glossier's first satellite brand, Play. "I think it was probably some investor that put the idea in Emily's head. If you could have satellite brands, imagine the opportunity: you can have a Glossier car. If you're in the right mood, you're like: Yeah, that's possible. Let's do it. Let's take over the world."

Weiss was all too willing to entertain large-scale ideas about how to scale Glossier. Not by something that she saw as a compromising decision, like having Glossier be sold at Target or department store beauty counters, but by bolder plans for growth. This was how the app was developed, and it's also how Glossier embarked on Play. The app suffered from flip-flopping and a decline in decisive decision-making. From the start, Play wasn't faring any better.

Glossier had launched with its mantra of skincare first, makeup second. And in 2018, makeup became its new category to conquer. Lipstick is the number one seller across the industry, and while Glossier had lip products, such as the balms and the sheer Generation G colors, they didn't have a proper lipstick. They started teasing Play ten days before the March 2019 launch with photos and videos. These suggested a sexy nighttime vibe, as if the products would be inspired by the refracted light of a disco ball, or at least the glittery kirakira Instagram filter. Their biggest single inspiration was an image of Diana Ross dancing with abandon at Studio 54, wearing tight jeans and a ripped tee that read "No Sweat." The marketing department was so effective at building up suspense that fans wondered if it would be music or sex toys.

In a sense, the fans were not alone. No one at Glossier knew what was going on with Play. "There was no real strategy," a former high-level employee said. The main inspiration was disco but the products were aesthetically confusing. Play's face glitter suggested the 1980s and its gel liners echoed Urban Decay and Hard Candy—cult brands of the 1990s. Or was it drawing on the early-aughts nostalgia of Weiss's own teen years?

In meetings, marketing and product development and creative teams overanalyzed ("to death," according to someone in them) whether Play was a part of Glossier or a separate brand. Did it need its own website? Its own pop-up stores? Questions made way for larger questions of whether Glossier was a brand that was going to launch a bunch of other brands. Play could have been the first of many brands Glossier would develop for new categories, instead of using the conglomerates' playbook of acquiring brands to fill niches, or a beauty incubator like Kendo, which developed Rihanna's Fenty Beauty and later skincare line, Fenty Skin. Play was all about color cosmetics, but there was the potential for another spin-off line for an older demographic. (Weiss did seem to be mulling it over in 2019 when she asked if I thought products targeting aging skin, such as retinol, should be their own line or just part of Glossier.)

"It went sideways," a high-level creative employee said. The time frame for the March 2019 launch seemed untenable to those employees assigned to it. The long hours added to the overall feeling of doom. People weren't just staying late, but lying on the floors, stressed-out from the pressure of wanting to do a good job, and crying in front of their coworkers. A member of the tech team said when they would play the game Werewolf (and "they" is definitely the tech team; in the world of Glossier, Weiss and her inner circle would never pass time that way), the role-playing game where someone gets murdered at night and the next morning players discuss who did it, "the moderator would change the setting from a medieval village in the woods to 'the night before the launch of Glossier Play, we're all just trapped here, and so-and-so is dead in the kitchen, with Cheerios all over the place.'"

The reaction was mixed at best even from eager customers. The small silicone spatula-shaped tool for applying the gel glitter was innovative, and the bright colors reminiscent of parrots or rainbows were joyful and sexy. But that wasn't necessarily what customers were looking for from Glossier. Someone wrote on the Glossier subreddit that "Glossier, to me, is that 'girl next door' look that's really wholesome. Their ads aren't sexualized. Glossier isn't really 'going out clubbing' makeup." Others complained that the lip color was goopy and broke easily, and the colored eye pencils and gels required too much practice to apply well. The packaging was splashy, with items wrapped in foil packs, but it was also an environmental sticking point. Customers also complained that Play's Glitter Gel was made with nonbiodegradable glitter; the company advised washing the product off with a cotton pad and its Milky Oil cleanser "to avoid getting glitter into the waterways." Play proved the point that Glossier's priorities were never sustainability, and things at Glossier changed only when enough customers spoke out.

After less than a year, Play was considered a failure and closed. The decision was made by Weiss to do it quickly and quietly, and the dedicated Instagram for the line was made private. The shoots, according to people who worked on Play, included photos never used ("there's a couple of Dropbox folders with a few $100,000 images that no one will ever see") and production cost over a million dollars. The unused custom packaging when they scrapped it was said to be worth around $100,000 at minimum. Weiss has never been one to comment on sales or failures, but she gave an interview to the trade publication *Business of Fashion* about the brand closing. "[We thought] why don't we create a different brand . . . so that it'll differentiate more intense makeup product from less intense makeup product. The realization we had was, 'Huh, we could have just launched more makeup products.'"

Aspects of Play were ahead of the curve. Play launched just before HBO's show *Euphoria*, whose Gen Z characters wear iridescent, super-pigmented, eye makeup–focused, glittery, crystal-accented looks that would have been easy to re-create with Play. (Then again, when retail employees drew stars on their faces with Play products, they got a stern email from corporate to stop being so loose with their makeup.)

Play was a strong indication that Glossier's leadership was thinking about market expansion more than creativity. They took their eye off the core of what Glossier was good at—simple makeup and skincare products—in favor of trying to develop more. The products were innovative, and some still sell for a hefty markup on eBay, but consumers didn't want to buy them from Glossier. They didn't feel like Glossier.

Inside Glossier, there were postmortem internal reviews to try to understand what went wrong, meetings where people were forced to discuss Play even though they complained over text that merely mentioning it triggered traumatic memories and joked they were in therapy over it. No one was willing to take accountability for the debacle.

12

"People would drool when they saw Glossier on my résumé," one former creative employee said. Recruiters wondered who the real brilliance was behind Glossier and weren't afraid of trying to poach them. Every fledgling beauty company, established beauty brand, and start-up wanted to hire alumni of the buzziest brand in the world.

One of Weiss's real talents was making brilliant hires. "It's like matchmaking," she said. She'd meet someone and see something special in them and tell them that she believed in them. She was a star and genuinely wanted everyone around her to be too. "Working there had such a cachet to it," said a middle manager. "At parties in New York, if you told people you worked there, even people from *Vogue* would have respect for that—they thought it was cool! You really wanted to keep that job."

Who wouldn't want to recruit the woman who named Boy Brow (Annie Kreighbaum) or the person who led the charge to develop Balm Dotcom (Alexis Page) or the genius behind Glossier's Instagram strategy (Eva Alt)? These stars became the Glossier diaspora. (Others called them the Glossier Mafia.) Or why not just start your own company? A very, very brief list includes Nick Axelrod-Welk, who left Into the Gloss shortly before Glossier launched; he moved to Los Angeles and co-founded his own minimalist body-care line, Nécessaire, which I admit I first purchased because I heard he was behind it. "You can't ignore the proliferation of DTC brands and DTC branding. I didn't want to create one, I didn't want the cuteness, the wink and the chatty subway ad personality of a DTC brand," he said. After leaving the day-to-day of that company, he helped the actor Courteney Cox launch the home products line Homecourt and became a vice president at United Talent Agency in its ventures department, connecting celebrity clients to simpatico companies. He also started a beauty news podcast called *Eyewitness Beauty* with Annie Kreighbaum, who herself went on to establish Soft Services, a body-care line, with another Glossier alumna, Rebecca Zhou. After Alexis Page developed the four original Glossier products, Boy Brow, and Milky Jelly Cleanser, she started her own company, advising brands such as Pat McGrath Labs and Urban Outfitters on product development. (The publication *Air Mail* called her "the most important person in beauty you've never heard of.") Eva Alt went on to consult, and Henry Davis launched his own incubator, Arfa. Diarrha N'Diaye, who worked in product development at Glossier (and prior to that, social media at L'Oréal), launched Ami Colé in 2021. "It is designed [with] Black women in mind. The messaging is: this is for you, images that look like you, your heritage story," she said. It sounded like a corrective to so many complaints that the darkest shade of some of Glossier's color products could barely work with olive skin.

Glossier had a young workforce. Often it was their first or second job out of college. Young employees typically have a high turnover rate, as they're ready to move or go back to school or try other careers. Another factor was that the company went back and forth so frequently about its focus, that frustrated staffers left in search of more stable office environments. Glossier was not unique in its turnover, but the hiring and musical chairs of these people was something the company got wrong. The problem was that Weiss thought talent was easy to replenish. She assumed anyone could be replaced with someone just as good, or better, but this ultimately led to the unraveling of the company.

Glossier had been a uniquely successful place for brilliant people to start careers, and they were hoping to cash in on their prize cow. That meant if they had animosity toward Weiss, they would be wise to say nothing. Many of those former employees are quite literally invested in Glossier. They own shares that most of them had to pay for with loans. They have an alumni Slack where they share advice on equity with each other and with current employees who are thinking of leaving. All the while I was interviewing these current and former employees, I was aware that there must be some reluctance to tell the truth, or at least show the company in a bad light. This book, more than one person told me, could have ramifications for the company's reputation. They were betting on the potential for Glossier to be worth a great deal of money whenever it does go public or is acquired in the future. "I would love for it to be a valuable liquidity event for me and former colleagues," one said.

Not that any of that is certain. The one thing former employees agreed on was trepidation about the future of the company. Paying for shares was expensive, and they all hoped they'd made the right bet and that the investment would be worth something. There is a psychology around a potential windfall that seems to corrupt or at least entice people. A tale as old as time! When you think you're sitting on a potential lottery ticket, it's hard not to spend the money in advance in your head. Three different alums confided they were counting on Glossier shares to pay for their children's higher education. Tech stocks like Amazon had a meteoric rise but took an unprecedented hit in 2022. Former employees who thought they were on-paper millionaires suddenly were not.

Then there was the vibe shift, "this realization that the last decade is over," according to the trend forecaster Sean Monahan. He originated the term in June 2021, and the phrase was made mainstream by a later article in *New York* magazine by Allison P. Davis. In an interview, Monahan explained it in reference to watching *The Andy Warhol Diaries* on Netflix: "Warhol talks about how a couple years into a new decade, things start to look and feel different. The quote is something like, 'There'll be new people and new faces and it takes a couple years into a decade for things to really get going. And that's when you decide who's going to make it into the future and who's going to be relegated to the past.'"

Into the Gloss and Glossier defined the aesthetic of the 2010s, but as the '20s came about, it started to feel stale, all the sans serif fonts and, yes, #glossierpink. Glossier was not the only company grappling with changing aesthetics. It was one of the most prominent brands that had fueled and been fueled by Instagram, along with Away luggage and Great Jones cookware and Allbirds shoes. What once felt fresh started to look the same and worse, like a cliché, the way virtually every Airbnb or café targeted to upwardly mobile millennials had the same vaguely anesthetized midcentury modern décor (the writer Kyle Chayka named it "AirSpace"). When discussing his realization about the vibe shift, Monahan said, "I think there was a time in the late 2010s where I just felt like everyone looked so boring, you know? You would walk around New York City, which used to have such great street style, and just be like, I can't tell if people are going to work or going to a party or going to the gym."

All of Glossier's design cohesion wasn't helping matters. The way Into the Gloss and later Glossier had popularized showing off beauty products—the classic flat layshot directly from above, or the shelfie, or the artful jumble on a nightstand—was considered a little passé. It was the same way that wearing head-to-toe designer looks straight off the runway lacked creativity at best and was the sign of a fashion victim at worst. Such was the power of Instagram that some brands designed their packaging to be matte just so it would look particularly beautiful on the app. The word "curate" was used so often to denote choosing that it became its own cliché. For brands, an internal question was often how they played a role in the life of a consumer.

For direct-to-consumer Instagram-forward companies and beauty companies alike, there were a few key creative agencies such as Red Antler or Partners & Spade. These full-service agencies could give a fledgling brand a design identity, complete with logo and color palette and positioning document, and point them to companies that did custom-designed packaging to stand out. They were considered so influential to success that they were DTC kingmakers.

When Weiss shopped Glossier around to certain large design firms for work, all the women at the agencies were excited. Everyone agreed the company had the potential to be even more massive than it was, especially flush with funding. Industry observers noted that some large agencies were reluctant to take on Glossier as a client because Weiss was seen as just wanting to hire someone to execute her unilateral vision. There was more than a little bit of misogyny in that idea of a diva founder with an uncompromising vision. But a top design agency can choose its clients and it doesn't want one that won't let it bring much to the table. Weiss was advised to stick to an internal team and remain in control.

One of the best summations of the consumer fatigue that was beginning to set in came from Teddy Blanks, who created a lot of era-defining graphic design, including the credits for the TV show *Girls*. He was interviewed in 2022 for the newsletter *Blackbird Spyplane* about the sameness of design. "There's been this dominant cursed advertising aesthetic for a few years now—the kind you see in timeline ads for DTC mattress brands or subway ads for food-delivery apps and hair-loss-prevention start-ups with no vowels or whatever—and I'm curious to hear you describe that aesthetic," Jonah Weiner, the cofounder of the newsletter, asked Blanks. "What tropes and clichés and design choices are we seeing when we see these ads?"

Blanks replied that it felt like the companies were making a concerted effort to be as inoffensive and congenial as they possibly could. "The adjectives I guess I'd use are very friendly, very soft colors, usually geometric sans serif faces in the Futura mold, but more contemporary." He also said that design cycles in and out of styles. So twenty years down the line, that aesthetic could in theory feel fresh again. But he also thought there was something malevolent in the branding. "Part of it is that it can't be divorced from the context of how all these brands and tech companies are being exposed as just another side of capitalism. There's this sense of evil lurking behind them, so the friendliness and softness can feel like a lie and oppressive. Whereas there's an honesty to Helvetica. It's a corporation: They are who they are."

The era of the Instagram influencer was a boon for perfectionists. But now, out were the painstakingly edited lives of Instagram influencers and in were the messy, slightly chaotic "real" girls of TikTok. The photo dump became popular— a collection of imperfect and casual images meant to reflect a mood or an event or nothing at all. The app TikTok went even further, becoming known as a platform whose fans tended to prefer a sense of authenticity, even if it was at the expense of being polished. The cold perfection of the shelfie and the carefully selected array of products that Into the Gloss and later Glossier helped codify started to feel artificial.

Consumer preferences also changed. There is a kind of seesaw between skincare and color cosmetics that shifts every decade or so. Glossier launched its minimalist line when skincare was already at the core of culture for several years. When Donald Trump won the 2016 election, skin-care routines were credited as a source of self-care, a phrase that shot to popularity in the wake of the surprising (to many on the left) election win. Many articles mentioned the late poet Audre Lorde's 1988 quote: "Caring for myself is not self-indulgence, it is self-preservation, and that is an act of political warfare." The mainstream media began to take note of skincare. "The obsession with skincare was mastur-batory in a certain way," said an executive at a large beauty company. "I think back to this 'women in film' class I took in college and there was a scene of a woman going shopping to treat herself and it's a metaphor for masturbation. You're feeling yourself, showing it off, luxuriating in that feeling and making sure other people see it. You know, 'Mmmmm, I'm going to put on oils now.'"

Competing brands like Kosas, Saie, Merit, Milk, Estée Edit, all took the Glossier playbook and ran with the chang-ing tide to varying degrees of success. A bigger threat was the seemingly endless number of celebrity-backed lines that came to cash in on the beauty gold rush just as Glossier was start-ing to struggle. There was an extremely low barrier to entry for a celebrity line to launch. Years ago, a celebrity want-ing to branch into a brand would have to convince someone who'd worked at Estée Lauder for a decade to leave and take a risk on them. Now celebrities could basically white-label a product. A lot of celebrity brands were created by incubators where a company fronts the money and expense to develop a beauty line and puts a celebrity's name on it in exchange for a stake in the company. There were famous women who tapped into a smart formula for what the customer wants: Rihanna's compelling narrative around shade range, or Gwyneth Paltrow's point of view about clean beauty.

If a consumer didn't feel a connection, they might move on to another brand. According to *Forbes*, only 7 percent of millennials, Glossier's base, self-identified as brand loyal. They could quickly age out of the brand. Glossier had one retinol product, Universal Pro-Retinol, but not much else for a demographic that is poised to move on to skincare targeting mature skin. Older fans of Glossier's makeup might try out the makeup artist Violette Serrat, a close friend of Weiss's, who launched a French-inspired line in 2021. Or they could seek out the makeup artist–led brands such as Bobbi Brown's line Jones Road, or Gucci Westman's Westman Atelier, with its luxurious packaging and creamy formulas for a grown-up version of no-makeup makeup, with a price tag to match.

What Glossier really needed to do to maintain relevance was to capture the attention of Gen Z. They were certainly curious about the brand: 37 percent of Glossier's website visitors are eighteen- to twenty-four-year-olds. That demographic was already being heavily courted by brands like Selena Gomez's Rare Beauty, which came out in 2020 with a message not of you-can-sit-with-us–style sunshine but of being "stigma-free." Gomez has spoken a lot as a star about mental health, and the shade names include Positive and Optimist and Gratitude. Or Glossier's younger fans might try skincare that was playful and reminiscent of the cartoonishness that Glossier steered away from, like the "acne acceptance" brand Starface. The line launched in fall 2019 with glow-in-the-dark star-shaped pimple patches that have proved to be hugely popular with the seventeen- to twenty-four-year-old demographic and was widely available at Target. Why try to sell the dream of beautiful skin when you could just throw on an adorably decorated pimple sticker and not try to fool anyone?

The bottom line was that beauty was a crowded and competitive market, and brand loyalty was slippery. And Glossier soldiered on with its pink packaging as if what worked in 2014 would work forever.

PART 3

THE LAST GIRLBOSS

My skin-care regimen is more extensive than I'm proud of. I'd recently learned the importance of letting each product "fully" absorb before applying the next, and while I did not spend forty-five minutes each night sitting in the bathroom awaiting transcendence, the layering approach I couldn't completely abandon left me plenty of time to consider my options. After a swipe of special water supposedly popular in France, I thought, I won't do it. After I cleansed a second time, with a cleanser beloved in Korea, I was pretty sure I wouldn't. After I used a scientific-looking dropper to apply serum to my nose to decrease redness and "purify," I thought, Great social revolutions are impossible without the feminine ferment. After a pat of stinging, expensive foam, the effects of which were unconvincing, I thought, Ha, that's funny. By the stroke of moisturizer, I was dewy and resolved: I had nothing to lose but my chains.

—LAUREN OYLER, FAKE ACCOUNTS

13

Despite a fantastic fourth-quarter sales trajectory, Emily Weiss's communications team was nervous in late 2019. There were panicked texts in the wee hours, worried huddles over pre-holiday drinks at a corner table at Le Coucou across the street from the old office at 123 Lafayette Street. Could Emily be in any danger? The question felt like sacrilege—Glossier was beloved by their community and seemed to be as flush with goodwill as it was with money. The problem at hand was one of paranoia.

The backlash against public-facing female founders was growing from a steady trickle of bad press to full takedowns of female leaders showing mismanagement, angry employees, and drama-filled internal struggles. Worse, the public was ravenous for these stories, and they had real consequences. It had started when Sophia Amoruso, who brought the #girlboss to the masses, faced a discrimination lawsuit in 2015 for allegedly firing pregnant employees. (It was settled in 2016 via arbitration.) Amoruso and Weiss had become friends, reposting each other on Instagram and seeming to delight as two female founders of consumer companies. In 2016, her company Nasty Gal filed for bankruptcy. The visionary designer Jenna Lyons left J.Crew in 2017 amid whispers that she'd become "too big" for the brand's khaki britches and that was why the retailer was floundering. Miki Agrawal, the always festival-ready founder of the successful period-underwear start-up Thinx, was ousted after accusations from employees that she sexually harassed them and was, in addition, generally very inappropriate at the office. Sheryl Sandberg of *Lean In* fame appeared in a 2018 report in the *New York Times* detailing how she oversaw an aggressive campaign against Facebook's critics. Then in December 2019 came leaked Slack messages from Steph Korey, the founder of the luxury luggage brand Away, revealing a workplace culture at odds with the cheerful ethos of the business.

The Away Slack messages caused a stir at Glossier, even though their products bore little similarity to luggage or period underwear. But it wasn't any of that, at least not yet, that concerned the communications team. Instead, a trend they'd been monitoring seemed to be gathering momentum. To found a beauty company is to be in a growing but pillar industry. If you can survive in beauty, you have a certain layer of protection; your company is strong. But the team at Glossier was still rightfully worried. The communications team decided it was time to call a meeting with Emily. They asked her if she had anything to worry about. Emily said no, but privately wondered if people were looking for prominent female CEOs to fail. She couldn't help but be caught up in the narrative.

The fairy tale of a safe working space for women was over. The Wing was all but rendered out of business during the early lockdown period of the pandemic, and was hit with a coincidentally concurrent *New York Times Magazine* story detailing negative experiences of women, many of them BIPOC, who worked service jobs for low wages at the clubs. By June 2020, Wing cofounder Audrey Gelman had stepped down, and by 2023, the building that housed its headquarters in Manhattan's East Village was for sale for $22.5 million. Two other highly visible, chic female founders whose companies shared customers and a pro-woman ethos with Glossier—Leandra Medine of Man Repeller (who was so close to Weiss at one point that she was one of the three dozen guests at her wedding in the Bahamas) and Christene Barberich from Refinery29—also stepped down in 2020 as the result of current and former employees exposing toxic workplace issues, most of them having to do with race.

The newsletter the *New Consumer* called the genre "girl-boss gotcha" exposés, "where female founders get publicly flogged for managerial flaws that range, depending on the situation, from petty nonsense to securities fraud. These stories perform well for their publications, are seen as 'telling truth to power,' and occasionally serve the broader public—see: Theranos—so they'll continue to be published." Dan Frommer, the author of the newsletter, was writing about the latest target, the cookware start-up Great Jones and the breakup of its founders. But he could have been writing about any of them. "Like many in the genre, this one is peppered with zinger quotes from anonymous ex-employees and cherry-picked gaffes, designed to be as embarrassing—or at least as unflattering—as possible," he wrote. "My disappointment with this piece in particular is that there's a potentially really interesting business story to be told here: The messy sophomore year of a hot start-up, culminating in a founder breakup and employee turnover."

Those exposed had no path forward but to repent. Some responses were better than others. Medine wrote in her own newsletter in 2021 about her integrity being publicly questioned. "The public performance of displaying integrity as a means to prove one's worthiness of any number of things (one among them maintaining a livelihood) has complicated the matter completely. And made it much more challenging for me to buy into the supposition that it could be divorced from good- or bad-ness," she wrote. "When I got canceled (canceled myself?) last June, I wanted to surrender my person to those who then seemed like the vanguards of justice, uncovering my badness in real-time. I drew a direct correlation between this badness and what I thought I should do to become better. This is what drove me to step back from my own company."

In October 2020, Gelman wrote an open letter saying that she had chosen a business model that was "a continuation, not a radical reimagination of the service industry," among other admissions. Gelman had a bit of the same issue of pivoting as Weiss. She was a native New Yorker who had grown up with Lena Dunham and had dated the controversial photographer Terry Richardson (she was said to have a tattoo of his name). All along the girlbosses' lives seemed at odds with the language of their businesses: We are your friend, but to be our friend, you need to literally buy something from us. Seeing photos of Audrey Gelman and Emily Weiss and Leandra Medine posing together in designer clothes outside chic Manhattan restaurants doesn't actually give the public the sense that they're reaching out beyond their social means. Like Weiss's, Gelman's allure was how connected and impossibly glamorous her life appeared. But the community she was selling was supposed to be about equality, revolution, feminism, accessibility. "She branded the whole thing to look like a vagina," a member told me. After the Wing's demise she decamped for upstate New York, was rumored to have been working in food service, and plotted her next retail concept, a Brooklyn store of cozy comforts based on a fictional English village. The business was all a bit high-concept, and came with a *Vanity Fair* profile showing her in overalls and naturally curly hair, a signal to all that she had turned down the glam. It felt like a folly, a girlboss who had become yet another wealthy woman with a vanity business. The intense branding of her store Six Bells showed the potential for some kind of scale, like this immersive world becoming a hotel. I thought she wanted it to become a planned community along the lines of something fans of Thomas Kinkade could live in.

Amoruso, who had been trying to reinvent herself as an investor and thought leader, had kept quiet about her own rise and fall until November 2022. She took to Twitter and defended herself in a series of posts. "I've been quiet for far too long re: the unfair slaughtering of female founders and 'girlboss culture,'" she wrote. "I did my best. I wrote a book that inspired the 500k+ readers who bought it." While many editors had reached out to her asking her to comment about it, she continued, she had declined them all. She didn't want to be further disparaged or seen as a whiner. "Is the takedown of female founders worth dissuading future women from starting businesses?"

Scrutiny of these companies was relentless and not without a little glee. A contingent of people are excited by founders failing because of the economic divide. These women have been given money and opportunity that's really not possible for the masses even though they are told it is in "inspirational" articles and self-help books like *The Secret*, or on the Goop website, or in guides to Mary Kay–style multilevel marketing sales.

It was a domino-falling period reminiscent of the string of so-called canceled men of the #MeToo era that began in 2018. But if #MeToo was offering a corrective to male abuse of power with public humiliation, was that really analogous to what was happening to the girlbosses? "The #MeToo campaign, as it evolved, was driven in no small measure by that faith—likewise Ms. Sandberg's *Lean In*, a 'movement' of free-standing C-suite aspirants, each of whom was instructed to defeat her 'internal obstacles' to get ahead as an individual rather than organize to defeat external forces," wrote Susan Faludi, author of *Backlash*, a book about how the media undermined feminist gains with its coverage. And it reminds me so much of the way the media seem to have built—and then torn down—this idea of the girlboss, so much that it is now an insult. "That ethic made it attractive to the professional class," Faludi noted, "but of little use to the great mass of working women." She mentioned that Sandberg's office reportedly declined a request to have her meet in a signature "Lean In Circle" for housekeepers organizing at a Hilton DoubleTree Suites hotel in Boston: "Isn't it good to fight the good fight on all fronts? Sure. But without a firm conviction about what's most important, fighting one battle can mean surrendering another. Should things be so either/or?"

"Girlboss" morphed from a term worthy of an eye roll to something more nefarious: shorthand for toxic white feminists. "Gaslight every moment, Gatekeep every day, Girlboss beyond words," the meme goes. Glossier's champion Kirsten Green weighed in, telling *TechCrunch*, "I truly believe the 'girlboss' term was created to celebrate an emerging wave of female leaders—which is still rare in business, and was even rarer around ten years ago when the phrase was popularized. However, I think it's time for all of us to move beyond gendered language when we talk about leadership, and instead focus on celebrating the qualities of great leaders regardless of gender: passion, integrity, focus, contentiousness [*sic*], and a willingness to grow and change with the needs of the company."

Culture had started turning against the girlboss. Glossier and other beauty companies were keenly aware of the need to show a more expansive and non-gender-specific version of beauty, as seen in the preferred pronoun stickers the editors wore at the Glossier showrooms and the corporate office's gender-neutral bathrooms. But there was also a nascent bimboism spreading from TikTok all the way to fashion, where Barbie-looking outfits prevailed. Sophie Haigney wrote in the *New York Times* that it was the antithesis of the mode of feminism that was dominant in the 2010s, a reaction to the hyperambitious girlboss who said you could have it all. "The girlboss was striving and succeeding in a male workplace; she was a female founder who also went to 6 a.m. yoga classes. She wore a chic dress and looked coiffed on Instagram. She was liberal and outspoken about her gender," she wrote. Bimboism surged when the girlboss fell from grace. "Girlboss aesthetics are simply cringe, for a generation steeped in internet irony. And so: No more Instagrams about rising and grinding. No more the Wing. No more straining to be smarter than the boys."

These female founders had done something right: they had captured the imagination of a younger generation, and had put women in business front and center in culture. But beyond the hype, their actual businesses hadn't accomplished much. Part of the problem was that there wasn't a lot to these companies in the end. Most of them didn't seem to think through the amount of commitment and innovation it takes to make a brand with longevity. Instead, they were all packaging and concept and targeted to a young demographic that might not have known better. Away luggage was not Tumi; Great Jones cookware was not Le Creuset; Hims and Hers were essentially Hair Club for Men where you could also get Viagra and medicine for yeast infections. Was Glossier just Mary Kay or Maybelline with better design? It's hard to compete with empires, especially when the new companies and their founders seemed, to the public, so out for themselves.

No one really liked the watered-down feminist idea of the #girlboss or wanted to be called one (with the exception of Amoruso, who had taken it to the bank). The supposed downfall of the girlboss was made so much worse by the pedestals onto which these women were shoved. Don't get me wrong: the pedestals benefit them . . . until they don't. That could be why Pat McGrath is notorious for rarely giving interviews. But in some ways signaling the end of the era of the girlboss was like saying female ambition was—*poof!*—out of style. Maybe it was, but probably not. There's a whole genre of bestselling books about how awesome and valuable failure can be. But when a woman fails, she's just a crazy bitch or an amateur. Either way, she had it coming. These women who were raised up as leaders were often young and inexperienced when they took on so much responsibility, which makes a great narrative, but what's the narrative for those who failed? Were they victims of the system? I think about how accessible they were made to seem, but accessibility can backfire. Parasocial relationships—following someone prominent via the public sphere, getting involved to the point where very real emotions arise and stick—are tricky. At some point one party, usually the regular person following it all, is left disappointed.

Outside funding also came with the pressure to scale the company no matter what. Look at a company like Augustinus Bader, which created a single cream in two formulations that was sold to fans as the only thing they needed to put on their faces. But soon Bader was coming out with oils, masks, haircare, even supplements. And Emily Weiss's detractors have said her strong suit is that she knows what she doesn't know and surrounds herself with smart hires and with a board, investors, and mentors to give her high-level advice. But I'm sure that not every founder has been so savvy or can take the ego hit to ask for help. Female founders are under unbearably hard pressure to be seen as powerful and perfect. Which is not to say that the bad behavior of the girlbosses or the behavior of their companies is okay—it's not; I believe they were terrible managers and behaved badly. Bad behavior is still a cardinal sin for women if it is exposed. No underlying problems with business or capitalism or celebrity culture or feminism were solved by the marketing of the girlboss. Just because the wave was led by women didn't make it fundamentally better.

Men in business are held to completely different standards. A man has to be truly, truly transgressive in his behavior to be fired, or lose a significant amount of money, or be publicly humiliated. There are countless less obvious but still insidious male targets. As Aliza Licht wrote in *Forbes* of people rushing to declare the girlboss dead, "Where are their White male counterparts who have failed as leaders, creating cut-throat environments or no social impact?"

There is no parallel fervor over Revlon chairman Ronald Perelman or BioSilk's Farouk Shami for being major conservative donors. Figures like Steve Jobs and Mark Zuckerberg are widely viewed as visionary heroes while admirers overlook or at most vaguely acknowledge their volatile personalities. In his book *The Everything Store*, Brad Stone wrote, "Andy Grove, the longtime CEO of Intel, was known to be so harsh and intimidating that a subordinate once fainted during a performance review," to say nothing of the mercenary tactics Amazon's Jeff Bezos used on competition. Elon Musk seems to be modeling himself on Kim Kardashian or Pamela Anderson, who admitted and stood behind their transgressions against society's norms, using them to gain fame. But Kardashian and Anderson didn't have shareholders. Even something as minor as Peloton CEO John Foley telling the *New York Times* in 2020 that he starts the day by taking forty sips of water from his sink would haunt a female founder for the rest of her life. It's a double standard to say the least.

Many women in leadership roles, whether we want to talk about it or not, will face similar backlashes. They, too, will have to (and should have to) deal with employee reckonings, and we need to show a way forward if society is going to come together. Plus, Weiss talked as if she was in it for the long haul. "L'Oréal has a male CEO, Estée Lauder has a male CEO, but the majority of beauty brands that those companies own are founded by women, so generally the woman is the CEO for a while, and maybe once the company gets bought or sold or enough time goes by, the female CEO ends up going away," she said in 2018. "I don't have any plans to go away anytime soon."

Weiss's guardedness and obfuscation of her personal life are what made her more resilient than the rest. Her foibles were far less out there than her cohorts' because her brand was not about being transparent about her life or making her personality her brand. What made Weiss feel like a cipher probably saved her career. She was the last girlboss standing. Which also made her a target.

14

Glossier's appeal was that it was more than just makeup—it was a part of customers' lives and values. Buying Glossier products was a statement about who you were in the world. The kind of moral affiliation that Weiss pioneered came with a huge potential upside, but also huge potential pitfalls. Glossier claimed to be inclusive, but the wider social definition of what inclusivity meant evolved faster than the company could have. Glossier and Weiss were not exempt from the mistakes of their cohort, nor were they spared from serious accusations of a racist work environment.

A group of about fifty former editors at Glossier showrooms started an Instagram account called @outtathegloss. They went public in the summer of 2020, stating that, as forward-facing retail employees, they found working at Glossier essentially like a backstabbing junior high where the queer and BIPOC were allowed to be victimized by customers, and that their LGBTQIA+ and BIPOC identities were trotted out to make Glossier seem more progressive than the C-suite level of leadership really was. Concerns included managers mixing up names of employees, low pay, that they weren't taken seriously.

And, of course, the lingering issue of shade range. The group never did respond to my requests for interviews, but they spoke to *Broadsheet* in August 2020, describing "a range of disturbing behavior: a group of customers who, they say, applied blackface with dark shades of concealer without any action from managers; visitors who touched Black employees' hair and skin and received apologies from managers if they complained after the employee asked them to stop; comments like a manager telling a Black employee interested in purchasing a designer handbag for resale that she 'couldn't afford it.'"

As it would turn out, none of these accusations would be toothless. I had seen the editors' tokenization firsthand, albeit in a way that was smaller-stakes. Look no further than the photo shoot that accompanied my *Vanity Fair* story to find Weiss seated amid a gaggle of pink-jumpsuit-wearing editors who were handpicked by her to ostensibly show diversity of race and gender in the company, albeit in a photogenic way.

Another time Weiss was in a meeting with the tech team when "she pointed out how 'we don't have any people of color in here,'" one former employee who was present recalled. When another employee, who was Asian, corrected Weiss and said they identified as a person of color, "Emily was like: 'Really? You identify as a person of color?' And she's like, 'Yes.'" (In June 2020, when @outtathegloss came to light, 43 percent of Glossier's corporate workforce identified as people of color, including 9 percent who identified as Black— and while 37 percent of their leaders and 60 percent of their board identified as people of color [Asians, Latinx], they had no Black representation at the leadership level.)

On May 30, following the protests over the murder of George Floyd, Glossier had pledged $1 million toward the fight against systemic racism in the United States: $500,000 in donations and $500,000 toward Black-owned beauty businesses. Glossier was small in size compared to conglomerates. Estée Lauder, the $18-billion-a-year company whose chairman, Ronald Lauder, was a major Trump donor, promised to boost Black hiring and donate $10 million over three years to the NAACP and similar organizations fighting racial injustice. Sephora was the first retailer to take the 15 percent pledge, which was a call to action by Brooklyn-based Black designer Aurora James for major retailers to carry 15 percent of their products from Black-owned companies. That was a much-needed corrective for Sephora, which in 2020 carried only seven Black-owned brands out of 290.

The @outtathegloss account highlighted that Glossier's initial response to the racial reckoning was imperfect; it was outward-facing rather than taking a hard look within to address racism that employees were experiencing every day.

Weiss and her team knew about @outtathegloss's issues with the company and launched an internal investigation, including asking every former retail employee to have conversations or share feedback. Some did, but not everyone. They had an action plan but also felt they couldn't realistically address every point @outtathegloss wanted. The team at Glossier knew it was highly unlikely that @outtathegloss, whose individual identities they never knew, would make itself public. The mood among those who knew about what was happening—this was during the pandemic lockdown and there was no office to gossip in—was sadness and a sense of responsibility. They wanted to make things right.

Weiss wrote her own open letter in response to her employees' concerns, accompanied by an action plan that included antibias training for all employees as well as changes to management policies and human resources. It wasn't enough to satisfy @outtathegloss, but it did seem to contain the crisis, and the account with its 10,000-plus followers stopped posting in December 2020.

The message she was sending was that she, who had tried so hard to build a brand around inclusivity, would not be defeated. Weiss stayed firmly in control but was privately rattled.

The Glossier allegations didn't take Weiss down for a few reasons. She was prepared. The @outtathegloss account surfaced two months after the first wave of allegations against female founders, and the company's very talented PR team had time to work out a plan and a response, should they too one day face a similar crisis.

Then there were the accusations themselves. Not all employees found the accusations indicative of a racist corporate culture. For an office Halloween party, one employee dressed up in a costume that highlighted a big fake butt that was meant for laughs. "I don't know if it was email or Slack or pulled aside, but someone said this wasn't okay, it makes other people feel uncomfortable," said an employee who was there. "I am sure that there were some inappropriate things that happened at Glossier that don't deserve to be minimized. But some of the Outta the Gloss stuff . . . I remember feeling kind of sad, because I don't think the office was run that way at all."

Glossier might have had such a large following that enough of their customers didn't know or care enough about racial bias in workplace culture to change their consumer habits or loyalty. Somewhere along the way, Weiss became an object of some criticism, but, crucially, she was never demonized.

Trying hard has always been Weiss's modus operandi, and she focused hard on the issue of race. But all those issues—racism, the degradation of working retail, working environments—are systemic problems that encompass all work. It's not for Weiss to solve single-handedly. Which is not to let her off the hook but rather to place her missteps in a larger context.

Weiss was right to try to make some public amends with Black Glossier fans—Black consumers have long outspent white women on beauty. Glossier sponsored *Verzuz* battles, Balm Dotcom appeared in the video for Saweetie and Doja Cat's "Best Friend," and the Spelman College chapter of the Black sorority Alpha Kappa Alpha wore Glossier sweatshirts in a stepping video. On other issues, her track record was more mixed. When Weiss posted a photo of her partner Will Gaybrick wearing a crystal on his nail complete with a caption wishing a Happy Pride to her sparkle princess, it was tone-deaf to the real political underpinnings of pride and her own and her partner's privileged position. Some of her LGBTQ+ staffers explained that they found it objectionable, and in response she edited it. They delayed the launch of Cleanser Concentrate so it didn't coincide with the verdict of the Derek Chauvin trial. Glossier was one of the first companies to sign on to Don't Ban Equality, a coalition of businesses advocating for reproductive rights, back in 2019. When *Roe v. Wade* was overturned in June 2022, Glossier responded that they were "incredibly saddened and disappointed" (language that sounded just a tad soft) by the news on an Instagram post and tagged places for donations. Internally, they changed policies for staff to cover travel and expenses potentially required for an abortion. They also gave staff time off to vote and, in September 2022, registered voters in store at an event with Olivia Rodrigo and purchased courtside signage for WNBA games prompting voter registration.

For change to happen at Glossier, it needed to happen on a foundational level. Glossier has held itself accountable to its mid-2020 promises of support for the Black beauty entrepreneur community by publicly identifying and promoting the sixteen recipients of their Grant Initiative for Black-Owned Beauty Businesses. The company received ten thousand applications over a two-month period.

One company that was chosen was Golde, cofounded by Trinity Mouzon Wofford in 2017 in a Brooklyn apartment. The brand makes superfood drinks and powders, like a turmeric blend, but has since branched out into skincare with face masks. "I am one of the biggest skeptics when it comes to . . . Black founders are overwhelmingly overmentored and underfunded. There's this perception that underrepresented founders need more coaching, but nobody wants to cut us a check," she said. She liked that the Glossier program came with a cash grant and one that she didn't have to jump through hoops for or wait long to get once she was told she'd made it to the program.

Each of the sixteen companies of her cohort was matched

with an advisor or mentor at Glossier. Hers was the head of the legal department, but she cycled through meetings with the company's supply chain and digital marketing units. Wofford saw it as a way to get access to experts she couldn't afford to hire as consultants to her own business. Golde was a team of two full-time employees and some part-time workers when they got the grant, so they worked a lot around hiring and building team structure—what salary comps would be or what an equity package might look like, building out career trajectories, how much money raises should be for promotions. "I've had a good amount of access to other inspiring founders and CEOs but it's difficult to get connected to those leaders, you're not going to get to talk to the head of marketing," said Wofford. "It was tactical in a way you usually can't go that deep with a founder because they have their hands in everything." She genuinely believed that Weiss set the tone and everyone wanted to be there. And they likely did. Helping fledgling companies in your field must certainly be rewarding. It makes for great storytelling. By 2022, grantees had gone on to win *Shark Tank* pitches, secure VC funding, and take on national and global wholesale partnerships.

Glossier's Instagram following had begun to decline after the @outtathegloss charges. According to Spate, a consumer trends data company, while Boy Brow remained Glossier's most searched-for product in 2022, searches for it declined 33 percent year over year. The company had overinvested in a hero product, particularly as the ideal full and bushy brow began to get slimmer, at least among celebrities and in makeup editorials. But what's more, searches for the brand's products overall were down 25 percent year over year, per Spate. Sales were also declining. For the 2021 holiday season, Glossier sales were down 22 percent from 2020, according to Earnest Research, and according to data from Bloomberg Second Measure, Glossier's US sales in 2021 were down 26 percent from the previous year. By mid-December 2021, Glossier had gotten most of the sales figures from that year and had enough data to crunch the numbers with an eye to next year's operating plan. The outlook for 2022 wasn't rosy. Around late winter 2022, there were layoffs announced at the company.

Glossier's identity was in crisis. Or, to quote the name of a Reddit thread: "Is Glossier in its flop era :(?"

"So this is gonna be the space," said Weiss as she set down a giant green crocodile Hermès Birkin bag that would conservatively sell for the high five figures. (And yes, I asked an expert in luxury goods if that number was correct because I'm nosy and thorough.) Glossier was betting big on retail for its post-pandemic future.

I was in Los Angeles in July 2021 for the first time since the pandemic had begun. The last time I had seen Weiss was over Zoom while interviewing her for this book months before. She had seemed distracted and was talking to me while smelling deodorant prototypes. I figured while I was in her new adopted city, I would try to interview Weiss and see the LA store she was working on opening. It was still a construction zone and involved a lot of imagination to see the Willy Wonka vision of what would come together. Nothing about that visit instilled a lot of confidence in where the company was headed.

Weiss was a few shades blonder and tanner than her New York self. I told her that LA Emily looked great, and she joked that she thought she was starting to look like she was in a hair metal band. She and Gaybrick had decamped to

Los Angeles during the pandemic, where she got engaged, bought a golden retriever puppy, and rented a house in Malibu. Some of her employees complained that she was leading a much better life than they were. But she wasn't the only executive at the company to leave New York.

We walked across a parking lot—or was it a courtyard?—to the retail flagship. It was on Melrose near La Cienega in West Hollywood, a busy spot, and between the store and the office took up almost the entire block. Giant letters would spell out G-L-O-S-S-I-E-R in the facade outside as a nod to the Hollywood sign. The whole thing was supposed to evoke Old Hollywood and the idea of dream factories as a destination that wasn't just about retail, but an experience.

The place was literally being built to nurture social media. The entrance would be dominated by a central atrium with the Glossier Globe, a round, rotating sculpture that recalled Gilmore D. Clarke's Unisphere built for the 1964 World's Fair in New York City. I looked at renderings of amphitheater seating and shades of marble and seventeen-foot-tall versions of Glossier's hero products Boy Brow and Cloud Paint. There were going to be mirrors with another of the brand's catchphrases, "You Look Good," adorning mirrors with ideal lighting for the selfies meant to be taken there.

Weiss took particular pride in the back-of-house section for the LA store being bigger than front of house, meaning the behind-the-scenes area for employees was larger than the customer section of the store. She showed me where there would be a wellness room and changing rooms where they would have freshly laundered pink jumpsuits available each shift. Caring about employees' physical and mental health was good business, but what went unsaid was that it was probably a bit of a corrective addressing the @outtathegloss group's call for changing working conditions. The new space was built to promote sensitivity about staffers' needs and health, and how customers interacted with them, particularly along the lines of race.

The pandemic had taken a toll on the company. In March 2020, Glossier closed their stores, and by June 2020 they furloughed retail teams—around two hundred people—in New York, Los Angeles, and London. Glossier began layoffs of their physical retail staff in August 2020. "Glossier actually handled it better than any company I read about," said one Los Angeles retail worker. "They kept us on payroll until August. They paid us normally until July and furloughed us until the end of August, and then we could file for unemployment and they gave us severance—even for part-time employees—and all of our sick and vacation hours." In an announcement in August 2020, Glossier predicted that its stores, which relied so heavily on high-touch interaction and kinetic energy, would likely be closed for the duration of the pandemic.

We were in an airy space that would be the LA offices for creative and marketing teams. "So it'll be like a hub, 'cause we're gonna take a future-of-work approach. That's, like, assuming people only want to come in three days a week. Although, yeah, I like coming in all the time," Weiss said. New York would continue to be the main office, Seattle a hub for the sizable tech team, and she envisioned a London office eventually.

I asked if she was moving back to New York and she told me she was looking for a place but planned to be traveling nonstop that year, opening retail locations in New York, Los Angeles, London. Glossier reopened its offices to those who wanted to work out of them in fall 2021 and had T-shirts printed that read: "I returned to the Glossier office and all I got was this shirt with old Glossier stickers on it." Glossier's retail strategy always prioritized experience and getting to play with products and try them on. Their pop-ups had fueled e-commerce sales. They bet that, instead of the pandemic making that a relic of the past, customers would be excited to return. The pandemic had been the rare time in major cities to negotiate a fairly cheap rate on retail leases. Opening beautiful, interactive spaces customers flocked to was what Glossier was good at.

So they went for more funding. I asked Weiss why, and she said, "The last round was really about just the success of the business and the brand and all the future opportunities," which is a very fun nonstatement about something as high-stakes as raising $80 million. Glossier closed its Series E round in 2021, led by Kelly Granat at Lone Pine Capital; existing investors also participated, including funds that have been with Glossier since its earlier rounds: Forerunner Ventures, Index Ventures, Thrive Capital, and the éminence grise Sequoia Capital. This Series E round gave Glossier a total funding of $266 million and valued the company at $1.8 billion, up from $1.2 billion in 2019. Venture capital firms raise new funds based on the success of past funds, so they like to see "markups" in valuation. One way to show that would be for Glossier to be acquired for a big premium. But in a situation where there is no exit in the form of an IPO or a sale in the immediate future, the firms still want to see new fundraising rounds at higher valuations so they can show paper gains to investors and raise new, big funds. Glossier was still on the treadmill of venture capital.

Outside, Weiss walked me through a passageway that would be called Glossier Alley, where a branch of the LA coffee chain Alfred would sell a Glossier Pink Latte and a Cloud Paint Honey Rose Donut. The Haas Brothers, the art-star sculptors (and brothers of the actor Lukas Haas), were designing the fountain. Glossier could have book launches or pop-up Italian-style fruit markets in the outdoor space.

The singer Olivia Rodrigo had just visited the construction site. A few months later she would be Glossier's first celebrity spokesperson, although the partnership lasted only eight months. Glossier was in talks with companies Weiss would only tell me off the record to occupy spaces in the complex. This was their version of Studio City, she said, their idea of what post-pandemic Hollywood coinciding with the rise of TikTok might be like. "I hope to make this a really inspiring and inspired place," she said. Things should have been, well, rosy.

But their new bronzer, Solar Paint, had launched the day before. "Have you tried it?" I asked an assistant who asked me if I wanted some kombucha for my tour. She was young, Black, and luminous. "I put it on my eyes actually," she said. But she was an employee, and, true to Glossier's aesthetic, not exactly the kind of person who needed the addition of makeup to look better.

Bronzer was something of a risk for a brand that had been criticized in its early days in particular for its limited shade range. Reviews had been mixed.

"Let's just collect ourselves," Emily said. We were in what appeared to be a hallway or alcove in the as-yet-to-open LA headquarters between the main room and a glassed-in conference room. Behind us the team working on the Seattle store was staring at live feeds of the construction happening over a thousand miles away. Weiss seemed distracted and admitted as much. "I'm in a funny mood right now and I don't know how much I'm gonna get through and there's so much I wanna share with you because this is so amazing. I might just call you tomorrow or something. I just want to make sure . . ." And then she asked me to turn my recorder off and told me what was really preoccupying her off the record.

I walked back to my hotel. Walking always feels strange in a car-culture city like LA where the sidewalks are fairly desolate, but I needed to collect my thoughts after that visit. I was frustrated with Weiss because I thought I was showing up for an interview, and she instead gave me a brief tour and then decided not to speak on the record. But I was also rattled because, while I can't say what Weiss said, the person I had spent time with appeared exhausted with her position in the world to the point of being defeated.

Things can change on a dime, even when it feels like a company is super flush with cash. When the Los Angeles store opened a few months later, Weiss came to the opening and greeted the excited showroom editors personally. But it was a different era for the company. New hires were fans—

but as fans, they had followed the @outtathegloss accusations. "I was wary and I was definitely open to asking about Outta the Gloss," said one retail employee who was interviewing in mid-2021. "I said, 'I want to know what you're doing for your employees.' They didn't specifically mention Outta the Gloss but said, 'We are revamping the retail experience and we are coming up with different paths for employees to take.'"

Not everything proved to be as dazzling in the Los Angeles store as the tour Weiss had given me suggested. The ballyhooed wellness room was basically a room with a chair to sit in during breaks. The elaborate social media–bait fountain was still under construction, so customers had to be told not to take photos of it. Once, the point-of-sale system went down for all the stores around the world that used it, but Glossier management decided to remain open, so editors had to welcome customers and then break the news that they could look around but not buy anything. That happened to be the day Olivia Rodrigo came in. "We were like, here, have a little pouch with some Balm Dotcoms," said one employee.

More cracks started to show. The editors had to park on the street, but they couldn't because they were not given enough break time to go and put more money in parking meters. So they ended up parking in lots that cost as much as $20 per day, or one whole hour of their pay. There was a company parking lot, but it was reserved for managers and corporate employees at the Los Angeles Glossier headquarters, where I had interviewed Weiss a few months before. Except that office never came to be, and they leased out that building.

The biggest sticking point was hours and wages for employees. Or lack thereof. Full-time retail employees had been hired for thirty to forty hours per week, according to their contracts. And those hours were reality when the Los Angeles store opened in the fall of 2021 and through the holiday season. But after that there was a big drop-off in consumer foot traffic. So the editors consistently had their hours shaved. Some editors said they would be scheduled for just thirty hours with long breaks they weren't getting paid for, or management would close the store quickly and not pay them fully for the estimated time to close. They would arrive early for a required long meeting and, rather than being paid for it, would be told to take two lunch breaks instead. Customer traffic wasn't all that the employees thought it would be. "We were told, 'It's just slow after the holidays, by March you'll get your hours back.' We were like, 'Go Glossier, whatever you need!'" one former employee recalled. The Los Angeles store had a daily goal of $25,000 to $30,000 in sales, but it wasn't always hitting those targets.

Some retail employees started to see, in the winter and spring of 2022, that they were scheduled for only three or four days a week and asked if they could be scheduled at the same times each week in order to get another part-time job. The cost of living in Los Angeles was not cheap. "We were always told, 'Due to the needs of the business, we can't accommodate this. The needs of the business, the needs of the business, the needs of the business,'" said one former employee mockingly. "They gifted us a lot of products and it was like, 'Hey, we're asking for more hours.' I don't need another

Balm Dotcom. I have enough Glossier to last a lifetime." But even after leaving she couldn't quit Glossier completely. She could never find anything that was better than Boy Brow or Milky Jelly Cleanser. "I hate that I love it. Even after everything, I am rooting for them. I think most of us are."

Emily Weiss was pregnant. She had her baby shower on a sunny weekend in late May 2022, held at the Los Angeles home of the marketing guru Richard Christiansen. His brand Flamingo Estate is known for purveying $350 jars of honey made from bees in Ai Weiwei's Portugal garden and a $75 bag of manure sold as "A Sack of Shit," as well as natural soaps and candles. Like Glossier, Flamingo Estate is Instagram gold, memeable, and adored by a devoted following. It's no wonder that when Weiss and Christiansen met after she moved to LA, they'd become fast friends. His house on the east side of the city was worth the long commute from Malibu for its setting: goats that occasionally wore cashmere sweaters and a kidney-shaped pool and climbing vines of jasmine. It was the perfect canvas for a chic baby shower. Friends came from across the country to celebrate Emily's impending transition to motherhood.

Just a few days later, on May 24, 2022, Weiss posted a note on Instagram and to the Glossier blog. She was stepping down from the CEO role, effective immediately, and Kyle Leahy, an alumna of Nike, Cole Haan, and American

Express, would be taking over. Included were photos of the two of them together at the Los Angeles store, with Weiss looking very pregnant and very golden (a follower noted, "She looks so good pregnant that it's honestly upsetting"). Weiss wrote in an elegiac but slightly removed tone:

> I've had the privilege of not just being Glossier's founder since 2014, but also its CEO—two roles that have brought me into communion with tens, hundreds, millions of the most inspiring people inside our company and around the world, building the foundations of this magical brand that has already, in a short time, changed a 100-year-old industry by flipping the paradigm from beauty as a "final destination," to beauty as a journey.
>
> At the same time, I've always thought of these titles as unique from one another: A founder is a forever identity, one that starts with a kernel of an idea and never ends. I will always be Glossier's founder. But a CEO is the champion that a company looks to, to lead it into tomorrow. From my observation, the greatest companies in the world understand this distinction and make sure that the CEO seat is always filled with the right person to take it where it needs to go for its brightest next chapter.
>
> Every year I reflect on Glossier, and specifically, the ever-evolving role of the CEO in our young company's lifecycle. I check in and ask myself the same question:

Am I the best person to lead the company, for where we are and where we're headed? And if not, who is? This year, as has often been the case with some of our proudest and most pivotal moments at Glossier, a person inspired a new direction: her name is Kyle Leahy, and I'm thrilled to announce that she's stepping up into the CEO role.

A few weeks after her post about leaving, in late June 2022, Weiss had her daughter, Clara Lion Weissbrick (the last name is a portmanteau of her and Gaybrick's last names). After her parental leave, I'd always assumed Weiss's next act as Glossier's CEO—"to lead it into tomorrow," as she wrote— would be to transcend the girlboss's pink ceiling to become the millennial version of Steve Jobs. In other words, to join that highest echelon of business fame that goes with becoming a household name whose every innovation is surrounded by hoopla. But something different seemed like it might be happening. At first I thought that leaving her CEO position meant she was renouncing her ambition for an unspecified period of time, one that might be longer than a traditional parental leave, wanting to devote herself fully to motherhood, which she had planned out so carefully from freezing her eggs a few years before. But Weiss would surely return to the helm of Glossier. Wouldn't she? Weiss could be a mother *and* a CEO. She could take time off and have a night nurse and a nanny and a housekeeper and a meal delivery service—all the assistance that powerful women have and many women who work as hard for less do not. Look no further than Kyle Leahy, who had a nine-month-old and another child at the time she took the CEO job at Glossier.

But Emily Weiss's exit had been in the works for some time.

She had always taken pains to separate her name from Glossier. From the brand's inception she'd underscored the fact that it was not called Emily Weiss and that what her customers were buying was something outside of herself. That was true but also completely false. Glossier was a group effort of a number of very talented people, but it was very much Weiss's brainchild, and as the founder and CEO she was able to make unilateral decisions.

Even after taking on investors, Weiss had autonomy because she still owned a large percentage of the company. Weiss has never shared what percentage of Glossier she retained.

"Oh, I can't," she scoffed when I asked right after the company achieved its unicorn status.

"You can't say that?" I asked.

"No, I guess I could," she said. "But I don't want to."

After Glossier's most recent round of Series E fundraising, venture capital funds and seed investors owned 63.23 percent of the company. According to several investors, it is standard to assume, with Glossier's middle-of-the-road packages, that 10 to 15 percent of the company went to employee equity, leaving Weiss owning roughly 20 percent of Glossier.

The Glossier board was supportive of Weiss back then because the company was working. No one was better at creating hype around the company she founded than Weiss was. She was the mind behind the brand and products. As she grew in her role as CEO, the board was willing if not eager to act as coaches and mentors, propping up any of her shortcomings. But building a brand is not the same as running a company.

The answer at first was to find a trusted number two for Weiss, which she had never really had, not in Nick Axelrod-Welk, and not in Henry Davis. Glossier wasn't just Weiss's first company but virtually her first job besides being an intern at *Teen Vogue*, working at Ralph Lauren as a teen, and assisting a freelance stylist at *Vogue*. An experienced second-in-command could do a lot for steering the company: scaling it and giving it some stability. Employees working outside of Weiss's creative expertise could report to this person. Having a leadership divide between the business and the creative side would not be unique to Glossier. Tech companies have done this with Sheryl Sandberg at Facebook or Eric Schmidt at Google. Plus having a second-in-command would work as a solid compromise for investors who wanted Glossier to have a better public narrative about its business foundations but who also might be skittish about what would happen to Glossier if Weiss left as CEO. Melissa Eamer was meant to take that trusted COO role, but the partnership between her and Weiss didn't work out. Eamer left her Glossier COO position over a reportedly tearful Zoom call in September 2020, after just one year.

Kyle Leahy was supposed to be the COO who stuck around. She and Weiss met over Zoom. A lot of initial meetings were still happening that way in April 2021, but the two women also happened to be many time zones apart. In Hawaii, where Weiss was on vacation, it was late at night. Leahy was living on the East Coast, taking time after leaving Cole

Haan, and entering the third trimester of pregnancy with her second child. They had met through mutual board members and executives, including the founder of Stitch Fix, Katrina Lake, who was on the Glossier board, and Ali Weiss, who was then Glossier's chief marketing officer. "And the mutual friends were like, you two should just meet. We had what we would both call a pretty magical first date," Leahy said.

She said what they were discussing was not initially about a job. "There was no role. . . . It was more like, 'Nice to meet you,'" Leahy said. "[She] was looking for a head of retail and I was helping provide candidates. And then we met and that started our conversations, and the atmosphere was kind of organic from there." What didn't add up to me was, if Leahy wasn't initially interviewing for a job, and a very critical one at that, then why was Weiss getting up in the middle of the night while on vacation to Zoom with her? "I don't know why," Leahy replied.

The two women kept in communication, and eventually Leahy signed on as Glossier's chief commercial officer. Her son was born in August 2021, and she started working at Glossier that November. According to former employees, Leahy had been hired to be COO and act as Weiss's maternity leave replacement, but it became increasingly clear that she was going to take over as CEO for the long term. "It was always in the conversation from when we first started talking . . . that was kind of part of the master plan," said Leahy. "But I would say more specifically, once I joined Glossier."

When Weiss met Leahy for the first time, she told Will Gaybrick that night at dinner that she thought Leahy was going to be the CEO, so stepping down was something Weiss will admit to being serious about for a long time. "Many months," she said. "I've always had no pride of ownership over being CEO. I've always been like, I happen to be CEO because I'm the founder. But as soon as it's time for . . . someone else is going to see about the business in the right way," she said. But finding that succession plan was one of the hardest things she had to do. Glossier was her baby. "Having the awareness to say, 'Hey, I think it's time.' And then to try and find a person. I think it's something like fifty percent of CEOs don't work out in the first year or something." I had certainly covered splashy new CEOs of struggling companies like Weight Watchers and American Apparel who were gone seemingly right after what I wrote about them had been published.

I had asked Nabil Mallick, of Thrive Capital and the Glossier board, if the decision to leave had been Weiss's. "Sometimes it can be distracting for a CEO of a rapidly scaling business to focus on what's important and you kind of need to focus," he said. "It is allowing a founder to slide back to things that she loves. It's something that should be normalized." He gave the example of John Foley of the exercise company Peloton not knowing how to be a public company CEO and staying on too long. There were other famous executives who exited their positions right around the time that Weiss did in mid-2022. Sheryl Sandberg announced she was leaving Facebook's parent company Meta in June 2022. Also in early June, Julie Wainwright, founder and CEO of the luxury resale company the RealReal, revealed that she would be stepping down from her position after eleven years.

"It was one hundred percent her decision to step down without a doubt," Mallick told me. What I wanted to know was how the news was relayed. Did she just announce it one day in an email to the board? Mallick said that the conversations happened with the board over a long time. "She met Kyle, worked with her for nine months, decided this is my person and she will carry the legacy."

The company line from Weiss, Leahy, Glossier's communications team, and even its board is that Emily Weiss made a shrewd decision. "I happen to sit on the board of a number of companies—Glossier, Vimeo, Skims, where I'm an observer—overarchingly the way female founders and CEOs get treated is something that's disappointing in so many ways," said Mallick. "Emily was so willing to make a smart decision for the right leader for the next chapter, and it's treated like the death of the girlboss."

Weiss did make the correct decision. But the story Glossier was telling about her stepping down was idealized. She made real mistakes. Even though Weiss's reputation survived the @outtathegloss accusations of poor leadership when it came to the company's treatment of labor and blind spots for race and class issues, she wasn't entirely unscathed. She made other missteps as CEO: the excuse that they were a start-up and that human resources were hard to put together; the constant changing of direction; the cliquishness of the office culture. The dominant narrative about Glossier in culture and social media and the news was one of bad tidings and lost momentum. Even her strength in product development was starting to be called into question, even among Glossier's fans. On TikTok, the user

@skylar.alyshia said, "At one point, they were everything. Then they really started slipping off everyone's radar and they quickly became so [irrelevant]. They weren't really releasing any new products and their shade range was honestly ridiculous."

The media ran with the narrative of decline. Headlines like "How Glossier Lost Its Grip," "What Went Wrong at Glossier?" and "How Can Emerging Beauty Brands Avoid Glossier's Stumbles?" sounded like the company's obituaries. Nothing seemed to be working. The most darkly humorous assessment of Glossier's problems was a tweet from someone named Carina Hsieh that made the rounds in August 2022, after Glossier makeup was found in a T.J.Maxx discount store: "I too am glossier makeup at tj maxx (hot and full of potential in 2017, not quite where I wanna be in 2022)."

Analysts and employees alike had assumed that Glossier was planning on going public as soon as 2021. But after the pandemic the IPO market has been dormant and forecast to only get worse. The sneaker brand Allbirds had struggled after its IPO in late 2021, including a March 2023 reported $101 million annual loss and a 13 percent drop in quarterly sales. Weiss was an Allbirds board member until late spring 2023, so she was painfully aware of their situation.

Meanwhile, Glossier had missed its moment to sell a few years back when the market was on fire and when beauty brands in particular (Drunk Elephant, Tatcha, Charlotte Tilbury) were being bought for billions of dollars. With Glossier's 2021 valuation of $1.8 billion, it was too big to sell for that kind of price in the current market. And the question was, was it even worth that much?

Lone Pine, the venture capital firm that had led Glossier's Series E round of funding in 2021, has to provide end-of-year valuations for the companies it invests in so that Lone Pine's own investors (those that aren't endowments or foundations) can properly file their taxes. For Glossier, a private company, Lone Pine must make an estimate. For 2022, its valuation of Glossier was marked down more than 30 percent since the last round. Private funds are not necessarily sufficiently conservative with markdowns, so it is possible that Glossier's valuation could be as low as 50 percent less than their $1.8 billion in 2021. The company might no longer be a unicorn.

Glossier was at a crisis point.

Weiss really had two roles at Glossier: as founder, to inspire the team on the creative level, and then as a chief executive. Those are completely different skill sets. "Every entrepreneur is unique. There are archetypes of founders. Some are more suited to be CEOs at whatever stage versus others. Your strength that led you to be successful may not be suited in the same role forever," said Kirsten Green of Forerunner. She added that it was hard to claim you're a start-up after a decade. "She didn't come in one day and say, 'I'm out,' and no one told her to get out." She said Weiss's departure was the result of many long conversations.

But it seems undeniable that Weiss's leadership had inhibited Glossier's success and growth. The rules of the game had changed. Glossier needed to professionalize. Weiss could stay on as CEO, albeit one with far less authority and much more supervision. Or she could leave voluntarily and craft her own compelling narrative around her departure.

Her farewell Instagram post was the start of that narrative. Now that she had left the position of CEO, the plan was for Weiss to return from parental leave as executive chairwoman, steering Glossier, as she wrote, into 2025, 2030, and beyond. It was year eight of what she called a hundred-year brand.

"I'll be able to focus more of my time as I did in the earlier days—supporting our brilliant leaders of creative, brand, product and retail," she wrote.

Kyle Leahy was chosen to be the adult in the room. "Emily is an amazing creative genius. She is a yin to my yang. I'm not a creative; I'm a businessperson," she said. That much is unimpeachably true—she is a seasoned executive who worked with boring but dependable consumer brands such as the Nike-owned shoe brand Cole Haan her whole career. She was never lumped in with the girlboss crowd, partly because her jobs had focused on operations and didn't fit in with the sexy narrative of a young woman founding a company. Leahy had also never courted the public. Even if she had, she wouldn't have had an easy platform from which to do so. She's not the founder of anything; she's a worker.

Leahy and I were meeting over coffee at Altro Paradiso, a Manhattan restaurant across from Glossier's offices that makes a good fennel salad. A publicist had joined us and it was late afternoon and mostly empty in November 2022, almost a year to the day since Leahy had originally joined Glossier. She was in New York City from Boston, where she's from; she and her husband, Michael, and two young children had moved back there during the pandemic. (According to a wedding announcement in 2016, the couple met on an online dating site in 2014.) Leahy had grown up a Clinique fan. She wanted Glossier to be "Clinique of the next generation, that type of name, accessible price point and people want to be a part of it."

Even though Leahy was roughly the same age as Weiss—thirty-eight when she took the CEO job—she seemed older. She was more polished but also more staid. Speaking to her was very different from speaking to Weiss. "One of the things Emily and I shared on Glossier was the belief in our shared perspective of the longevity of brands," Leahy said. She talked like that, the way I imagine a graduate of Harvard Business School, which she is, would. (Though I did find it surprising she wasn't aware that there was a case study of Glossier by her alma mater, but another alumna of the same school said that wasn't a red flag because the 2018 study was already dated.) She used phrases like "values-based" and "target sectors" and "mosaic of our team" and "operational muscle." She went through each talking point smoothly and said all the right things: that they're a hundred-year brand; that they have the potential to be a household name; that they need to ground themselves in strategy and execution.

But first Glossier, and by extension Leahy, had uncertain times to contend with: unprecedented inflation, a looming recession, a land war in Europe, a pandemic in its latter stages but far from over. The beauty industry is considered a stable industry. So much so that there's a name for the so-called Lipstick Effect, the idea that in tough economic times, consumers tend to spend more on small luxuries. It's the lift that's so easy to get from buying a tube of red lipstick. Leonard Lauder said that was what made that industry recession-proof. According to McKinsey in 2022, cosmetics is the only category that has grown year over year purely from an increase in consumption (and not inflation).

Glossier's new CEO was well aware of the volatile climate. "What that's doing to consumer sentiment, the business landscape, the speed with which the markets have adjusted, I think all those things, you know, weigh heavily on anyone who's leading a company." She said there were "hard decisions to protect the business and optimize for the future." This was as close as she would get to talking about laying off about eighty people in the summer of 2022, which was one of the first things she had to do as CEO.

Kyle Leahy doesn't seem very cool. That's likely a good thing. I wrote in my notes at the time that "she will be a traditional leader for a company that prided itself on not being traditional." Part of that involved homing in on what Glossier really is, a beauty brand. "Kind of eliminating the distractions that maybe took our eye off the ball. I think refocusing on that core and saying, like, 'Let's go back to the thing that makes Glossier so special,'" she said. "We're not a tech company, we're not a DTC company. DTC is a channel. It's not a value proposition. We're a beauty company. I believe we have a multibillion-dollar business here easily on our hands. I genuinely believe, in 2030, this will be the next household name in beauty."

The company had identified two target customer demographics for Glossier going forward. There were the "polished naturalists," who were the core no-makeup makeup beauty routine customers. And then there were the "conscientious trendsetters," who tended to skew younger, more Gen Z, and were more interested in shopping aligned with their values, which was why Glossier was in the process of reformulating some of its products—Boy Brow, Balm Dotcom—to be vegan. What the two cohorts had in common was that they were both looking to Glossier for essentials, not trend-driven products. The larger plan was to recenter the core tenets of the brand— makeup, skincare, fragrance, body, merchandise—and amplify them. Leahy wanted, simply, to get more Glossier to more people.

What Leahy would have to show to be a successful leader was whether the business was profitable or whether it was growing. Glossier has never been forthcoming about those kinds of numbers. When asked for sales figures in late 2022, a Glossier publicist wrote that "marketing investments are going further—we are driving 20–40 percent growth, while spending 50 percent less on paid marketing efforts than last year, trends which we are planning to continue into next year. We've driven more efficiency as a result of investing in influencer marketing in a much larger way. . . . When we say 'influencers' we aren't necessarily referring to celebrity talent or social media personalities: to us, an influencer is someone with an interesting beauty story to tell."

Glossier wanted to reintroduce itself. I was skeptical until I thought about myself in college discovering MAC Cosmetics at department stores in the late '90s. That was well over a decade after they were an independent brand in Toronto with their own stores. It didn't matter that I hadn't been aware of the RuPaul Viva Glam campaign or was yet to be educated in the company's progressive politics; it was new and exciting to me as I was a late adolescent going to parties and doing makeup for the first time in the bathroom with my friends, dabbing on shimmery silver eye shadow and red lip gloss. It felt like it belonged to us. The same could be said of Glossier.

Slowly the conversation around Glossier had turned into one of reinvention. Social media had changed, constantly migrating to different apps and fads, but Glossier wasn't entirely left behind. The perfume You went viral on TikTok in June 2022 after a user called @bitcoin_papi shared a post talking about the reactions she'd received when wearing the fragrance, including being stopped on the street and receiving a poem about it written by a man she'd gone on two dates with. The post received over 500,000 likes. In late 2022, Glossier came out with its first two brand collaborations, a toothbrush with the Italian toothpaste brand Marvis and a limited-edition Balm Dotcom with Swiss Miss that sold out in five weeks. In November 2022, I watched videos of fans from the opening of the new store in Williamsburg, which had been in the press for its 600-person lines that formed around several Brooklyn city blocks to get in. When they introduced the reformulated vegan Balm Dotcom in February 2023, Glossier sold $1 million worth in its first week.

Then Glossier announced that after so many years of being direct-to-consumer, the brand would enter into a retail partnership. It was going omnichannel. Beauty retailers were more important than ever: in 2021, a full 44 percent of American internet users said they began shopping for beauty products at a beauty retailer's website versus 16 percent in 2019; only 9 percent began shopping on a brand website in 2021, down from 18 percent in 2019. Before the Sephora announcement, industry prognosticators wondered which third-party retailer Glossier would go with: Ulta (which had outposts in Target), CVS, or even Walmart. In an article in the *Business of Fashion*, this decision was compared to the basketball player LeBron James taking his talents to the Miami Heat: "James took the traditional path to success and left his hometown team for the Miami Heat, which manufactured one of the greatest basketball teams of the 2010s. Weiss, who built her brand the unconventional way—with no help from a leading beauty retailer—is now choosing the traditional path to success: Sephora."

On February 23, 2023, Glossier debuted in 600 Sephora stores in the United States and Canada. All Sephora employees wore Glossier pink T-shirts that day. "Could just be me, but seeing the brand's tightly edited skincare and makeup in the context of Sephora's vast beauty repertory reminds me what a good value a few of my favorites like Lash Slick, Boy Brow, and After Baume are. If the intended effect was a re-up, it worked," the fashion journalist Laura Reilly wrote in her newsletter *Magasin*. The gondola—Sephora-speak for its shelving units—had on the top shelf Glossier's hero products: Boy Brow, You perfume, Milky Jelly Cleanser, Cloud Paint for blush, the primer Future Dew. (The company did make a big deal out of getting to break the rules at Sephora and display their perfume with their other products, as opposed to in the fragrance section—a coup for them.) Glossier was previously only available either to people who were willing to buy makeup and skincare online sight unseen or to the relative few who could go to a metropolitan area, usually stand in a long line, and then shop in a store. Allowing themselves to spread into retail gave the brand a kind of reboot. For a swath of people venturing into a Sephora, Glossier will be a new brand to discover. Shoppers already in the know (the ones who made "Glossier" one of Sephora's most searched-for terms) could buy it from Sephora in order to boost their VIB points in Sephora's loyalty program, which adherents are as fanatic about ascending as Delta SkyMiles fans are about trying to get diamond status. Sephora was not yet carrying Glossier outside the United States and Canada. There are entire foreign markets, such as Asia and South America, that may be hard to crack but represent millions of potential customers for Glossier to win over. There was still ground to cover, and room to grow.

It's possible the younger Weiss, if she could have looked forward to this moment, might in her naïveté have seen Glossier going to Sephora as a failure. But avoiding that turned out to be impossible. After all, even her beloved lifestyle brands Apple and Nike are sold in other stores besides their own. So are brands such as Chanel and Cartier, which retain a kind of wide hold on the imagination. That didn't have to be an admission of defeat for her or women in business or feminism. It didn't have to be a victory or a downfall. I realized what I wanted for Weiss was to, under pressure to give up her post in the face of Glossier's challenges, decide at the last minute not to hire an outside CEO and to double down on her authority. If that sounds like a fantasy, it sort of is. It's the plot, I realized, of the 2015 movie that Robert De Niro and Anne Hathaway made with Nancy Meyers, *The Intern*. It's not real life.

The real question is what Glossier will look like now that it is no longer aspiring to be a tech company, and no longer has a CEO aping a tech-founder mentality. Glossier never became a tech company. They finally gave up on the app that never was and used an established software—Shopify—for their sales. In fact, whenever Glossier strayed from its core, things didn't work out. The brand is not going to look or feel the same as it did with the first launch. Their challenge now is to show that the ephemeral, emotional, resonant, creative energy of the brand can also make Glossier a household name and legacy; that they can capture the moment and also be evergreen. There are products beyond personal care the company can move into. If Glossier created a world that fans wanted to live in and, for better or worse, be friends with, what could those products be? Could Weiss's dreams of a bra or a hotel (or the fan's suggestion of a tampon) become real?

There was before Glossier, there was the disruption of Glossier, and there's the Glossier of now. Glossier could be acquired and be a huge brand within a conglomerate. Glossier could wait out the market and IPO and become a massive stand-alone business, or even start acquiring other brands, becoming the next iteration of L'Oréal or Estée Lauder. It could stay private and grow at its own pace. The real opportunity for Glossier is to prove that it can move away from the girlboss narrative, the perceived downfall, the Glossier pink—all those clichés—to its next phase. And Into the Gloss and Glossier can finally prove that they were always supposed to be bigger than Emily Weiss.

But someone has to be there for that Glossier magic. Leahy is well aware of that. As we sat together talking, she called it the je ne sais quoi and rubbed her fingers together in a vaguely European way. The company needs to recapture that elusive sense of authenticity, which is difficult to do with so few early hires left at Glossier. The cool has to come from somewhere. It can't all be extracted from Weiss.

17

The biggest flaw in Weiss's self-creation narrative of Glossier was that she really only allowed for a narrative of success, that the company's trajectory was up and up and up. Weiss had done something so many people aspire to do: be paid well, have the means to finance their dreams, have fame and autonomy. If she were a man, she would probably take a lot more credit. Glossier's motto "You can sit with us" is a fantasy, pure and simple. But she allowed that idea to be taken too literally. That idea that Glossier is your friend, and the company that employs you is your friend, and capitalism is your friend, is not fair to the consumer. And it's a single trick—if you try to monetize that, you'll lose because you must maintain constant likability or you'll be attacked. I'm not sure there's a male CEO who has had to deal with that in the way that Weiss's cohort has.

But she was not willing to admit how difficult it was to maintain that smiley veneer when it mattered. Which is why, when the company started to show signs of struggles, people were so thrilled to follow the story of Glossier's fall from grace. It's also why her departure was so shocking.

In early November 2022, after our last in-person meeting in October, I got an email from Emily Weiss. "I think another interview makes sense, and I'd like to move forward with speaking on the record," she wrote. I knew this would be our final interview and I wanted to hear, in her own words, why she'd left. What did leaving the only real job she had held as an adult feel like? Now that she no longer had to maintain the role of the leader, she could show some vulnerability.

Once again the two of us were at the Crosby Street Hotel, this time on a Sunday, sitting at a relatively discreet corner table. "I'm trying to think back to when I was doing Into the Gloss, I don't think we had voice notes. I remember it being more complicated than that, in 2010," she said. We were talking about voice memos and recording on iPhones because Weiss had chosen to record this conversation. It's well within the rights of anyone I interview, but it has never happened before to my knowledge. It's the kind of thing I imagined only happened when interviewing high-level politicians. "We're living in two different worlds where you're spending every day writing your book and I'm spending every day being like, 'There's a book being written about me,'" she said. That's why she was recording me—she was anxious.

Weiss had gone back and forth with me all morning about timing due to her daughter's nap and feeding schedule, so I knew we had one hour at the most. Neither of us was very hungry. We both ended up ordering chicken apple sausage. She poured maple syrup on hers. Was that a southern thing? I asked, knowing that she had spent her early childhood in

Georgia before her family settled in Connecticut. "I think it's a me thing," she said. She was again dressed casually in a button-down and sneakers and no obvious makeup, and commented that her life had changed entirely. She had not worn a pair of high heels in three years. ("I literally go into my closet now and I look at all my old shoes. I'm like, 'Do I just get rid of all of these?'") Instagram, she said, was no longer something she was constantly refreshing. "Instagram I feel like was so different, where the more time I would go on Instagram, the better I felt. Although that's kind of changed. I feel like now Instagram doesn't make me feel good, but sad."

She called her role at Glossier a steward of the brand. That's been a trendy word to throw around about founders and CEOs lately, that one should be the steward of the brand, not be the brand. ("Why Leaders Should Create a Culture of Stewardship," "Stewardship: The Core Compass of Real Leaders," and "Inspiring Stewardship" are a few such headlines.) In her case, being a steward was an unspoken rejoinder to her business fame; she wanted to be seen as steering the brand, not being the brand. Leahy used the word "steward" too when talking about Weiss's role as executive chairwoman: "She allows us to kind of steward our business for the next chapter."

Weiss knew her career was at a crossroads and had made a decision. Leaving the CEO title was not easy. "That was an incredibly vulnerable moment. I mean, of course you're feeling a little bit like sending your kid to college. You have to truly have faith and trust in people," she said. I asked her if there was any frustration or self-doubt. Was she struggling? Sure, she said. That's the nature of the relentless pace of being a CEO. "I've been burnt-out. It's part of the job." The decision to leave was an open conversation, not an announcement. The board hadn't changed; they were committed to Glossier and, she said, they were her sounding board. "I need to do everything I can to let it blossom and become all that it can be for people. And so I think that attitude has just enabled me, whether it was the rejection from venture capitalists or countless other hurdles or trials and tribulations," she said.

Her answers were truly amazing exercises in obfuscation. The way she spoke felt like she was running for office: inane, plotless, a banal word salad. I asked how she'd changed from the time she founded Into the Gloss until she stepped down as CEO nearly twelve years later. "I wish I could say," she said, and looked at the clock on her phone. "I'm enjoying this, but I probably have five or so." I repeated the question—I wanted the most I could get from five minutes: How have you changed? "Let me see how much more time I have," she said. I tried again. "How have you changed as a leader over the course of Glossier?" I asked.

Weiss responded almost robotically, "Have you read *Shoe Dog*? So I love this just not even as a business book, just as I'm shocked it hasn't been a movie. *Shoe Dog* would be such an amazing movie." I had to stop myself from saying the story of Glossier could also be an amazing movie. "That was such a great example of a founder . . . that's not what I'm trying to say. What am I trying to say? There's no replacement for learning along the way," she said. "I would say I'm very much—what's that phrase?—the beginner's mindset. I've always had a beginner's mindset and the learning curve is hugely steep with how fast Glossier has grown. It's all about trying to continue to be the best, to be a steward of the company. What was the question?"

The question, I said, was whether there were moments when she felt like she had to change how she related to the employees, or the press, or how people perceived her. "There are moments for sure. I think it's interesting to think about how the definition of professional has changed what is being professional and how to be professional. And it's such an interesting question too as a woman because there's such a double standard," Weiss said. So did she feel pressure to project professionalism? "It's less pressure to project professionalism and there's more a realization that you are held to a different standard as a woman than a man in your behavior and in your attitude because women are expected to be all things. They're expected to be very nice, very smiley. . . . I think women are held to different standards. And so I think there have been moments where I've really felt that. I just read an article about a company this week that did layoffs and basically they were applauding the CEO for the way in which he exhibited kindness in the email that was sent to employees about the layoffs."

After a full hour of going round and round in circles, she seemed both unable and unwilling to tell me one real thing about power or money or success or hardship. Instead, all I had was jargon. What has ever gone wrong? I asked. "You need another half an hour, you need forty-five minutes," Weiss said. "But thank you." And she was off upstairs to nurse her daughter.

As I walked home, I thought back to the way Weiss introduced Glossier to her readers and fans, just eight years prior. Then she was able to use real language. "Freedom is being more or less okay with wherever you're at, at any given point in your life or your day or your hour, be it really sucky or really great or somewhere in between," she wrote. It sounded the way people spoke to each other, but there was rhythm and polish to it and it was clear. It might not have been great writing, but it was good writing. The way she communicated her thoughts both to me ("no pride of ownership") and to the public via her Instagram announcement about leaving the CEO role ("a CEO is the champion that a company looks to, to lead it into tomorrow") felt irrevocably different. She had changed by spending way too much time around the patois of business school graduates and tech bros. But also Glossier had changed—grown, evolved—and she had to remake herself to fit in.

She was a completely different person when she launched Into the Gloss and, later, Glossier than she had been when she was working at magazines. She went from somebody who thought her taste and good eye and overall perspective and ability to commentate on beauty were enough to start a buzzy website that would strengthen her own career to somebody who thought she could disrupt an entire industry. And did.

Weiss's career will be whatever she wants it to be. She turned thirty-eight in 2023. She could stay in her role at Glossier or do some kind of next act. Gwyneth Paltrow was thirty-six when she launched Goop, around the same age Lorne Michaels was when he left *Saturday Night Live* for a few years in the early 1980s, before returning. Steve Jobs left Apple in his early thirties and again in his early forties, and returned both times. Martha Stewart was in her early forties in 1982 when *Entertaining* came out. Weiss could return to Glossier, the way Bob Iger returned to Disney. Or she could put her effort into something else and prove to be a creative visionary. Unlike Bobbi Brown or any other founder who left their namesake company but whose name continued on without them, haunting their old brand like a ghost, Weiss could move on a bit more seamlessly to whatever she will do next.

Weiss started out as a starry-eyed innovator, a girl for whom nothing had ever gone wrong. She wasn't a Rockefeller, exactly, but to most Americans she might as well have been. She was pretty, connected, thin, tall. She dripped with privilege. But she was also smart. And, crucially, she was willing to put in the work. She had a solid idea—Into the Gloss—that came at exactly the right time. That was all hers. But Weiss sometimes fell into an internalized misogynist trap of not taking credit for her ideas, as if Glossier were a craft project, a manifestation of her vision boards. That's because luck plays a huge role in Weiss's trajectory. And luck can be scary to discuss because it can't be bought or controlled. You can only set up all the right conditions for it, which can involve a lot of hard work, though not always. People don't like talking about luck the way they don't like talking about privilege: because it makes it seem like they haven't "earned" everything. But I don't think it has to be a luck or hard work thing, but rather an *and*.

Weiss seemed to be born That Girl with the outsize drive and ambition who chose that senior quote in 2003 from Calvin Coolidge about persistence and determination. She lived up to those ideals as much as anyone can of what their teen selves want them to be. Weiss has an electricity that viewers of *The Hills* felt from a few brief scenes. She deserves every bit of praise for Glossier's phenomenal success as a brand. Unlike so many businesses founded by well-bred people with good connections, Weiss never saw her company as a vanity business. She didn't treat it like one, either.

So many founders like Weiss are larger-than-life. That is a quality that is seductive to someone like me who is interested in telling stories, and makes them good at their jobs. Steve Jobs saw the potential for a Mac computer. There were certainly other personal computers that had come before, but none of those were able to spark the consumer imagination the same way. Weiss saw that there was a market for a beauty brand that was sunny and easy to afford but had a sheen of exclusivity and cool. When I walk down Ludlow Street to the corner of Canal Street in New York City, the buildings' exteriors are lined with wheat-pasted ads. A lot of them these days are for beauty companies. They all look like Glossier.

Glossier fans wanted the brand and Weiss to be everything, and they both had to come back to earth. This is not a story of a poorly managed company or a sociopath in charge, like so many of those business books in her living room. Weiss is not a villainous figure, but she is also not the philosopher-genius she aspired to be. Rather, she is a woman who was learning on the job, who was calling the shots from the beginning of Into the Gloss until she stepped down as CEO of Glossier. She built a company that will last, and she deserves all the credit for that. So who is she? Weiss is a complicated woman who is admired more than she is liked.

Spring Street

In what felt like a divine joke, Glossier's new flagship store in SoHo was previously an Amazon 4-Star store. I visited it once before to buy clothes hangers. Or at least, that was supposed to be the errand of the day. Instead, I was distracted by seven thousand square feet of wall-to-wall products and started to pick up plush dog toys and blank notebooks and ultimately left empty-handed. The Amazon store was closed in 2022 when the company decided to shift focus toward grocery and fashion ventures.

In the retail cycle of life, Glossier had made the space its own. One room had a mosaic that echoed NYC subway tiles depicting one of the elaborate floral arrangements so endemic to the brand, with "You Look Good" etched into it. Across from the mosaic was a giant mirror ready for fans' selfies. In the room next door were a photo booth for friends to pile into and a claw-machine arcade game to win G-shaped cookie cutters and hair clips.

It turns out Glossier succeeded as a lifestyle brand. The store had as much merchandise stocked as skincare and makeup. Shoppers had the opportunity to buy a limited-edition 2022 beach bag previously available only at the Miami store, a water bottle from the Seattle store, and a very coveted black-on-black Glossier hoodie exclusive to Manhattan.

In the days leading up to the Glossier opening, the brand was inescapable in New York City. The marketing efforts included MTA banner wraps, Glossier-branded MetroCards, a pop-up coffee truck, and pink newsstands scattered around the city. The team even made a publication that looked like an alt weekly, complete with guides to a day in SoHo and, in true Glossier fashion, products matched to each horoscope.

The Glossier store was bookended on Spring Street by two other businesses known for long waits to get in: the TikTok favorite Jack's Wife Freda restaurant and the legacy bistro Balthazar. But when Glossier opened on February 16, 2023, the longest lines were for them.

I went that opening day, getting in line in below-freezing weather. "I want to get the candle," a college-aged girl wearing head-to-toe pink told her friend, who was wearing Ugg boots.

"I wish they made sweats," the other one moaned. "That would be so cute."

"So cute," her friend cooed back to her.

I couldn't stop thinking of the time in 2019 when I went to the Glossier Manhattan flagship with Weiss and how it hadn't exactly been a celebrity experience. Some customers, like a trio of teens studying at the School of American Ballet, had recognized the brunette in the black dress standing in the back and shyly said hello or took selfies, but most people seemed not so much to wish to leave her alone as to have no idea who she was. Weiss had taken that as a very good sign, surveying the room and smiling at her anonymity: "It's more than me." And it's true that no one looked out for her in line, or even mentioned her, that opening day in 2023.

One of the offline editors with short, dyed-red curly hair and a thick Bronx accent, wearing a giant red puffer jacket over her pink jumpsuit, sprayed You on those of us waiting for around ten minutes in line. She told us that someone had come to line up at 1 a.m. "Now, that's dedication," she said. At first that seemed odd, considering that the customer could just get in a taxi and, twenty minutes later, be at the Glossier store in Williamsburg to get whatever she wanted. She was incentivized to go to SoHo—the brand was giving away some gifts to the first customers—but her reasons for waiting were larger than that.

Leahy described the Glossier customer as willing to stand in a long line for the retail store, even though she can buy Boy Brow online, because "I want to come experience it. I want to touch, feel it. I want to, you know, be part of it." The physical in-store experience is an emotional one for Glossier's fans. It's a virtual one, too, where fans can gather content for their online lives and show off the fact that they went there, they made it, they, to use the words Glossier prints on its mirrors, look good.

Glossier built the ultimate hype machine, and it's one that fans are still obsessed with. Glossier's fans will age up and maybe never grow out of Glossier, but the company will also keep getting new ones. Name another decade-old company that has lines out the door every weekend.

Behind me were a very small girl, around middle school age, and her mother, who was drinking a coffee. The girl kept up a constant patter as their place in line drew closer to the entrance. "I'm really excited," she said. "Isn't it really pretty?" She wanted to stock up on the Wild Fig flavor of Balm Dotcom and thought her mom should get the new deodorant.

"I'm gonna take so many pictures!" she said. By then she was almost at the front and started hopping up and down in anticipation of being let in.

"Okayyyy, it's coming soon," said her mother, amping up her daughter's already off-the-charts excitement. "Are you ready?"

Author's Note

The first email I sent when I started reporting this book in 2021 was to Emily Weiss and her Glossier communications team. This book was conceived as a larger narrative about the beauty industry but Glossier was going to be the central narrative. I soon learned that Glossier was more than enough to be the story. It was *the* story.

Weiss and I sat down four times for interviews exclusively for this project. Once was in spring 2021 over Zoom. The others were in person: one interview was in Los Angeles in the summer of 2021 and two were at the Crosby Street Hotel in New York City in the fall of 2022, the content and tenor of which are all described in detail in the narrative of this book. I had also interviewed Weiss for a *Wired* profile in 2016 and a *Vanity Fair* profile in 2019, plus many additional times as a source over the past decade.

In the course of reporting from winter 2021 until the winter of 2023, I have spoken to more than two hundred sources, including current and former employees, board members, investors, industry competitors, members of the media, and Weiss's acquaintances and childhood friends. Some of these names and their contact information were provided by Weiss. Not everyone was able to speak to me about Glossier and its founder on the record, so anonymity was given so that people felt safe and comfortable talking freely about their experience and perspectives on Glossier and Emily Weiss. Each interview helped me illuminate a person, a company, and a part of business and cultural history.

Dialogue, emails, text messages, and DMs in this narrative were taken from audio files, video recordings, or transcripts, or were recounted or described by sources. Some quotes are condensed and edited for clarity.

Acknowledgments

This book is the result of the tireless work of my agent, Jen Marshall, at Aevitas Creative Management; my editor, Julia Cheiffetz; and the whole team at One Signal Publishers: Abby Mohr, Falon Kirby, and Jolena Podolsky.

Margaux Weisman, Courtney Rubin, Glynnis MacNicol, and Jamie Johns gave me such generous guidance and direction. Drew Zandonella-Stannard and Paul McAdory helped with additional research, and Caryl Espinoza Jaen fact-checked this book.

I want to thank my parents, Alyson Kennedy and Paul Meltzer, for their continued support.

Finally, I am grateful for Emily Weiss's willingness to participate in this project. I am indebted to everyone who took time to speak to me for this book, whether it was on the record or anonymously.

Notes

THE CROSBY

1 *"beauty Disneyworld":* Rachel Strugatz, "Glossier Gets a Makeover," *New York Times*, February 15, 2023, https://www.nytimes.com/2023/02/15/style/glossier-gen-z-make-up-skin-care.html.

2 *They called her the Superintern: The Hills*, season 2, episode 5, "One Big Interruption," aired February 12, 2007, on MTV, https://www.mtv.com/episodes/4buxb1/the-hills-one-big-interruption-season-2-ep-5.

2 *the site had more than 200,000 unique visitors:* Imran Amed, "The Business of Blogging | Into the Gloss," *Business of Fashion*, November 26, 2012, https://www.businessoffashion.com/articles/technology/the-business-of-blogging-into-the-gloss/.

2 *she was initially passed over by about a dozen venture capitalists:* Eric Johnson, "Full Q&A: Glossier CEO Emily Weiss on the 'Art and Science' of the Beauty Business," Vox, January 16, 2019, https://www.vox.com/podcasts/2019/1/16/18185512/glossier-ceo-emily-weiss-beauty-makeup-interview-podcast-recode-decode-kara-swisher.

2 *Glossier had a billion-dollar valuation:* Olivia Carville, "Glossier Is NYC's Newest Unicorn with $1.2 Billion

Valuation," Bloomberg, March 19, 2019, https://www
.bloomberg.com/news/articles/2019-03-19/glossier-is-nyc
-s-newest-unicorn-with-1-2-billion-valuation?leadSource
=uverify%20wall.

3   *Glossier was valued at $1.8 billion:* Alexandra Mondalek and
Rachel Strugatz, "Glossier Raises $80 Million Series E, Valuing
Company at $1.8 Billion," *Business of Fashion,* July 6, 2021,
https://www.businessoffashion.com/articles/beauty/glossier
-raises-80-million-series-e-valuing-company-at-18-billion/.

4   *"So was Mr. Jobs smart?":* Walter Isaacson, "The Genius of
Jobs," *New York Times,* October 29, 2011, https://www
.nytimes.com/2011/10/30/opinion/sunday/steve-jobss
-genius.html.

8   *"Every journalist who is not too stupid or full of himself":*
Janet Malcolm, "The Journalist and the Murderer—I,"
New Yorker, March 13, 1989, https://www.newyorker.com
/magazine/1989/03/13/the-journalist-and-the-murderer-i.

10   *an industry that generates more than $500 billion globally:*
Emily Gerstell et al., "How COVID-19 Is Changing the
World of Beauty," McKinsey & Company, May 5, 2020,
https://www.mckinsey.com/~/media/McKinsey/Industries
/Consumer%20Packaged%20Goods/Our%20Insights
/How%20COVID%2019%20is%20changing%20the%
20world%20of%20beauty/How-COVID-19-is-changing
-the-world-of-beauty-vF.pdf.

10   *predicts that number will reach $800 billion . . . ; we spend
more on beauty than any other country:* Pamela N. Danziger,
"6 Trends Shaping the Future of the $532B Beauty
Business," *Forbes,* September 1, 2019, https://www.forbes
.com/sites/pamdanziger/2019/09/01/6-trends-shaping-the
-future-of-the-532b-beauty-business/?sh=62825199588d.

10   *six of them made their fortunes at least partially in beauty:*
Ariel Shapiro, "The Richest Self-Made Women Under 40,

Including Rihanna, Maria Sharapova and Kylie Jenner," *Forbes*, October 13, 2020, https://www.forbes.com/sites /arielshapiro/2020/10/13/the-richest-self-made-women -under-40-including-rihanna-maria-sharapova-and-kylie -jenner/?sh=4c128c8236b3.

11   *"with varying degrees of knowledge of the landscape":* Rachel Strugatz, "Emily Weiss Is the LeBron James of Beauty," *Business of Fashion*, February 20, 2023, https://www.business offashion.com/articles/beauty/glossier-nyc-soho-flagship/.

CHAPTER 1

18   *Her father was an executive for the global shipping company:* Alexandra Jacobs, "Emily Weiss: The Beauty Guru for Millennials," *New York Times*, March 10, 2015, https:// www.nytimes.com/2015/03/11/fashion/emily-weiss-of-into -the-gloss-creates-a-skincare-line.html.

19   *"I wore a tulle and velvet fifties gown":* Emily Weiss, "Treasure Hunt," *Teen Vogue*, December 2005/January 2006.

23   *years before Weiss, was Soon-Yi Previn:* Frederick M. Winship, "Working Girl," *People*, October 14, 1995, https://www.upi .com/Archives/1995/10/14/People/2969813643200/.

26   *sometimes both, in the case of Paley:* Grace Mirabella and Judith Warner, *In and Out of Vogue* (New York: Doubleday, 1995).

27   *Consider the case of the actor Chloë Sevigny:* Kara Jesella and Marisa Meltzer, *How* Sassy *Changed My Life* (New York: Faber and Faber, 2007).

30   *Weiss said in an interview:* "Live Episode! Glossier: Emily Weiss," NPR, *How I Built This*, November 26, 2018, https:// www.npr.org/2018/11/20/669783899/live-episode-glossier -emily-weiss.

34   *she wrote on* Vogue's *website:* Emily Weiss, "The Verdict's In: *Vogue* Editors on Their Perfect Fall Pants," July 2010,

http://www.vogue.com/voguedaily/2010/07/the-verdicts
-in-vogues-editors-on-their-perfect-fall-pants/gucciwe10
-vo-ds16001/ (URL page discontinued).

CHAPTER 2

43 *Into the Gloss had over 200,000 new users per month:* Imran
Amed, "The Business of Blogging | Into the Gloss,"
Business of Fashion, November 26, 2012, https://www
.businessoffashion.com/articles/technology/the-business-of
-blogging-into-the-gloss/.

44 *Lancôme spent $5,000 to be their first advertiser:* "Live Episode!
Glossier: Emily Weiss," NPR, *How I Built This,* November 26,
2018, https://www.npr.org/2018/11/20/669783899/live
-episode-glossier-emily-weiss.

48 *A Harvard Business School case study:* Jill Avery, "Glossier:
Co-Creating a Cult Brand with a Digital Community,"
Harvard Business School Case 519-022, January 2019
(revised October 2019), https://www.hbs.edu/faculty/Pages
/item.aspx?num=54905.

50 *"Unlike the valued book club reviewer":* Cynthia Ozick,
"Literary Entrails: The Boys in the Alley, the Disappearing
Readers, and the Novel's Ghostly Twin," *Harper's,* April
2007, https://harpers.org/archive/2007/04/literary-entrails/.

CHAPTER 3

53 *Green began by investing modestly:* Leena Rao, "Meet the
Woman Funding the Valley's Hottest Shopping Startups,"
Time, July 19, 2017, https://time.com/collection-post
/4832819/kirsten-green-american-voices/.

61 *It costs about $1.5 million from marketing to staffing:* Lauren
Indvik, "How to Launch a Beauty Brand for $1.5 Million,"
Vogue Business, January 1, 2019, https://www.voguebusiness
.com/beauty/how-to-launch-a-beauty-brand-for-1-5-million.

62   *Jamie Siminoff... rejected by seventy VCs:* Alejandro
     Cremade, "These Entrepreneurs Were Rejected Hundreds of
     Times Before Bringing in Billions," *Forbes*, February 5, 2019,
     https://www.forbes.com/sites/alejandrocremades/2019/02/05
     /these-entrepreneurs-were-rejected-hundreds-of-times-before
     -bringing-in-billions/?sh=7a1e05e05c67.

CHAPTER 4

68   *Clinique... came onto the market in 1968:* Laurie Brookins,
     "Eye On: Carol Phillips and the Creation of Clinique,"
     Clinique (website), https://www.clinique.com/thewink/eye
     -on-carol-phillips.

71   *wrote a BuzzFeed reporter:* Nitasha Tiku, "Inside Glossier,
     the Beauty Startup That Reached Cult Status by Selling
     Less," BuzzFeed News, August 25, 2016, https://www
     .buzzfeednews.com/article/nitashatiku/inside-glossier-the
     -beauty-startup-that-just-happens-to-sell.

73   *left Into the Gloss in mid-2014:* Emma Sandler, "Welcome
     to the World of the Glossier Mafia," Glossy, September 28,
     2020, https://www.glossy.co/beauty/welcome-to-the-world
     -of-the-glossier-mafia/.

78   *McGhee told* Glamour*:* Teryn Payne, "Glossier Just Made
     Its Shade Range Way More Inclusive for Women of Color,"
     Glamour, January 29, 2019, https://www.glamour.com/story
     /glossier-skin-tint-shade-range-expansion.

82   *Hyland coined the term "millennial pink":* Véronique Hyland,
     "Why Is Millennial Pink Suddenly So Popular?," *The Cut*,
     August 2, 2016, https://www.thecut.com/2016/07/non-pink
     -pink-color-trend-fashion-design.html.

85   *"Any woman who counts on her face is a fool":* Zadie Smith,
     On Beauty (New York: Penguin Books, 2006).

86   *In the 1990s, third-wave feminists championed:* Melena Ryzik,
     "A Feminist Riot That Still Inspires," *New York Times*,

June 3, 2011, https://www.nytimes.com/2011/06/05/arts/
music/the-riot-grrrl-movement-still-inspires.html.

88 *Dove's Campaign for Real Beauty from 2005:* Mary McCall,
"The Dove Campaign for Real Beauty: An Embodiment
of Postracial Rhetoric," *Peitho* 23, no. 1, Fall 2020, https://
cfshrc.org/article/the-dove-campaign-for-real-beauty-an
-embodiment-of-postracial-rhetoric/.

91 *Glossier's pink hoodie had a pre-sale wait list of 10,000 names:*
Victoria Turk, "How Glossier Turned Itself into a Billion-
Dollar Beauty Brand" *Wired* (UK edition), February 6,
2020, https://www.wired.co.uk/article/how-to-build-a-brand
-glossier.

92 *"Train to be a model, or just look like one!":* Sue Carlton,
"Tampa's Barbizon USA Continues the 'Be a Model or Just
Look Like One' Legacy," *Tampa Bay Times*, March 25, 2022,
https://www.tampabay.com/news/business/2022/03/25
/tampas-barbizon-usa-continues-the-be-a-model-or-just-look
-like-one-legacy/.

94 *"One of the most superlative accounts of beauty-related futility":*
Charlotte Shane, "I Think About This a Lot: Emily Weiss's
Wedding Prep Routine," *The Cut*, April 3, 2018, https://www
.thecut.com/2018/04/i-think-about-this-a-lot-emily-weisss
-wedding-prep-routine.html.

94 *"4:00–4:15 wash face . . . clear mind":* Bill Murphy Jr., "This
Ex-CEO's Insane Morning Routine Is the Most Tragic
Example I've Ever Seen," *Inc.*, December 6, 2021, https://
www.inc.com/bill-murphy-jr/this-ex-ceos-insane-morning
-routine-is-most-tragic-example-ive-ever-seen.html.

CHAPTER 5

98 *Jonathan Glick, the CEO of Sulia . . . "Mediata":* Jonathan
Glick, "Rise of the Platishers," Vox, February 7, 2014, https://
www.vox.com/2014/2/7/11623214/rise-of-the-platishers.

101 *A New York Times writer described the scene:* Alexandra Jacobs, "Emily Weiss: The Beauty Guru for Millennials," *New York Times,* March 10, 2015, https://www.nytimes.com/2015/03/11/fashion/emily-weiss-of-into-the-gloss-creates-a-skincare-line.html.

104 *"Research shows that as women get older":* Alex Abad-Santos, "The Death of the Girlboss," Vox, June 7, 2021, https://www.vox.com/22466574/gaslight-gatekeep-girlboss-meaning.

CHAPTER 6

115 *she showed up to a Proenza Schouler fashion show:* Kali Hays and Allison Collins, "Glossier on the IPO Path," *Women's Wear Daily,* March 1, 2018, https://wwd.com/beauty-industry-news/beauty-features/glossier-beauty-company-ipo-1202589159/.

117 *known for having a friendship with Snoop Dog:* Paige Strout, "How Snoop Dogg Inspired Martha Stewart to Start Her Own Marijuana Farm," E! News, July 13, 2022, https://www.eonline.com/news/1337835/how-snoop-dogg-inspired-martha-stewart-to-start-her-own-marijuana-farm.

121 *"AWOK" sign-off:* Chioma Nnadi, "The Story Behind Anna Wintour's Secret 4-Letter Word," *Vogue,* August 16, 2017, https://www.vogue.com/article/vogue-sticker-anna-wintour-awok-secret-four-letter-word.

CHAPTER 7

134 *It was a similar lineage:* Shira Li Bartov, "Former Google Employee Reveals the Dark Side of Tech Company Perks," *Newsweek,* March 14, 2022, https://www.newsweek.com/former-google-employee-reveals-dark-side-tech-company-perks-1687898.

138 *According to a 2017 paper by the* Vanderbilt Law Review: Randall S. Thomas, Norman Bishara, and Kenneth

J. Martin, "An Empirical Analysis of Non-Competition Clauses and Other Restrictive Post-Employment Covenants," *Vanderbilt Law Review* 68, no. 1 (revised September 6, 2017), Vanderbilt Law and Economics Research Paper No. 14-11, https://papers.ssrn.com/sol3/Papers.cfm?abstract_id=2401781.

CHAPTER 8

143 *Boy Brow had a 10,000-person wait list:* Lindsay Colameo, "Why the World Can't Stop Buying Glossier Boy Brow," Zoe Report, April 12, 2019, https://www.thezoereport .com/p/why-glossier-boy-brow-is-the-brands-best-selling -product-of-all-time-17003437.

147 *"Maybe my eyebrows are more famous than I am?":* Nitasha Tiku, "Inside Glossier, the Beauty Startup That Reached Cult Status by Selling Less," BuzzFeed News, August 25, 2016, https://www.buzzfeednews.com/article/nitashatiku /inside-glossier-the-beauty-startup-that-just-happens-to-sell.

148 *Hailey Bieber . . . has made the glazed-doughnut look her signature:* Aamina Khan, "Hailey Bieber's 'Glazed Donut' Skincare Routine and Go-To Products," Byrdie, January 11, 2022, https://www.byrdie.com/hailey-bieber-glazed-donut -skincare-routine-5180257.

149 *her favorite product was Glossier Ultralip Tinted Balm:* Laura Regensdorf, "The Glossier Sale Is Here—with Product Picks by Jenna Lyons, Donni Davy & More," *Vanity Fair*, May 26, 2022, https://www.vanityfair.com/style/photos/2021/06 /glossier-sale-product-recommendations.

149 *Glossier grew by 600 percent year over year in 2016:* Emily Canal, "How This Beauty Blogger Created a Cult Brand (and Raised $34 Million)," *Inc.*, December 5, 2017, https://www.inc.com /emily-canal/glossier-2017-company-of-the-year-nominee.html.

150 *those reportedly had a combined wait list of 30,000:* Tiku, "Inside Glossier."

153 *They tried a representative program in summer 2016:*
Jenni Avins, "Glossier Is Building a Multimillion-Dollar
Millennial Makeup Empire with Slack, Instagram, and
Selfies," *Quartz*, December 1, 2016, https://qz.com/847460
/glossier-girls-emily-weiss-on-how-glossiers-customers
-became-its-most-powerful-sales-force.

156 *In 2018, Glossier won the FiFi:* Charles Manning,
"Fragrance Foundation Honors Tom Ford, Gets
Embarrassed, Censors Bottle," *Fashion Week Daily*,
June 13, 2018, https://fashionweekdaily.com/fragrance
-foundation-tom-ford-fucking-fabulous/.

CHAPTER 9

159 *There was a Series A round in November 2014:* Kim-Mai
Cutler, "Glossier Raises $8.4M Led by Thrive to Take
on Beauty and Cosmetics with Verticalized Approach,"
TechCrunch, November 17, 2014, https://techcrunch
.com/2014/11/17/glossier/.

160 *The money allowed them to expand . . . Series A had been
8/10:* Emily Weiss, "How We Raised Our Latest Round
of Funding," Into the Gloss, November 2016, https://
intothegloss.com/2016/11/glossier-series-b-funding
-announcement/.

161 *wrote Eric Liaw:* Eric Liaw, Roseanne Wincek, and Louise
Ireland, "IVP Just Got Glossier," IVP News, November
30, 2016, https://www.ivp.com/news/blog/ivp-just
-became-glossier/.

162 *The Series C round added $52 million in investment:* Connie
Loizos, "The Beauty Company Glossier Just Closed on a
Whopping $52 Million in Fresh Funding," *TechCrunch*,
February 22, 2018, https://techcrunch.com/2018/02/22
/the-beauty-company-glossier-just-closed-on-a-whopping-52
-million-in-fresh-funding/.

162 *Bloomberg reported that Glossier had crossed into $100 million in revenue:* Janine Wolf and Kim Bhasin, "Inside Glossier's Plans to Shake Up Your Makeup Routine," Bloomberg, August 30, 2018, https://www.bloomberg.com/news /features/2018-08-30/millennial-makeup-brand-glossier -shakeup-makeup-routine?leadSource=uverify%20wall.

163 *when it averaged 50,000 visitors per month:* Alex Comeau, "Glossier SVP Takes Us Inside Their 360 Customer Journey," *Adweek,* August 27, 2019, https://www.adweek.com/inside-the -brand/glossier-vp-takes-us-inside-their-360-customer-journey/.

164 *Émile Zola used it as the setting for his 1883 book:* Émile Zola, *The Ladies' Paradise* (Berkeley: University of California Press, 1991).

164 *"I longed to be in a crowd of busy women shopping":* Barbara Pym, *Excellent Women* (New York: Penguin Classics, 2006).

164 *In the 1984 movie the assertive Muppet Miss Piggy . . . applies some makeup to perk her up: The Muppets Take Manhattan,* directed by Frank Oz, 1984.

172 *A Harvard Business School case study quoted Weiss:* Jill Avery, "Glossier: Co-Creating a Cult Brand with a Digital Community," Harvard Business School Case 519-022, January 2019 (revised October 2019), https://www.hbs.edu /faculty/Pages/item.aspx?num=54905.

174 *sending online marketing and customer acquisition costs through the roof:* Brad Bergan, "Apple's Privacy Changes Have Cut $278 Billion from 4 Big Tech Firms," Interesting Engineering, February 3, 2022, https://interestingengineering.com/culture /apples-privacy-cut-278-billion.

174 *Large retailers take 60 percent of the MSRP:* Cheryl Wischhover, "It Costs $2.50 to Make Lipstick—Here's Why You're Charged So Much More," Racked, May 30, 2018, https://www.racked.com/2018/5/30/17392668/beauty -product-pricing-stowaway-cosmetics.

174 *Glossier reached a valuation of $1 billion in March 2019:* Kate
     Clark, "Glossier Triples Valuation, Enters Unicorn Club
     with $100M Round," *TechCrunch*, March 19, 2019, https://
     techcrunch.com/2019/03/19/glossier-triples-valuation
     -enters-unicorn-club-with-100m-round/.

175 *an investor in Apple, Google, PayPal:* Sequoia Capital, Our
     Companies, https://www.sequoiacap.com/our-companies/.

CHAPTER 10

178 *"The world was the same as it had been . . . yet I was
     worth $178 million":* Phil Knight, *Shoe Dog* (New York:
     Scribner, 2016).

178 *Glossier was one of just twenty-one female-led companies that
     were christened unicorns in 2019:* Carmen Ang, "On the
     Rise: 2019 Set a Record for New Female-Led Unicorns,"
     Visual Capitalist, November 10, 2020, https://www
     .visualcapitalist.com/on-the-rise-2019-set-a-record-for-new
     -female-led-unicorns/.

178 *Others in Glossier's class included Away, Rent the Runway,
     and the RealReal:* Natasha Mascarenhas, "Female-Founded
     Unicorns Are Being Born at an Unprecedented Rate in 2019,
     Data Shows," Crunchbase News, June 5, 2019, https://news
     .crunchbase.com/venture/female-founded-unicorns-are
     -being-born-at-an-unprecedented-rate-in-2019-data-shows/.

178 *Less than 2 percent of venture capital investment:* Dominic-
     Madori Davis, "Women-Founded Startups Raised 1.9% of
     All VC Funds in 2022, a Drop from 2021," *TechCrunch*,
     January 18, 2023, https://techcrunch.com/2023/01/18
     /women-founded-startups-raised-1-9-of-all-vc-funds-in
     -2022-a-drop-from-2021/.

179 *Charlotte Tilbury, Sequoia's first beauty investment, was sold:*
     Sarah Butler, "Spanish Puig Snaps Up Charlotte Tilbury
     Makeup Empire," *Guardian*, June 4, 2020, https://www

.theguardian.com/business/2020/jun/04/spanish-puig-snaps
-up-charlotte-tilbury-makeup-empire.

179 *Unilever bought Tatcha for an estimated $500 million:*
Stephanie Saltzman, "Unilever Acquires Skin-Care Brand
Tatcha for a Reported $500 Million," Fashionista, June 10,
2019, https://fashionista.com/2019/06/unilever-tatcha
-acquisition.

179 *Shiseido bought Drunk Elephant for $845 million:* Marci
Robin, "Beauty Giant Unilever Just Bought Tatcha for an
Estimated $500 Million," *Allure*, June 11, 2019, https://www
.allure.com/story/unilever-buys-tatcha-estimated-valuation.

184 *Glossier announced that it had acquired Dynamo:* Quinn
Mason, "Dynamo Reveals Acquisition by Glossier as the
Beauty Empire Announces US$52 Million Series C,"
Montreal in Technology, February 28, 2018, http://www
.montrealintechnology.com/dynamo-reveals-acquisition
-by-glossier-as-the-beauty-empire-announces-us52-million
-series-c/.

184 *Keith Peiris, a former product manager . . . . [Vavrasek] as
the chief people officer:* Courtney Rubin, "Last Girlboss
Standing," *Bustle*, April 18, 2022, https://www.bustle.com
/politics/glossier-emily-weiss-profile.

CHAPTER 12

193 *Others called them the Glossier Mafia:* Emma Sandler,
"Welcome to the World of the Glossier Mafia," Glossy,
September 28, 2020, https://www.glossy.co/beauty
/welcome-to-the-world-of-the-glossier-mafia/.

196 *[Monahan] originated the term in June 2021:* Allison P. Davis,
"A Vibe Shift Is Coming," *The Cut*, February 16, 2022,
https://www.thecut.com/2022/02/a-vibe-shift-is-coming.html.

197 *the writer Kyle Chayka named it "AirSpace":* Kyle Chayka,
"The Subway That Sunk," The Verge, August 2016, https://

www.theverge.com/2016/8/3/12325104/airbnb-aesthetic
-global-minimalism-startup-gentrification.

201 *only 7 percent of millennials, Glossier's base, self-identified as brand loyal:* Michael Osborne, "Brands Need to Step Up Their Game to Win Over Millennials," *Forbes*, September 26, 2017, https://www.forbes.com/sites/forbesagencycouncil/2017/09/26/brands-need-to-step-up-their-game-to-win-over-millennials/?sh=592743f1b321.

201 *37 percent of Glossier's website visitors are eighteen- to twenty-four-year-olds:* Emma Sandler, "Why Glossier's New Flagship Store Is a 'Homecoming' for the Brand," Glossy, February 16, 2023, https://www.glossy.co/beauty/why-glossiers-new-flagship-store-is-a-homecoming-for-the-brand/.

CHAPTER 13

207 *faced a discrimination lawsuit in 2015 for allegedly firing pregnant employees:* Rachel Zarrell and Stephanie McNeal, "Nasty Gal Employees Describe the Company Environment as 'Toxic' After New Lawsuit," BuzzFeed News, June 9, 2015, updated June 10, 2015, https://www.buzzfeednews.com/article/rachelzarrell/nasty-gal-a-horrible-place-to-work-if-youre-pregnant#.quyJ31zk6.

207 *settled in 2016 via arbitration:* Kayleen Schaefer, "What Comes After Scandal and Scathing Reviews? Sophia Amuroso Is Finding Out," *Vanity Fair*, April 26, 2017, https://www.vanityfair.com/style/2017/04/sophia-amoruso-girlboss-netflix-nasty-gal.

207 *In 2016, her company Nasty Gal filed for bankruptcy:* Valeriya Safronova, "Nasty Gal's Path to Bankruptcy," *New York Times*, November 11, 2016, https://www.nytimes.com/2016/11/11/fashion/nasty-gal-sophia-amoruso-bankruptcy.html.

208 *Miki Agrawal [of Thinx] . . . was ousted after accusations from employees:* Noreen Malone, "Sexual-Harassment Claims

Against a 'She-E.O.,'" *The Cut*, March 2017, https://www
.thecut.com/2017/03/thinx-employee-accuses-miki-agrawal
-of-sexual-harassment.html.

208 *in December 2019 came leaked Slack messages from Steph
Korey:* Zoe Schiffer, "Emotional Baggage," The Verge,
December 5, 2019, https://www.theverge.com/2019/12
/5/20995453/away-luggage-ceo-steph-korey-toxic-work
-environment-travel-inclusion.

209 *By June 2020, Wing cofounder Audrey Gelman had stepped
down:* Katherine Rosman, "Audrey Gelman, the Wing's
Co-Founder, Resigns," *New York Times*, June 11, 2020,
https://www.nytimes.com/2020/06/11/style/the-wing-ceo
-audrey-gelman-resigns.html.

209 *housed its headquarters in Manhattan's East Village was for
sale for $22.5 million:* Clio Chang, "The Wing's Office (and
Furniture) Is for Sale," Curbed, March 2, 2023, https://
www.curbed.com/2023/03/the-wing-former-headquarters
-furniture-sale.html.

209 *Christene Barberich from Refinery29—also stepped down in
2020:* Katie Robertson, "Refinery29 Editor Resigns After
Former Employees Describe 'Toxic Culture,'" *New York Times*,
June 8, 2020, updated September 8, 2020, https://www
.nytimes.com/2020/06/08/business/media/refinery-29-christene
-barberich.html.

212 *"The #MeToo campaign, as it evolved" . . . wrote Susan Faludi:*
Susan Faludi, "Feminism Made a Faustian Bargain with
Celebrity Culture. Now It's Paying the Price," *New York
Times*, June 20, 2022, https://www.nytimes.com/2022/06/20
/opinion/roe-heard-feminism-backlash.html.

213 *Kirsten Green weighed in, telling* TechCrunch: Amanda
Silberling and Anita Ramaswamy, "How the Myth of the
'Girlboss' Harms Emerging Women in Tech," *TechCrunch*,

June 3, 2022, https://techcrunch.com/2022/06/03/girlboss
-era-myth-toxic-harms-women-tech-startups-ceo-founder/.

213 *Sophie Haigney wrote in the* New York Times*:* Sophie
Haigney, "Meet the Self-Described 'Bimbos' of TikTok,"
New York Times, June 15, 2022, https://www.nytimes
.com/2022/06/15/opinion/bimbo-tiktok-feminism.html.

216 *"Where are their White male counterparts who have failed
as leaders":* Aliza Licht, "Girlboss May Be Over, but the
Woman Founder Is Here to Stay," *Forbes,* July 15, 2020,
https://www.forbes.com/sites/alizalicht/2020/07/05
/girlboss-may-be-over-but-the-woman-founder-is-here-to
-stay/?fbclid=IwAR1VepGKTsYEn3ivl0JAJeIgOhL3Wj
_gzBPyFGx0wjuEfqnw8DghtRk5pMg&sh=6924f1be78cc.

216 *"Andy Grove, the longtime CEO of Intel":* Brad Stone,
The Everything Store: Jeff Bezos and the Age of Amazon
(New York: Little, Brown, 2013).

216 *Even something as minor as Peloton CEO John Foley:* Paige
Darrah, "How John Foley, Peloton Co-Founder, Spends His
Sundays," *New York Times,* December 11, 2020, https://www
.nytimes.com/2020/12/11/nyregion/coronavirus-peloton
-john-foley.html.

CHAPTER 14

220 *they spoke to* Broadsheet *in August 2020, describing "a range
of disturbing behavior":* Emma Hinchliffe, "Former Glossier
Employees Say They Faced Racism at the Brand's Retail
Stores," *Fortune,* Broadsheet, August 18, 2020, https://
fortune.com/2020/08/18/former-glossier-employees-say-they
-faced-racism-at-the-brands-retail-stores/.

220 *In June 2020, when @outtathegloss came to light, 43 percent of
Glossier's corporate workforce identified as people of color . . . no
Black representation at the leadership level:* Jeena Sharma, "How

to Apply for Glossier's Black-Owned Beauty Grants," *Nylon*, June 12, 2020, https://www.nylon.com/beauty/applications-for -glossiers-black-owned-beauty-business-grant-are-now-open.

221 *Estée Lauder . . . promised to boost Black hiring . . . Sephora was the first retailer to take the 15 percent pledge:* William P. Lauder, "The Estée Lauder Companies Commits to Racial Equity," Estée Lauder Companies, June 10, 2020, https:// www.elcompanies.com/en/news-and-media/newsroom /company-features/2020/elc-commits-to-racial-equity.

221 *which in 2020 carried only seven Black-owned brands out of 290:* "Sephora Takes 15 Percent Pledge FAQ," Sephora, June 11, 2020, https://newsroom.sephora.com/sephora -takes-15-percent-pledge-faq/.

225 *According to Spate . . . searches [for Boy Brow] declined 33 percent year over year:* Liz Flora, " Beauty and Wellness Briefing: The End of an Eyebrow-First Era," Glossy, May 3, 2022, https://www.glossy.co/beauty/beauty-wellness -briefing-the-end-of-an-eyebrow-first-era/.

226 *Glossier sales were down 22 percent from 2020, according to Earnest Research:* Rachel Strugatz, "How Glossier Lost Its Grip," *Business of Fashion*, January 28, 2022, https://www .businessoffashion.com/articles/beauty/how-glossier-lost-its-grip/.

CHAPTER 15

229 *In March 2020, Glossier . . . furloughed retail teams . . . physical retail staff in August:* Cara Salpini, "Glossier Lays Off Retail Employees, Closes Stores for the Rest of 2020," Retail Dive, August 10, 2020, https://www.retaildive.com/news /glossier-lays-off-retail-employees-closes-stores-for-the -rest-of-2020/583218/.

230 *closed its Series E round in 2021 . . . up from $1.2 billion in 2019:* Alexandra Mondalek and Rachel Strugatz, "Glossier Raises $80 Million Series E, Valuing Company at

$1.8 Billion," *Business of Fashion*, July 6, 2021, https://www
.businessoffashion.com/articles/beauty/glossier-raises-80
-million-series-e-valuing-company-at-18-billion/.

CHAPTER 16

243 *Sheryl Sandberg announced she was leaving Facebook's parent
company Meta in June 2022:* Bobby Allyn, "In Surprise
Move, Sheryl Sandberg Leaves Facebook After 14 Years,"
NPR, June 1, 2022, https://www.npr.org/2022/06/01
/1102479732/in-surprise-move-sheryl-sandberg-leaves
-facebook-after-14-years.

243 *Julie Wainwright . . . would be stepping down from her position:*
Ezreen Benissan, "The RealReal's Julie Wainwright Steps
Down as CEO," *Vogue Business*, June 8, 2022, https://www
.voguebusiness.com/companies/the-realreals-julie-wainwright
-steps-down-as-ceo.

245 *"How Glossier Lost Its Grip":* Rachel Strugatz, "How Glossier
Lost Its Grip," *Business of Fashion*, January 28, 2022, https://
www.businessoffashion.com/articles/beauty/how-glossier
-lost-its-grip/.

245 *"What Went Wrong at Glossier?":* Jacqueline Kilikita, "What
Went Wrong at Glossier?," Refinery29, February 1, 2022,
https://www.refinery29.com/en-us/2022/02/10854189/what
-happened-to-glossier.

245 *"How Can Emerging Beauty Brands Avoid Glossier's
Stumbles?":* Rachel Brown, "How Can Emerging Beauty
Brands Avoid Glossier's Stumbles?," Beauty Independent,
February 3, 2022, https://www.beautyindependent.com
/how-emerging-beauty-brands-avoid-glossier-stumbles/.

245 *"I too am glossier makeup at tj maxx (hot and full of potential
in 2017, not quite where I wanna be in 2022)":* carina hsieh
@carinahsieh, Twitter, July 23, 2022, 2:48 p.m., https://
twitter.com/carinahsieh/status/1550915775971696641.

245 *Allbirds had struggled after its IPO:* Matthew Kish, "Allbirds Stock Crashes After the Company Said It Lost $101 Million Last Year and Quarterly Sales Fell Well Below a Year Ago," Business Insider, March 10, 2023, https://www.businessinsider.in/retail/news/allbirds-stock-crashes-after-the-company-said-it-lost-101-million-last-year-and-quarterly-sales-fell-well-below-a-year-ago/articleshow/98529085.cms.

248 *there's a name for the so-called Lipstick Effect:* Emily Gerstell et al., "How COVID-19 Is Changing the World of Beauty," McKinsey & Company, May 2020, https://www.mckinsey.com/~/media/McKinsey/Industries/Consumer%20Packaged%20Goods/Our%20Insights/How%20COVID%2019%20is%20changing%20the%20world%20of%20beauty/How-COVID-19-is-changing-the-world-of-beauty-vF.pdf.

249 *According to McKinsey in 2022, cosmetics is the only category that has grown:* Kari Alldredge et al., "How US Consumers Are Feeling, Shopping, and Spending—and What It Means for Companies," McKinsey & Company, May 4, 2022, https://www.mckinsey.com/capabilities/growth-marketing-and-sales/our-insights/how-us-consumers-are-feeling-shopping-and-spending-and-what-it-means-for-companies.

251 *the reformulated vegan Balm Dotcom . . . sold $1 million worth in its first week:* Rachel Strugatz, "Glossier Gets a Makeover," *New York Times*, February 15, 2023, https://www.nytimes.com/2023/02/15/style/glossier-gen-z-make-up-skin-care.html.

251 *in 2021, a full 44 percent of American internet users said they began shopping for beauty products . . . down from 18 percent in 2019:* Sky Canaves, "US Beauty Ecommerce 2022," Insider Intelligence, May 25, 2022, https://www.insiderintelligence.com/content/us-beauty-ecommerce-2022.

252 *"James took the traditional path to success and left his hometown team for the Miami Heat":* Rachel Strugatz, "Emily Weiss Is the LeBron James of Beauty," *Business of Fashion*, February 20, 2023, https://www.businessoffashion.com /articles/beauty/glossier-nyc-soho-flagship/.

252 *the fashion journalist Laura Reilly wrote in her newsletter Magasin:* Laura Reilly, "To Shop Is to Err, to Err Is to Be Human," *Magasin*, February 28, 2023, https://www.magasin .ltd/p/093-to-shop-is-to-err-to-err-is-to.

CHAPTER 17

263 *Gwyneth Paltrow was thirty-six when she launched Goop:* Pilar Guzmán, "The 'Secret Sauce' Behind Gwyneth Paltrow's Success," *Condé Nast Traveler*, September 22, 2015, https:// www.cntraveler.com/stories/2015-09-22/the-secret-sauce -behind-gwyneth-paltrow-success.

263 *around the same age Lorne Michaels was when he left* Saturday Night Live: Brian Boone, "The Untold Truth of *SNL's* Forgotten Season," Looper, January 27, 2023, https://www .looper.com/83835/untold-truth-snls-forgotten-season/.

263 *Steve Jobs left Apple in his early thirties and again in his early forties, and returned both times:* Luke Dormehl, "Today in Apple History: Steve Jobs Leaves *and* Rejoins Apple," Cult of Mac, September 16, 2022, https://www.cultofmac .com/445723/today-in-apple-history-steve-jobs-leaves-and -rejoins-apple/.

263 *Martha Stewart was in her early forties in 1982 when Entertaining came out:* "Party at Martha's: Stewart's Tips for 'Entertaining,'" NPR, December 5, 2011, https://www.npr .org/2011/12/05/143008159/party-at-marthas-stewarts-tips -for-entertaining.

About the Author

Marisa Meltzer is a journalist based in New York whose work has appeared in the *New York Times*, the *New Yorker*, *Vanity Fair*, *Vogue*, and more. She is the author of *Glossy* and three previous books. Find out more at MarisaMeltzer.com.